DATE DUE

DEMCO 38-296

OTTO LUENING

Otto Luening. *Photo courtesy of Columbia University Office of Public Information.*

OTTO LUENING

A Bio-Bibliography

RALPH HARTSOCK

Bio-Bibliographies in Music, Number 35
Donald L. Hixon, Series Adviser

Greenwood Press
New York • Westport, Connecticut • London

Library of Congress Cataloging-in-Publication Data

Hartsock, Ralph.
    Otto Luening : a bio-bibliography / Ralph Hartsock.
        p.   cm.—(Bio-bibliographies in music, ISSN 0742-6968 ; no.
35)
    Includes bibliographical references and index.
    ISBN 0-313-24320-4 (alk. paper)
    1. Luening, Otto, 1900- —Bibliography.   2. Luening, Otto, 1900-
—Discography.   I. Title.   II. Series.
    ML134.L86H4   1991
    016.78′092—dc20   90-22926

British Library Cataloguing in Publication Data is available.

Library of Congress Catalog Card Number: 90-22926
ISBN: 0-313-24320-4
ISSN: 0742-6968

First published in 1991

Greenwood Press, 88 Post Road West, Westport, CT 06881
An imprint of Greenwood Publishing Group, Inc.

Printed in the United States of America

The paper used in this book complies with the
Permanent Paper Standard issued by the National
Information Standards Organization (Z39.48-1984).

10 9 8 7 6 5 4 3 2 1

In memory of my father

Norval Milton Hartsock
1914-1979

Contents

Preface

This volume is meant to provide a concise bibliographic guide to the life and career of Otto Luening, American composer, educator, conductor, and flutist. Many of his works have not been performed outside the northeastern United States, and it is the author's hope that this volume will lead to more frequent performances of the chamber music and other compositions of Luening.

It consists of four main sections:

1) a brief **Biography**;

2) a list of **Works and Performances**, complete to 1986, arranged in chronological order, and subarranged alphabetically. This was prepared with the assistance of Dr. Luening and Emily Good. It includes basic bibliographical data and information on the premiere and selected performances. In entries where the information is incomplete, that data is unknown. Each work is denoted by the mnemonic "W" followed by a numeral indicating its chronological position (for example, *Kentucky Concerto* is numbered W143), and the performances of that work are identified by successive lower-case letters (W143a, W143b, W143c, etc.);

3) a **Discography**, arranged alphabetically by title. Due to the low number of available recordings, both commercially-produced and selected privately-released recordings are included. Each title is denoted by the mnemonic "D" followed by a numeral indicating its alphabetical position (for example, *Fantasy in Space* is numbered D7), and each issue of that work is identified by successive lower-case letters (D7a, D7b, D7c, etc.);

4) a **Bibliography** of writings by and about Luening covers the years 1921 to 1989. These are prefixed with the mnemonic "B". B1-B34 are the *Bibliography by Luening*, while B35-B625 are the *Bibliography about*

Luening. Articles and books from multiple sources will be differentiated by successive lower-case letters (e.g., various editions of *Music Since 1900*, by Nicolas Slonimsky are numbered B542a, B542b, B542c)

In addition, there are two appendixes, an **Alphabetical List of Compositions** and a **Classified List of Compositions**. An index, which includes titles, subjects, and personal, corporate and geographical names, concludes the volume.

Compositions of Luening are thus arranged in three groups:

(1) Chronologically in the **Works and Performances**;
(2) Alphabetically, without genre grouping, in **Appendix I** and the **Index**;
(3) Alphabetically, by genre, in **Appendix II**.

It is hoped that this volume will bring a greater awareness of the contributions to contemporary American music made by Otto Luening.

Acknowledgments

For Bibliographic Assistance: Mary Lou Allen, St. Louis Public Library; R. Amelan, Jerusalem Post; Natalie Anderson, Ipswich Public Library, Massachusetts; Sandra Batzli, Urbana, Illinois; Marsha Berman, University of California, Los Angeles; Sharon Bidwell, Louisville Courier-Journal; Helen Bisbee, Grand Rapids Public Library; Dorothy Bognar, University of Connecticut; Kathy Breidenbach, Westport Public Library, Connecticut; Rebecca O. Bridges, Margaret Chase Smith School, Sanford, Maine; Pamela Bristah, Manhattan School of Music; Myrna Brown, Denton, Texas; Brunswick Times-Record, Maine; Dave Burke, Louisiana State University; Richard D. Burbank, University of Illinois; Frances R. Burdette, South Bend Public Library, Indiana; Maria Calderisi Bryce, National Library of Canada; Eileen Carrier, Bennington College; Seamus G. Connolly, The Chapin School, New York; Ineke Constantine, Consulate General, Netherlands; Salome Cory, Congregation Emanu-el, New York; Carol Dunn, SUNY--New Paltz; Virginia L. Enos, University of Hawaii, Manoa; Pozzi Escot, Wheaton College, Massachusetts; Mary Findley, George Washington University; Catherine Gerhart, University of Washington; John Gibbs, University of Washington; Emily Good, ISAM/New York Public Library; Gary L. Good, Milwaukee Symphony; Jean Gordon, Urbana Free Library; Laura E. Gowdy, Illinois State University; Michael Gray, U.S. Information Agency; Sidney Grolnic, Free Library of Philadelphia; Iselin Gunderman, Geheimes Statsarchiv Preussischer Kulturbesitz; Rosalinda Hack, Chicago Public Library; Steve Hanna, Eastman School of Music; Deborah Hayes, University of Colorado, Boulder; Sharon Herfurth, Dallas Public Library; Florence W. Hoffman, Denison University; Laura Hollerman, Newington, Connecticut; Iwona Jankowski, Universite de Moncton, New Brunswick; Ellen Johnson, University of Kansas; Pamela Juengling, University of Massachusetts; Virginia Kellogg, Texas Tech University; Margaretta Keith, Lenox Library Assoc.; Faith Kindness, Wheaton College, Massachusetts; Charles King, University of Arizona; Dorothy T. King, East Hampton Library; Janet Kinzer, Arlington County Public Library, Va.; Elinor Kotzen, Spoleto Festival U.S.A.; David W. Kraeuter, Washington and Jefferson

Acknowledgments

College; Karl Kroeger, University of Colorado, Boulder; Dixie M. Lanning, Bethany College, Lindsborg, Kan.; Anna Large, Jacksonville University; Charles Lindahl, Eastman School of Music; John P. Luidens, Holland Historical Trust; Carlton Lowenberg, Lafayette, California; Jerry McBride, Middlebury College; Diane Majors, California State University, Fresno; Jim Mann, St. Louis Symphony; Michael Meckna, Ball State University; John Mielke, SUNY, Albany; Rebecca Mitchell, University of Wisconsin, Parkside; Holly E. Mockovak, Harvard University; Tina Mudgett, Ripon College; Margaret Neu, Corpus Christi Caller-Times; Vivian Perlis, Yale University; Barbara Peterson, BMI; Catherine Phinizy, Connecticut College; Lois Price, Vermont State Symphony; Edwin A. Quist, Peabody Conservatory of Music; Sarah B. Ransom, Vassar College; Susan Ravdin, Bowdoin College; Wendy J. Richards, Central Washington University; Eero Richmond, American Music Center; Steve Roehling, Charleston County Lib., S.C.; Marty Rosen, University of Louisville; William Schimmel, New York; Peter Schubert, Barnard College; Dorothy Selby, St. Martin Parish Lib., Louisiana; Joel Sheveloff, Boston University; Martin A. Silver, University of Calfornia, Santa Barbara; Tinsley E. Silcox, University of Tenn., Knoxville; Scott Skelton, Houston Public Library; Robert Skinner, Southern Methodist University; Richard Smiraglia, Columbia University; Carol Smith, Kalamazoo College; Dorman Smith, University of Arizona; P. Sonnenberg, South African Library; Jean Stamm, Saratoga Springs; Gael B. Stein, St. Johnsbury Athanaeum, Vermont; Keith Stetson, University of California, Berkeley; Steven L. Sundell, University of Wisconsin, Madison; Stephen Toombs, Case Western Reserve University; Carol Tucher, American Museum of Natural History; Merle vonWettberg, Colgate University; Fred Tulan, San Francisco; James Whittle, University of Alberta; Christina Wilson, Stratford Public Library, Ontario; Ross Wood, Wellesley College; Jason S. Wright, Omaha Symphony; Nancy Kobialka Zavac, University of Miami.

Libraries which sent materials freely for loan: Allegheny College; Allentown College; Arizona State University*; Auburn University; Bucknell University; California State University, Fullerton; California State University, Hayward; California State University, Los Angeles; Carnegie Library, Pittsburgh; Central Arkansas Library system; Connecticut College; Dallas Public Library; Eastern New Mexico University; Eastman School of Music; Free Library of Philadelphia; Hamilton College; Indiana University; Indiana University of Penn.*; Ithaca College; Mesa Public Library, Ariz.; Miami University, Ohio; Milwaukee Public Library; New Mexico State University; Northern Illinois University; Ohio State University; Peabody Conservatory of Music; Penn. State University*; Southern Baptist Theological Seminary, Louisville; Southern Illinois University; Southern Methodist University; Stephen F. Austin State University; Texas Christian University; Texas Tech University; University of Arizona; University of California, Irvine; University of Cincinnati; University of Colorado, Boulder; University of

Georgia; University of Illinois*; University of Kansas*; University of Louisville; University of Montana; University of New Mexico*; University of North Texas*; University of Northern Colorado; University of Oklahoma; University of Tennessee; University of Texas, Austin; University of Utah; University of Vermont; University of Western Ontario; University of Wisconsin, Parkside; University of Wisconsin, Milwaukee; Wake Forest University; Washburn University; West Chester University; Western State College; Whittier College; Witchita State University. * Library's collections used.

For Data Entry and Support: Janet Hartsock.

For Editorial Support: Don Hixon, University of California, Irvine; Dorman Smith, University of Arizona.

OTTO LUENING

Biography

Otto Luening was born June 15, 1900, in Milwaukee. He was one of seven children of Eugene and Emma Luening, a family with a rich musical heritage. His mother, Emma, was a singer, and his father, Eugene, was a singer, conductor and pianist who had studied at the Leipzig Conservatory, later singing in performances conducted by Richard Wagner. For nearly thirty years (1879-1904), Eugene Luening directed the Milwaukee Music Society.

This upbringing greatly influenced Otto, who early showed musical interest and talent. He was essentially self-taught at piano, though his father began to supervise his practice in a casual manner when Otto was about four years old. By age six, young Otto had composed *Little Miniature Pieces* (W1), a waltz for piano. However, for the next six years, Otto's father discouraged him from a musical career because "an artist's life is too difficult in the United States."[1]

In 1912, the family moved to Munich, where Otto studied flute with Alois Schellhorn. His talents astounded even his own father. At age 15, he was the youngest student at the Staatliche Hochschule für Musik, where, in addition to flute lessons, he studied piano with Josif Becht. After secretly composing a set of piano pieces in 1916, he played them within earshot of his father. Eugene, unaware of the origin of the music, asked whose music it was. Otto credited it to Max Reger (1873-1916), whereupon his father launched into a discourse on the fine music of Reger. Afterwards, Otto revealed that the music was his own. His concert debut as a flutist occurred on March 27, 1916. On December 18 of that year he made his debut at the Akademie der Tonkunst in Munich with Handel's *Sonata in G minor for Flute*.

The following year, when the United States entered the World War, Otto and his sister, Helene, moved to Switzerland, where the composer continued his musical studies at the Zurich Conservatory with Philipp Jarnach (1892-1982), a pupil of Ferruccio Busoni (1866-1924). Luening later had an opportunity to study privately with Busoni, a futurist, largely self-taught, and a "curious mixture of impressionism, aloofness, and withdrawal from 'reality.'"[2] It was in Zurich that Luening studied with composer-conductor Volkmar Andreae (1879-1962), who directed the Tonhalle Orchestra from 1906 to 1949, championing new music of Anton Bruckner, Richard Strauss, Gustav Mahler, and Claude Debussy. Beginning in 1917, Luening was a percussionist and flutist in this Zurich Tonhalle Orchestra. During that year he made his conducting debut in Zurich, directing a Viennese operetta. He later conducted the Tonhalle Orchestra in Grieg's *Piano Concerto*, with Ernst Weilemann as pianist.

Under the stage name of James P. Cleveland, Otto Luening was an actor and stage manager for the James Joyce English Players Company during 1918 and 1919. The pseudonym was used because Luening sometimes had conflicting duties as a member of the opera and symphony orchestras, also in Zurich.

Returning to the United States in 1920, Luening settled in Chicago, playing flute in the Stratford Movie Theatre Orchestra, teaching, arranging hymns of Homer Rodeheaver (1880-1955), and conducting choral societies. He helped found the American Grand Opera Company, conducting its first performance of an all-American opera in November of 1922, Charles Wakefield Cadman's *Shanewis*.

In the early 1920s, Luening studied harmony, theory, and counterpoint with the foremost authority on Bach at that time, Wilhelm Middelschulte, who used Bernhard Ziehn's (1845-1912) approach to composing. While most theorists based harmony upon laws of physics, Ziehn advocated a chromatic/enharmonic system which pointed toward the harmonies of Scriabin and Schoenberg. Busoni, among others, considered his 'enharmonic law' as futuristic, in that it "affirms that 'every chord tone may become the fundamental.'"[3]

In 1924, Luening's *Sextet* (W32) was presented to the newly formed committee of the United States section of the International Society for Contemporary Music. One member, Howard Hanson, later offered Luening a position as coach and assistant conductor in the Opera Department at the Eastman School of Music. Luening also served as assistant conductor, then conductor, of the Rochester American Opera Company. While studying conducting with Eugene Goossens (1893-1962), he developed an ability to sight-read scores.[4]

On April 19, 1927, Luening married Ethel Codd, a Canadian-born concert singer with whom he made several recital tours between 1928 and 1941. In 1928, Ethel and Otto Luening spent a year performing and composing in Cologne, Germany. In 1930, he received a Guggenheim Fellowship that lasted through 1931. This enabled him to compose the opera *Evangeline*, based on the poetry of Henry W. Longfellow.

From 1932 to 1934, Luening taught ear training, sight singing, harmony, counterpoint, and music history at the University of Arizona in Tucson, where he reorganized the theory and composition department. Later, he moved to Bennington College in Vermont, then a women's college, where he was chairman of the Music Department until 1944. He discovered a music faculty with a narrower set of experiences than his previous ones. It was here that Luening began an active advocacy of American and avant-garde music. His leadership in the Bennington Composers Conferences brought many composers to that campus, including Carl Ruggles, Aaron Copland, Henry Cowell, and Paul Hindemith.

During the Bennington years, Luening became involved with the Works Projects Administration music program from 1935 to 1939. In addition to granting employment to performers, the WPA program promoted new American compositions, many of which were performed at the 4000 concerts held each month.[5] Some of Luening's music reached audiences this way, with the composer conducting several concerts. In 1941, with Alan Carter, Luening founded the Vermont Festival of the Arts, held at Middlebury. This became known in some circles as the Green Mountain Festival.

From 1944 to 1959, he was musical director of the Brander Matthews Hall at Columbia University. There, he conducted the premieres of such works as Gian Carlo Menotti's *The Medium* (May 8, 1946), Virgil Thomson's *The Mother of Us All* (May 7, 1947), and his own opera, *Evangeline*, the following year. He also, from 1944 to 1964, taught at Barnard College in New York. In 1949, he joined the faculty of Philosophy at Columbia University.

During this period, Luening was active in the promotion of new American music. He assisted Henry Cowell in *New Music*, a quarterly publication of modern music compositions, which was founded in 1927. From 1937 to 1942, he succeeded Cowell in the leadership of *New Music Quarterly Recordings*, founded in 1934, which issued recordings of works by Aaron Copland, Wallingford Riegger, Carlos Chavez, Luening, and others. He was a co-founder of the American Music Center in 1940 and served as its chairman until 1960. Between 1945 and 1951 Luening was president of the American Composers Alliance. In the 1950s, along with Douglas Moore and Oliver Daniel, Luening founded Composers Recordings, a record producer dedicated to twentieth century music, and served as its president from 1968 to 1974.

It was at Columbia University that Otto Luening became actively interested in electronic music. Busoni had earlier introduced Luening to the concepts of electronic sound production. In 1952, Luening recorded flute sounds, transforming them on magnetic tape, to produce *Fantasy in Space* (W148). He later collaborated for ten years on several compositions with another composer interested in electronic music, Vladimir Ussachevsky.

With Ussachevsky of Columbia University and Milton Babbitt and Roger Sessions of Princeton, Luening was a co-founder and co-director of the Columbia-Princeton Electronic Music Center, which began operation in 1959. This was the same year in which Otto and Ethel were divorced. Later that year he married Catherine Johnson Brunson, a pianist. She had received her M.A. from Columbia University in Musicology, and was a teacher at the Packer Collegiate Institute in Brooklyn.

In 1965, the Wisconsin legislature, in a joint resolution, recognized Luening's contributions to twentieth century American music. The resolution says in part:

> Luening's career has "included key contributions to the most important stages in the development of a mature and creative American music--the exploitation of native materials such as hymn-and-fuguing tunes; organization of opera, symphony and chamber recitals throughout the nation; formation of the American Composers Alliance which for more than 25 years has aided outstanding creative composers to publish and distribute their music to the public; and most recently, development of electronics as a musical medium which is our century's major contribution to the creative resources of musical culture ...."
> *"Resolved by the assembly, the senate concurring,* That Otto Luening be congratulated on his outstanding achievements in and contributions to our musical culture...."[6]

Luening has also received honorary degrees from a number of colleges, including Wesleyan University of Connecticut and Columbia University.

Even following his retirement from Columbia University in 1968, Luening was very active in the American music scene, and espoused a philosophy that "turning people out at 65, 70, or 85 is a social waste."[7] He was also featured in *50 Plus*, a layperson's magazine for those over age fifty.[8] He displayed energy which reporter John Zinsser found nonindicative of the composer's age. Luening was professor of composition at the Juilliard School of Music from 1971 to 1973. In 1984 he was a featured speaker at a program of the Brookdale Institute on Aging and Adult Human Development, entitled "Creativity in the 80s."

Because of his attitudes toward his position as a teacher, Otto Luening has had a more subtle impact upon the world of music than that of many composers. Many of his compositions were for youth ensembles or commissioned by schools (W132, W197, W262-W263) Other works for young performers included *Six Short and Easy Piano Pieces* (W70), *Ten Pieces for Five Fingers* (W132), and *Pilgrim's Hymn* (W137). Otto Luening was the coordinator of the Silver Burdett series "Making Music Your Own." He later assisted in the production of a filmstrip demonstrating the processes of electronic music generation, illustrating these with his *Moonflight* (W213; B203). Many other of his works are easy pieces or exercises (W123, W136, W141, W207) Leonard Bernstein conducted a Young Person's Concert with *Concerted Piece for Tape Recorder and Orchestra* (W180). Jacob Avshalamov conducted the Portland Junior Symphony Orchestra in *A Poem in Cycles and Bells for Tape Recorder and Orchestra* (W158)

His music varies in style, a characteristic also found in the multistylistic compositions of one of his teachers, Ferruccio Busoni. Luening's styles encompassed diatonic, serial, polytonal, improvisatory, and electronic music.

Serial techniques are utilized in the *Piece for String Quartet* (W5), written in 1914. The *Sextet* (W32) is a polytonal composition from 1917. In 1923, his *Trio* (W42) instructed performers to improvise on fixed pitches. One of the first symphonic pieces recognizing William Billings is Luening's *Prelude to a Hymn Tune* (W108), composed in 1937. He composed much electronic music, some in collaboration with Vladimir Ussachevsky, including *Rhapsodic Variations for Tape Recorder and Orchestra* (W159), and *A Poem in Cycles and Bells for Tape Recorder and Orchestra* (W158). He also composed electronic music on his own, including *Synthesis* (W192), *Moonflight* (W213), and *Gargoyles* (W183). His *Louisville Concerto* (W143) in a style reminiscent of Rossini appeals to a wide audience while it allows performers to enjoy their individual parts.

7

Variation form is one upon which Luening capitalized, including *Thema con Variazione* (W27), *Variations on Christus der ist mein Leben* (W34), *Variations on the National Air "Yankee Doodle"* (W48), *Variations for Harpsichord* (W120), *Rhapsodic Variations for Tape Recorder and Orchestra* (W159), and *Gargoyles for Violin Solo and Synthesized Sound* (W183).

Themes of Native Americans are introduced in such works as *Fantasia Brevis for Clarinet and Piano* (W101). Composed in 1936, it includes a fast section with a motive influenced by Native American music. Other compositions using these themes are *Potawatomi Legends for Chamber Orchestra* (W240) and *Potawatomi Legends No. 2, for Flute Solo* (W233).

A noticeable aspect of Luening's music is stylistic variety, even within a single composition. *Music for Orchestra* (W51), his first orchestral composition, was composed at age twenty-three. His opera *Evangeline* (W85) encompasses almost two decades of stylistic development. Luening's variety is particularly apparent in the orchestral works with tape. *Sonata in Memoriam Ferruccio Busoni* (W162), a composition which spanned eleven years reflects a wide variety of expression symbolizing the influence of its dedicatee.[9]

If we examine Luening's stylistic development over the years we see that his early works show a definite German influence, specifically those songs from 1915-1918 (W7, W8, W11, W13, W14, W20), carrying on the tradition of Robert Schumann (1810-1856). Piano parts are kept subordinate to flexible vocal melodic lines, while never being merely backgrounds. This German influence is obscured by the later songs with English and American texts, The Whitman songs (W60, W68, W74, W80, W83, W98, W103, W199, W272) tend to be more dramatic in nature. New acoustic settings appeared in the *Emily Dickinson Song Cycle* (W125). Some acquaintance with his numerous songs is crucial to an understanding of his music--the way he allows the vocal lyricism to dominate the compositions. Vocal and instrumental pieces from 1925 to 1952 were composed in a "modern idiom but based on Romantic texts."[10]

The works of Luening's early adulthood included the *Sextet* (W32) of 1918, and *String Quartet No. 1* (W38) of 1919. These works "exhibit polytonality and nontonal writing ... [being] 'objective chamber works.'"[11] The quartet, with a clarinet obbligato in the final movement, is a work in which Busoni was "extremely interested."[12] The second movement contains twelve-tone writing which Luening had originally composed at age 14. The final movement contains several polytonal passages. These early works, plus the *Sonatina for Flute and Piano* (W36) are "highly contrapuntal, often tonal, with overt atonality, polytonality and incipient serialism."[13]

8

This period of linear manipulation drew to a close in the late 1920s, when he became interested in acoustic harmony. This concept uses the overtone series as a source of harmonic materials, becoming the harmonic-dissonant norm for the piece. This approach eventually led him to compose electronic music, noted earlier. "The roots of Luening's style of the 1950s and 1960s, like those of other modernists, can be found in his work in the 1920s and 1930s."[14]

The *Trio* (W42) for violin, cello, and piano, in one movement, includes bitonality based on the harmonic series. Some serial techniques are used, such as retrograde and inversion, without the music being strictly serial itself. This work received mixed reviews after its premiere in Chicago on October 26, 1922. The influence of organist and theorist Wilhelm Middelschulte is evident in Luening's *Introitus* for organ (W40) (1921), *Sonata for Violin and Piano No. 2* (W46) (1922), *Chorale Fantasy for Organ* (W43) (1922), and *Music for Orchestra* (W51) (1923), his first orchestral composition. The latter has an Ivesian, American style, as described by the composer: "It was linear and used melodic lines that were constantly being transformed. It was alternatively tonal, atonal, and bitonal."[15]

Luening studied Vedanta, theosophy, yoga, and became a vegetarian. The strongest effect, the composer says, of the theosophical and Indian studies was found in his *The Soundless Song* (W52) (1923)[16] In his *Trio for Flute, Violin and Soprano* (W57), the last movement consists of pitches only, allowing the performers the choice of rhythms, dynamics, and phrasing.

Symphonic Fantasia no. 1 (W56) was originally entitled *Symphonic Poem.* Combining all earlier styles of Luening, it is lyrical and expressively romantic. Critic James Lyons describes this as:

> "monothematic. The opening five measures presented all of the material, which is thenceforth transfigured continuously, with successive climaxes involving ever more intensity of orchestration. The closing section is signaled by a dance-like tune in the oboe that subsequently [metamorphoses] into a broad lyric statement by the orchestra. A review of initial material brings the work to an end."[17]

In 1926, Robert Mamoulian, of the Eastman School of Drama, invited Luening to write music to *Sister Beatrice* (W59), a play in three acts by Maurice Maeterlinck. Mamoulian described the production as "a synthesis of drama and dance."[18] The music was suggestive of the early Gregorian style, although the play was set in the early fourteenth century. Luening wrote this by attending all rehearsals, improvising at the organ, and writing the acceptable parts into the score. The final score was well-coordinated and very precise in its cues.

Otto Luening

The *Serenade for Three Horns and Strings* (W62), commissioned by Eugene Goossens, was romantic, tonal, and melodious. Luening writes that his *String Quartet No. 2* (W53) was "rejected by several contemporary musical societies and quartets because of its difficulties, apparently no problem for the present generation of performers." Composed in 1923, it was premiered forty-two years later, in 1965.[19] Luening describes his String Quartet No. 3 (W72) as "linear in orientation [with] horizontal and vertical triadic formulations"[20], while it was considered by some reviewers as an enigma, abstract and dissonant. But after a recording in 1975 by the Sinnhoffer Quartet (D43a), a critic wrote "the piece has a lucid classical clarity."[21] With a conventional first movement, this quartet's next section is a set of variations on a twelve-tone theme, while not being "Schoenbergian." *Fantasia for Organ* (W78) combines early American hymn tunes and gospel hymns from the turn of the century.

Luening's opera, *Evangeline* (W85), based on the poetry of Henry W. Longfellow, went through continuous revision for almost two decades. This caused a great deal of variety in the highly lyrical score. Colored by Acadian folk music, Swedish hymns, Native American music, and Catholic Church music in its arias, choral scenes, dances, and instrumental interludes, it has an eclectic American folk identity. The variety of styles encompassed and the 18 years of composition and revision make the opera an index to the musical language of Luening, and one of his most important works.[22] Through a grant from the Alice M. Ditson Fund, the opera was premiered on May 5, 1948 at Columbia University under the musical direction of the composer. It has been revived several times, including a performance at the Acadian Bicentennial Festival in St. Martinville, Louisiana, on October 28, 1955.

Meanwhile, Luening composed *Two Symphonic Interludes* (W96). After a performance in 1936, a *New York Herald Tribune* critic wrote:

> Mr. Luening's brief *Interludes* reveal him as a follower of the modern school, who, while making discreet use of the harmonic innovations of our day, is not oblivious to the fact that music, to be attractive, must have sustained melodic interest as well as dissonant harmonies.[23]

The following year Luening composed a *Prelude to a Hymn Tune by William Billings* (W108). This "may well have started the current interest in the original music of Colonial America." The theme, Billings' *Hymn to Music*, is rich and vigorous. The original theme is stated by the winds, then the strings. This is followed by variations with a "sudden shift to dissonant harmonies."[24]

10

His choral music is widely sung. *Alleluia* (W130) has been described as a "spirited religious work, moderately conservative ... with genuine dynamic thrust."[25] *Tiger's Ghost* (W147) was sung on the tours of the De Paur Infantry Chorus. The New Calliope Singers recorded *Lines from a Song for Occupations* (W199; D18a), and commissioned another, *Lines from the First Book of Urizen and Vala* (W247).

During the 1940s and 1950s his acoustic experiments resulted in a long list of chamber music. There was a further increase in Luening's output of chamber music during the 1960s and 70s.

The flute played an integral part in the compositions of Otto Luening, consisting of five suites for flute solo (W138, W156, W186, W196, W214), three short sonatas for flute and piano (W110, W222, W204), and suites for flute and soprano (W105, W272). In addition, flute sounds are the basis of many of the electronic and tape compositions (W148, W149, W150, W158, W213) However, while the flute was a predominant instrument for the compositions of Luening, one finds a lyrical oboe line in many of his works (W56, W144, W159), including the conclusion of *Rhapsodic Variations for Tape Recorder and Orchestra* (W159).

Electronic music became an active interest of Otto Luening at Columbia University. In 1952 he recorded flute sounds, transformed them on magnetic tape, to produce *Fantasy in Space* (W148). Its success is due, in part, to a solid structure, good melodic lines, and cohesively fused harmonies.[26] Reverberation was used in this and in *Low Speed* (W150). When a tone is repeated, it creates several layers of sound. Luening describes these as two "impressionistic, virtuoso pieces." The latter is described as "an exotic composition that took the flute below its natural range, but with certain acoustic combinations and the help of [Peter] Mauzey's reverberation box, the flute was made to sound like a strange new instrument."[27]

These works, plus *Invention in Twelve Tones* (W149), were given their premieres on October 28, 1952, in an historic concert at the Museum of Modern Art, with Leopold Stokowski conducting. While some reviewers referred to this music as "vaporous, tantalizing, [and] cushioned,"[28] others felt the pieces for tape recorder were "frankly experimental and not too encouraging."[29] Also included were works by another composer interested in electronic music, Vladimir Ussachevsky.

In December of 1952, Luening and Ussachevsky were invited to give a live interview demonstration on Dave Garroway's television news program, *Today*. Luening recounts that "we were met at the studio be a member of the Musicians Local 802, who asked if I had a union card. I said, 'No, but if any flutist in the

11

union can improvise the program, I will be glad to have him take over.' This settled the matter."[30]

Incantation (W153), a collaboration with Vladimir Ussachevsky, was the result of a commission by Leopold Stokowski for the CBS radio program, "Twentieth Century Concert Hall". It used a variety of sound sources, including woodwind instruments, voice, bell sonorities, and piano.[31]

The two composers collaborated during the next ten years on several compositions. *Rhapsodic Variations for Tape Recorder and Orchestra* (W159) is the first work to combine the sound of live performers with magnetic tape. Its taping technique is reverberation, an artificial prolongation of sound. It includes sounds derived from the flute, piano, and percussion. Commissioned by the Louisville Orchestra, it premiered March 20, 1954. After the premiere, there was a controversy surrounding *Rhapsodic Variations* reminiscent of that experienced by Stravinsky's *Rite of Spring* in 1913. The concert master, Sidney Harth, wrote a letter to the editor "No Tape Recorder Fan," hoping *Rhapsodic Variations* was not only the first work of its kind, but also the "last". His hope was that "the tape recorder is not here to stay. It can never replace the human, and is a most imperfect and impersonable artist."[32] But others, such as Calvin W. Bisha took issue with Harth, Bisha citing the philosophy of commissioned works.[33]

Later that year the Los Angeles Philharmonic premiered another collaborated composition, *A Poem in Cycles and Bells for Tape Recorder and Orchestra* (W158). It has been described as a fusion of Luening's *Fantasy in Space* (W148), using flute sounds, and Ussachevsky's *Sonic Contours*, using piano sounds. *Concerted Piece for Tape Recorder and Orchestra* (W180) was commissioned by Leonard Bernstein and the New York Philharmonic. Carter Harman describes this as the "third and one of the most attractive results of ... collaborations, as its frequent public performances attest."[34] The work has a recurring five-note theme in the first section which was composed by Luening. This is one of sophisticated sounds. Those of the second part, composed by Ussachevsky, are more percussive, and include sounds resembling short wave communication and telegraph. This composition evoked varied responses from the critics. One critic describes it as a "sensible musical effort," utilizing new sound techniques and vivid new timbres.[35] Another critic, however, thought that this was a "poor synthesis or antithesis of live and prefabricated music ... [a] venture ... as hazardous as the combination of a symphony orchestra and a jazz band."[36]

As with others who dared to be different by infusing new elements into the music, Luening had his share of critics; some were harsh, describing his new music as "uninspired nonsense,"[37] while others did not understand the new directions he was taking. But a mere fifteen years after *Rhapsodic Variations*, Luening's electronic works were considered conservative by some. When a Luening piece was played at a European festival of avant-garde music in about 1969, a Romanian critic grumbled "We did not come here to listen to Waldteufel and Tchaikovsky."[38] Another critic described it thus:

> This work represented a "more conservative, neo-Romantic trend in electronic music. In fact, it is only superficially related to the kind of fusion of live and tape pieces which became common in the late fifties. In general, the conservative style continued at Columbia through" the late 1950s.[39]

Additional compositions with Ussachevsky included *Of Identity* (W157) in 1954, the Orson Welles production *King Lear* (W164) in 1956, and *Back to Methuselah* (W168) in 1958. *Of Identity* was commissioned by the American Mime Theatre, and composed at the MacDowell Colony, using a projector to synchronize the music. Luening, in the *Unfinished History of Electronic Music*, recalls:

> The problem was that there was a voltage drop at certain times, but Ussachevsky, with mathematical meditations that I do not understand to this day, timed the score accurately enough so that we could deliver it just before dress rehearsal, and it worked.[40]

Orson Welles had desired an abstract sound score for his production of *King Lear*. "Welles came to our (Luening's and Ussachevsky's) studio to listen to our basic sound materials.... After five minutes' listening, Welles, who has an extremely musical ear, said, 'This is the greatest thing to have happened in the theater since the invention of incandescent lights.'"[41] The *Suite* was also featured at an International Conference of Composers, held in Stratford, Ontario, during August of 1960. Luening and Ussachevsky were joined in this conference by Hugh LeCaine of Canada, Josef Tal of Israel, Edgard Varèse, and Luciano Berio.

Compositional collaboration was not limited to Vladimir Ussachevsky. Luening and Halim El-Dabh, an American composer of Egyptian birth, jointly wrote *Diffusion of Bells* (W187) and *Electronic Fanfare* (W181).

Theatre Piece No. 2 (W165) combined orchestral and electronic music with modern dance. Written for the Jose Limon Dance Company and Doris Humphrey, this "Concerto for Light, Movement, Sound and Voice" contained "weird and boldly experimental effects." It began with an "eerie ostinato" and had what were called "bizarre sonorities" with what some viewed as unusual mutations of the human voice.[42]

13

Gargoyles for Violin Solo and Synthesized Sound (W183), another of his many subsequent non-collaborated compositions, has a formal structure of a theme and variations. It displays "contrast on the one hand ... and unity on the other,"[43] by juxtaposing the lyrical sound of the violin against the complex and brilliant sounds of the tape. Unity and continuity are exhibited by symmetry, balance in design, and linear counterpoint. Like *Rhapsodic Variations for Tape Recorder and Orchestra* (W159), *Gargoyles* had a variety of reactions. One reviewer observed "after some semblance of a dance on the Moog, the violin entered with a passionate recitative. The rest was chaos. It sounded suspiciously like an avant-garde gypsy fiddler playing at a Parisian sidewalk cafe, while high above the gargoyles of Notre Dame vomit amplified obscenities."[44] Another critic comments that the traditional style of *Gargoyles* "is aggravated by the banality of the musical composition." Beginning with sounds of a "very bad organ," followed by a triplet rhythm in the electronic part, the violin plays a "stylistically inconsistent melody--Romantic, lyrical, and broodingly Russian."[45] Yet some described this piece as "cogently delineated and beautifully projected."[46]

Another composition for violin and tape is *Duo Concertante* (W184), subtitled "A Day in the Country." It includes a tape with such sounds as "the noise of a crowd [and] the sing-song of an auctioneer."[47] The violinist plays a set of folklike variations.

Other electronic works composed by Luening alone were *Synthesis* (W192) for tape and orchestra, and *Sonority Canon* (W191), for four solo flutes and thirty-three flutes on tape. *Variations on Fugue and Chorale Fantasy* (W224), for organ and electronic tape includes electronic doubles based on recorded segments of his *Fugue for Organ* (W221) and *Chorale Fantasy for Organ* (W43). Each of the five sections of the fugue is followed by an electronic double, each pair having different characteristics.[48]

During the late 1950s and 1960s he continued to compose orchestral and chamber music for conventional instruments as well as to experiment in electronics. *Suite for Double Bass and Piano* (W155) (1953) is described as a spicy work which uses the instruments' lyric flavor.[49] *Wisconsin Suite* (W160), composed in 1954, has been described as "a sort of *Prairie Home Companion* of tunes recalled from the composer's childhood. The music alternated between plush modal chorales for the strings and tart polytonal clashes for the winds."[50]

Luening also composed a piano piece to remember his teacher, the *Sonata in Memoriam Ferruccio Busoni* (W162), begun in 1955, and completed in 1966. The first movement resembles a French overture, followed by a slow-moving melodic "Dramatic Scene," and a "Burlesque" with Alberti bass. The final movement, "Fantasia," displays Luening's multistylistic composing, including melodic, contrapuntal, and rhythmic variety.[51] *Lyric Scene for Flute and Strings* (W171), another composition in memory of Ferruccio Busoni, is described by its composer as "written in the Neo-Classic style, befitting a work in memory of Busoni."[52]

Suites for Flute Solo No. 3-5 were recorded on the album, *Flute Possibilities*. His third suite (W186) was composed in 1961, followed by the fourth (W196) in 1963, and the fifth (W214) in 1969.

> In the *Suites* I wished to build a bridge from the nineteenth century to the exciting new flute sounds of today. Each of the seven movements in *Suites III* and *IV* consists of a sonority form contrasting with all the others. *Suite V* has four movements; Preamble, March Ceremony, Reception, and Conversations. The intervallic relations, integrated with tempo, rhythm, and dynamics bring out the certain acoustic characteristics of each movement. The contrasting sound images balance and give an impression of the flute's manifold possibilities."[53]

Don Henahan describes *Sonata for Violin Solo no. 3* (W220) of 1970 as a "freely serial piece in eight movements."[54] The composer describes this piece as predominantly linear, "its origins ... from an awareness of the complex relationships between partials that exist in the harmonic series."[55]

The *Wisconsin Symphony* (W230), composed in 1975 includes periodic use of electronic music, Ivesian variations, and a retrograde version of "On Wisconsin." *Potawatomi Legends for Chamber Orchestra* (W240) (1980) fuses elements found in Arthur Farwell's pentatonicism, Igor Stravinsky's bitonality, a cowboy theme from Aaron Copland, and the pandiatonic humor of Virgil Thomson.

Because of his position as a teacher, the impact of Otto Luening has been quite profound. During his tenure at Columbia University, his influence was especially felt by several of today's younger composers. Luening's catholic thinking in the juxtaposition of musical styles is evident in a partial list of his pupils who are composers of widely varied stylistic inclinations: Ezra Laderman (1924-) has an intense, romantic, and traditional style. "Luening encouraged him to free himself from the most rigid aspects of atonality and to develop the long lyrical line which would become characteristic of his compositions."[56]

Seymour Shifrin (1926-1979) composed long lyrical lines with fragmentary interjections, mixing metrical regularity with rhythmic dislocation. Charles Wuorinen (1938-   ) is noted as a virtuostic pianist, and as a conductor and co-founder of the Group for Contemporary Music. Wuorinen's earlier music had conventional tonal sources, and exhibited a keen sense of relation among pitch, duration, timbre and structure. Some compositions are of the twelve-tone technique, while others are realized on the RCA Synthesizer.

Chou Wen-chung (1923-   ), a Chinese civil engineer, who completed Varèse's *Nocturnal*, later fused Chinese traditional and sophisticated western style. Chou's *And the Fallen Petals* (1954) includes "Varèse-like intervallic structures and dynamic gestures and sonorities."[57] He also assisted Luening in the composition of *Theatre Piece No. 2.*[58] Wendy Carlos (1939-   ), formerly Walter Carlos, was an early experimenter in electronic music, best known for *Switched-on-Bach*.

Charles Dodge (1942-   ), a student of Luening and Chou, directs the Center for Computer Music at Brooklyn College, CUNY. His *Earth's Magnetic Field* is a musical rendition of the effect of solar radiation on the magnetic field surrounding the earth. Argentine born Mario Davidovsky (1934-   ) began to work at the Columbia-Princeton Electronic Music Center in 1960. He is best known for compositions combining live instrumental performance with recorded electronic sounds, and in particular for the *Synchronisms nos. 1-8.*[59] Since 1981, he has been director of the Columbia-Princeton Electronic Music Center.

Luening's conception of a composer and his community is much broader than usual. His approach to a commission includes considering the tastes and abilities of performers, plus musical backgrounds of the intended audiences. *Suite no. 5 for Flute Solo* (W214) is "an experiment in contemporary 'music for use,'" and has been used at a wedding.

> Composers do not write music for themselves. It is meant to be performed and listened to by others, too.[60]

As a composer of the twentieth century, Luening has given this philosophy of the function of contemporary music:

> I believe that the music of our time will necessarily reflect in part the complexities and pattern of our age. It seems to me that a composer who is unaware of the most recent developments in his art and who does not use them when there is an artistic need for the use of such material, is turning his back on his own age. This was never done in the periods of music which we venerate; I mean the Romantic movement of the last century and the Classical period before that. I do not feel that a composer need necessarily turn his back on everything that has been done before. That would be very unwise and bizarre. He needs to have the courage to explore and the desire to formulate those musical ideas which come to him because he is living today and not living in the memories and reminiscences of the glorious days of old.[61]

This is reiterated in the Preamble to his autobiography, *The Odyssey of an American Composer*:

> When I was fifty-two, Leopold Stokowski introduced my electronic music (or "tape music," as it was called then) at a concert for a distinguished audience at the Museum of Modern Art in New York. To my surprise this event immediately catapulted me into the rarefied atmosphere of the international avant-garde. I won many new friends. But they knew little about my early musical career and were not particularly interested in it.
>
> Many of my old friends and associates looked on my venture into the world of electronic sound as a caper from which they hoped I would soon recover. When I tried to acquaint both new and old friends with those parts of my career they knew nothing about--even then, more than a quarter-century ago, I was "explaining" myself--I was asked repeatedly why I was not content to be either a traditionalist who moves slowly forward or an avantgardist who never looks back. Why, I was asked, would I want to combine such drastically opposed points of view?[62]

Luening has contributed to the repertoire of flute music, and integrated electronic and orchestral music, illustrating the manner of collaboration with three other composers. His educational influences have been felt at Eastman School of Music, the University of Arizona, Bennington College, Barnard College, and Columbia University. He has been a conductor of opera in Chicago, Rochester and

New York, and has been active in contemporary music advocacy, particularly with the Bennington Composers Conferences at Bennington College. He was a co-founder of the American Composers Alliance, American Music Center, Composers Recordings Inc., and the Columbia-Princeton Electronic Music Center. His earlier work in *New Music Quarterly Recordings* helped to bring much contemporary music to the public. Luening has contributed to the repertoire for children, not only by his compositions for school orchestras and easy pieces for keyboard, but also by his contribution to the Silver Burdett series "Making Music Your Own."

Even in the 1950s, critic Oliver Daniel assessed Luening's contribution as follows:

> Otto Luening is like a mythical character who at some point in his life begins to grow younger. After having established his reputation as a solid and perhaps even academic composer he has suddenly burst forth to produce with Vladimir Ussachevsky some of the most avant-garde music of our time. He has expanded his musical interest toward the field of electronics, producing music made of tape-recorded sound quite unlike any music that has preceded it.[63]

Finally, Otto Luening has given this advice for those interested in contemporary music and composition:

> Novelty and tradition, methodology and complete freedom, systems and automation are by themselves not enough to bring music to new heights.
>
> Only if we develop a sense of responsibility and a deep desire to bring human satisfaction to large numbers of individuals can our vision become penetrating enough to draw on the greatness of the past, add to it our new findings, and move forward into the future that even now promises beautiful new experiences as yet undreamed of.[64]

As stated earlier, Otto Luening has been a pioneer. He was among the first to experiment with electronic sound, as found in his *Fantasy in Space* (W148). He has fused orchestral and electronic elements in *Rhapsodic Variations for Tape Recorder and Orchestra* (W159), the first composition for such a combination. There has been collaboration with Vladimir Ussachevsky, Ernst Bacon, and Halim El-Dabh. His stylistic variation makes Otto Luening one of the transitional composers of the twentieth century.

NOTES

1. B21, p. 42.

2. Larry Sitsky, "Busoni, Ferruccio," in John Vinton, *Dictionary of Contemporary Music* (New York: Dutton, 1974), p. 112.

3. Siegmund Levarie, "Ziehn, Berhnard," in *New Grove Dictionary of American Music* (London: Macmillan, 1986), v. 4, p. 594.

4. B21, p. 277.

5. B21, p. 379.

6. B168.

7. B525, p. 33.

8. B620, p. 50.

9. B419, p. 44.

10. B575, p. 125.

11. B575, p. 125.

12. B21, p. 183.

13. B577, v. 3, p. 124.

14. B575, p. 125.

15. B21, p. 253.

16. B21, p. 241.

17. D51a, Jacket notes.

18. B21, p. 271.

19. D42a, Jacket notes.

20. D43a, Jacket notes.

21. B21, p. 279.

22. B70, p. 4.

23. "Recordings," *American Composers Alliance Bulletin*, 2, No. 3 (October 1953), 8.

24. "Recordings," *American Composers Alliance Bulletin*, 2, No. 3 (October 1953), 8.

25. B156, p. 19.

26. B274.

27. B22, p. 16.

28. B259, p. 6; B517, p. 330.

29. B202, p. 8.

30. B22, p. 17.

31. B22, p. 17.

32. B265.

33. B76.

34. D2a, Jacket notes.

35. B107, p. 17-18.

36. B174, p. 377-378.

37. B144.

38. B209.

39. B398, p. 203.

40. B29a. p. 135.

41.   B29a. p. 135.

42.   B437, p. 14.

43.   B317, p. 43.

44.   B563, p. 18.

45.   B398, p. 234-235.

46.   B105.

47.   B322,p. 17.

48.   D10, Jacket notes.

49.   B112, p. 202.

50.   B91, p. 7.

51.   B63.

52.   *Arlington Civic Symphony Program*, October 25, 1964, p. 11.

53.   D46a, Jacket notes.

54.   B273, p. 25.

55.   D41a, Jacket notes.

56.   Philip Friedheim, "Laderman, Ezra," in *New Grove Dictionary of American Music* (London: Macmillan, 1986), v. 3, p. 3.

57.   Edward Murray, "Chou Wen-chung," in *New Grove Dictionary of American Music* (London: Macmillan, 1986), v. 1, p. 437.

58.   B29a, p. 138.

59.   Lester Trimble and Noel B. Zahler, "Davidovsky, Mario," in *New Grove Dictionary of American Music* (London: Macmillan, 1986), v. 1, p. 582.

60.   B2, p. 9.

61. "Recordings," *American Composers Alliance Bulletin*, 2, No. 3 (October 1953), 8.

62. B21, p.1

63. B167, p. 18.

64. B29a, p. 145.

Works and Performances
(W1-W272)

1906

W1.   *Little Miniature Pieces*
           For piano.

1907

W2.   *Theme with Variations*
           For piano.

1913

W3.   *Piano Piece*

W4.   *Waltz*
           For piano.

1914

W5.   *Piece for String Quartet* (4 min.)

W6.   *Trio for Women's Voices* (2 min.)
        Soprano, mezzo-soprano, and alto.

1915

W7.   *An dem Traume* (3 min.)
        Soprano and piano; Text by Peter Cornelius.

W8.   *Der Eichwald* (3 min.)
        Soprano and piano; Text by Nikolaus Lenau.

W9.   *Fantasie Stücke*
        For piano.

W10.   *Piece for Organ* (3 min.)

W11.   *Septembermorgen* (3 min.)
        Soprano or tenor and piano; text by Eduard Morike.

W12.   *Four Short Piano Pieces*

W13.   *Wir Wandeln alle den Weg* (3 min.)
        Soprano and piano; Text by Friedrich von Bodenstadt.

1916

W14.   *Two Songs for Soprano and Piano* (4 min.)
        Soprano and piano; Old German sacred texts.

1917

W15. *Cum Sancto Spiritu* (4 min.)
      Vocal fugue for SATB.

W16. *Doppelfugue* (9 min.)
      For string quartet.

W17. *Fugue for Piano.*

W18. *Gavotte for Cello and Piano.* (3 min.)

W19. *Gavotte for piano.*

W20. *Three Songs for Soprano and Piano or Small Orchestra* (6 min.)
      Songs for soprano or tenor and piano, composed 1917-1922; version
      for soprano and small orchestra completed 1927.
      In Weihnachtszeiten = At Christmastime (3:00) / text by Hermann
      Hesse -- Noon Silence (1:30) / text by William Sharpe -- Venilia
      (1:30) / text by William Sharpe.

   Premieres:

   W20a. 1924 (February 19): Chicago; Helene Luening, soprano; Otto
          Luening, piano.

   W20b. 1926 (December 30): Rochester, New York; Ethel Codd (Luening),
          soprano; Rochester Little Symphony; Howard Hanson, conductor.

   Performances:

   W20c. "At Christmastime": 1933 (January 12): San Francisco; Fairmont
          Hotel; Ethel Luening, soprano; Otto Luening, piano.

   W20d. "At Christmastime": 1980 (December 1): New York; Manhattan
          School of Music; Group for Contemporary Music.

Otto Luening

W21.   *Minuet for Cello and Piano*. (3 min.)

W22.   *Mysterium* (3 min.)
             Soprano or tenor and piano; text by Ernst Frey.

W23.   *One Step for Piano*.

W24.   *Piano Piece*.

W25.   *Requiescat* (2 min.)
             Soprano and piano; text by Oscar Wilde.

W26.   *Sonata for Violin and Piano No. 1* (12 min.; American Society of
             University Composers, 1974)
                 Previous publisher: American Composers Alliance, 1952.

         Performances:

    W26a.   1921 (December 9): Chicago; Rudolph Mangold, violin; Otto
                 Luening, piano.

    W26b.   1979 (April 1): Kenosha, Wisconsin; University of Wisconsin at
                 Parkside; S. Eden Vaning, violin; Barbara English Maris, piano.

W27.   *Thema con Variazione* (15 min.)
             For piano.

W28.   *Three Swiss Folk Songs* (3 min.)
             Arrangement for SATB.

1918

W29.   *Choral Vorspiel zu Christus der ist mein Leben* (1 min., 30 sec.)
       For organ.

W30.   *Fruhling* (2 min.)
       Soprano or tenor and piano; text by Hermann Hesse.

W31.   *Fuga a tre voci in C minor* (3 min.)
       For piano.

W32.   *Sextet* (20 min.; Highgate Press, 1976; Bardic Edition, 1988)
       Flute, clarinet, horn, violin, viola, violoncello.
       Previous publisher: American Composers Alliance, 1958.

   Premiere:

   W32a.   1921 (April 30): Zurich; Freie Orchestervereinigung; Hans
           Zimmerman, conductor.

   Performances:

   W32b.   1921 (December 9): Chicago; Members of the Chicago Symphony.

   W32c.   1980 (November 20): New York; Carnegie Recital Hall;
           International Society for Contemporary Music.

   W32d.   1981 (May 3): Kenosha, Wisconsin; University of Wisconsin at
           Parkside; An ensemble conducted by Scott Mather.

   W32e.   1981 (November 11): Milwaukee, Wisconsin; Wisconsin
           Conservatory of Music, sponsors; faculty members were probably
           performers.

   W32f.   1983 (July 9): New Paltz, New York; State University of New York.

   W32g.   1986 (June 3): New York; Whitney Museum; International Society
           for Contemporary Music.

W33. *Slumbersong* (45 sec.)
      For piano.

W34. *Variations on Christus der ist mein Leben* (4 min.; Highgate Press)
      For 4 horns.

W35. *Vater unser im Himmelreich* (1 min., 30 sec.)
      Mixed chorus, SATB.

1919

W36. *Sonatina for Flute and Piano* (5 min.; New Valley Music Press, 1976)
      Previous publisher: American Composers Alliance, 1952.

   Premiere:

   W36a. 1924 (February 19): Chicago; Otto Luening, flute; Flora Zygman,
          piano.

W37. *Fugue for String Quartet* (4 min.)

W38. *String Quartet No. 1* (1919-1920) (Clarinet obligato; 40 min.; Highgate
      Press)

   Premiere:

   W38a. 1922 (February 14): Chicago; Rudolph Mangold, 1st violin;
          Members of the Chicago Symphony.

   Performance:

   W38b. 1924 (March): Berlin; Roth Quartet.

W39. *Wie sind die Tage* (2 min.)
      Soprano or tenor and piano; text by Hermann Hesse.

1921

W40.   *Introitus*
           For organ.

   Premiere:

     W40a.   1921 (July 17): South Bend, Indiana; Notre Dame University,
             Wilhelm Middelschulte, organ.

W41.   *Music for Piano--A Contrapuntal Study* (5 min., 30 sec.; Highgate Press)

W42.   *Trio for Violin, Cello and Piano* (17 min.; Highgate Press, 1952)

   Premiere:

     W42a.   1922 (October 26): Chicago; Rudolph Mangold, violin; Bruno
             Steindel, cello; Ella Spravka, piano.

   Performances:

     W42b.   1934 (November): Bennington, Vermont; Bennington College;
             Mariana Lowell, violin; Margaret Aue, cello; Gregory Tucker,
             piano.

     W42c.   1982 (April 2): Kenosha, Wisconsin; University of Wisconsin at
             Parkside; Oriana Trio (Elaine Skorodin, violin; Harry Sturm, cello;
             Carol Bell, piano)

1922

W43.   *Chorale Fantasy for Organ* (8 min.; World Library Publications)
           Previous publisher: American Composers Alliance, 1952.

   Premiere:

     W43a.   1922: South Bend, Indiana; Notre Dame University; Wilhelm
             Middelschulte, organ.

Performances:

W43b. 1960 (April 21): New York; St. Paul's Chapel; Ralph Kneeream, organ.

W43c. 1960 (May 5): New York; Columbia University; Ralph Kneeream, organ.

W43d. 1960 (July 6): New York; Columbia University; Ralph Kneeream, organ.

W43e. 1971 (May 9): San Francisco; Fred Tulan, organ.

W43f. 1971 (August 18): San Francisco; St. Mary's Cathedral; Fred Tulan, organ.

W43g. 1971 (November 24): Cambridge, Mass.; Harvard University; Fred Tulan, organ.

W44. *Coal Scuttle Blues* (8 min.; Associated Music Publishers, 1944)
For two pianos; With Ernst Bacon.

Premiere:

W44a. 1946 (March 3): New York; Times Hall; Elizabeth Mulfinger, Ernst Bacon, pianos.

Performances:

W44b. 1982 (April 2): Kenosha, Wisconsin; University of Wisconsin at Parkside; Carol Bell, August Wegner, pianos.

W44c. 1986 (June 3): New York; Whitney Museum; International Society for Contemporary Music.

W45. *Enigma Canon* (4 min.)
Mixed chorus, SSAATB; Theme by Johann Sebastian Bach.

W46.   *Sonata for Violin and Piano No. 2* (15 min.; Highgate Press)
             In one movement.

Premiere:

W46a.   1927: Rochester, New York.

W47.   *Transcience* (About 2 min.; American Composers Alliance)
             Soprano and piano; Text by Sarojini Naidu.

W48.   *Variations on the National Air "Yankee Doodle"* (6 min.)
             For piccolo and piano.

1923

W49.   *Concertino for Flute and Chamber Orchestra* (20 min.; C. F. Peters,
             1969)
                 For flute, harp, celeste and strings.

Premiere:

W49a.   1935 (January 30): Philadelphia; Otto Luening, flute; Chamber
             Orchestra of Philadelphia; Isadore Freed, conductor.

Performance:

W49b.   1986 (February 2-3): Cleveland; Cleveland Chamber Symphony;
             Edwin London, conductor.

W50.   *Legend for Violin and Piano* (6 min.)
             1923-1924.
             Previous publisher: American Composers Alliance, 1952.

W51.   *Music for Orchestra* (18 min.; Highgate Press)

    Premiere:

W51a. 1978 (May 23): New York; Alice Tully Hall; American Composers Orchestra; Gunther Schuller, conductor.

W52.   *The Soundless Song* (25 min.; Highgate Press)
    Soprano, flute, clarinet, 2 violins, viola, cello, dancers, and light; songs also for soprano and piano; Text by Luening.

    Premiere:

W52a. 1944 (February 13): New York; New York Public Library; Maria Maximovitch, soprano; Hellmut Baerwald, piano.

    Performances:

W52b. 1981 (November 11): Milwaukee, Wisconsin; Marlee Sabo, soprano, with string quartet, flute, clarinet and piano.

W52c. 1984 (May 8): New York; Manhattan School of Music; Danielle Woerner.

W53.   *String Quartet No. 2* (9 min.; C. F. Peters, 1976)
    In one movement. Dedicated to Philipp Jarnach.
    Previous publishers: American Composers Alliance, 1952; Galaxy, 1965.

    Premiere:

W53a. 1965 (December 13): New York; Columbia University; Jean Benjamin Quartet for the Group for Contemporary Music.

    Performances:

W53b. 1971 (October 20): Munich; Sinnhoffer Quartet.

W53c. 1976 (February 8): New York; National Arts Club; Blue Hill String Quartet.

1924

W54.   *Two Bagatelles for Piano* (2 min.)

W55.   *Sonata for Cello Solo No. 1* (6 min.; Highgate Press, 1952)
         Previous publisher: American Composers Alliance, 1952.

Performances:

W55a.   1955 (March 1): Munich; Milton Forstat, cello.

W55b.   1963 (March 11): New York; Columbia University; Joel Krosnick,
         violoncello.

W56.   *Symphonic Fantasia No. 1* (9 min.; American Composers Alliance;
         Galaxy, 1963)
         For orchestra, with percussion, harp, celeste, piano, and organ.
         Former title: *Symphonic Poem.*

Premiere:

W56a.   1925 (November 25): Rochester, New York; American Composers
         Concerts; Rochester Philharmonic Orchestra; Howard Hanson,
         conductor.

Performances:

W56b.   1935 (October 16): New York; Brooklyn Symphony Orchestra of the
         WPA; Franco Autori, conductor.

W56c.   1986 (February 28): New York; McMillin Theater; National
         Orchestra of New York; Efrain Guigui, conductor.

W57.   *Trio for Flute, Violin and Soprano* (6 min.; Highgate Press; Galaxy, 1960)
       Without words.

Premiere:

W57a.   1957 (March 18): New York; Music in Our Time Series; no performers listed.

Performances:

W57b.   1957 (April 8): New York; YMHA Kaufmann Auditorium; Otto Luening, flute; Max Pollikoff, violin; and Matilda Nickel, soprano; in "Music in Our Time" series.

W57c.   1983 (May 10): New York; Manhattan School of Music.

1926

W58.   *Hymn to Bacchus* (3 min.)
       For piano.

W59.   *Sister Beatrice*
       Intermedia for organ, alto, mixed chorus. For 3 act play by Maurice Maeterlinck, translated by Paul Horgan.

Premiere:

W59a.   1926 (January 15): Rochester, New York; Kilbourn Hall; Performers from the Eastman School of Dance, Rochester, New York; Martha Atwell, Sister Beatrice; Rouben Mamoulian, theater director.

1927

W60.   *Gliding O'er All* (1 min.; G. Schirmer; Rights reverted to composer)
         Song for soprano and piano; Text by Walt Whitman.
         Also published with W76 and W64 by Schirmer as *Three Songs*,
         1944.

   Premiere:

   W60a.   1944 (February 13): New York; New York Public Library; Maria
           Maximovitch, soprano; Hellmut Baerwald, piano.

W61.   *If That High World* (3 min.; Arrow Music, 1941; C. F. Peters, 1964)
         Women's chorus, SSA a cappella; Text by Lord Byron.

   Performances:

   W61a.   1952 (May 4): New York; Three Choir Festival, Temple Emanu-el;
           University Singers and Emanu-el Choir; Otto Luening, conductor.

   W61b.   1953 (March 4): Lindsborg, Kansas; Bethany College; S.A.I. Chorus;
           Norma Wendelberg, probable conductor.

   W61c.   1976 (February 19): Baton Rouge; Louisiana State University; LSU
           A Cappella Choir; Victor Klimash, conductor.

   W61d.   1987 (March 7): New York; Gregg Smith Singers; Gregg Smith,
           conductor.

W62.   *Serenade for Three Horns and String Orchestra* (8 min.; Highgate Press)
         Commissioned by the Rochester Philharmonic.

   Premiere:

   W62a.   1928 (January 12): Rochester, New York; Rochester Philharmonic
           Orchestra; Eugene Goossens, conductor.

Performance:

W62b.   1928 (March 19): Rochester, New York; Rochester Philharmonic Orchestra; Howard Hanson, conductor.

W63.   *Sun of the Sleepless (So Gleams the Past)* (2 min., 30 sec.; R. D. Row Music; Rights reverted to composer)
Women's chorus, SSA a cappella; Text by Lord Byron.

Performances:

W63a.   1938 (May): Bennington, Vermont; Bennington College; University Women's Chorus.

W63b.   1952 (May 4): New York; Three Choir Festival, Temple Emanu-el; University Singers and Emanu-el Choir, Otto Luening, conductor.

W63c.   1954 (December 5): New York; Temple Emanu-el; Emanu-el Choir.

1928

W64.   *Auguries of Innocence (To See the World in a Grain of Sand)* (1 min.; G. Schirmer; RRTC)
Song for soprano and piano; Text by William Blake.
Also published with W76 and W60 by Schirmer as Three Songs, 1944.

Performance:

W64a.   1953 (August 25): Bennington, Vermont; Bennington College; Ethel Luening, soprano; Lionel Nowak, piano.

W65.   *The Birth of Pleasure* (Highgate Press)
Song for soprano and piano; text by Percy Bysshe Shelley.

W66.   *Eight Piano Pieces* (Galaxy)
        Chorale -- Humoresque -- Intermezzo I -- Intermezzo II -- Prelude
        No. 1 "Starlight." -- Prelude No. 2 "The Philosopher." -- Prelude No.
        3 "Introspection." -- Prelude No. 4 "To the Warriors."

W67.   *Infant Joy* (1 min.; G. Schirmer; Highgate Press)
        Song for soprano and piano; Text by William Blake.

W68.   *Locations and Times* (1 min.; Highgate Press)
        Song for soprano and piano; Text by Walt Whitman.

    Performance:

    W68a.   1949 (January 12): Hartford, Connecticut; Institute of Contemporary
            American Music, University of Hartford; Margaret Burtaine,
            soprano; Elizabeth Warner, piano.

W69.   *A Roman's Chamber* (1 min.; Highgate Press)
        Song for soprano and piano; Text by Percy Bysshe Shelley.

    Performances:

    W69a.   1949 (January 12): Hartford, Connecticut; Institute of Contemporary
            American Music, University of Hartford; Margaret Burtaine,
            soprano; Elizabeth Warner, piano.

    W69b.   1981 (May 3): Kenosha, Wisconsin; University of Wisconsin at
            Parkside; Martha Dodds, soprano; Barbara English Maris, piano.

W70.   *Six Short and Easy Piano Pieces* (5 min.; Bradley Publications, 1980)

W71.   *Songs of Experience* (4 min.; Highgate Press, 1986)
        Bass-baritone and piano; text by William Blake.
        Hear the Voice of the Bard -- Earth's Answer.

Performance:

W71a.   "Earth's Answer": 1958 (November 21): Poughkeepsie, New York;
        Skinner Recital Hall, Vassar College; Marvin Hayes, bass-baritone;
        Lalan Parrott, piano.

W72.   *String Quartet No. 3* (17 min.; C. F. Peters, 1978)
        Dedicated to Oliver Daniel.
        Previous publisher: American Composers Alliance, 1952.

Premiere:

W72a.   1937 (September 19): Saratoga Springs, New York; Yaddo Festival.

Performances:

W72b.   1945 (April 25): Rochester, New York; Gordon String Quartet
        (Jacques Gordon, Walter Hagen, violins; Kras Malno, viola; Gabor
        Rejto, cello).

W72c.   1971: Munich; Sinnhoffer Quartet.

W73.   *To Morning* (1 min., 30 sec.; Highgate Press)
        Song for soprano and piano; Text by William Blake.

Performance:

W73a.   1949 (January 12): Hartford, Connecticut; Institute of Contemporary
        American Music, University of Hartford; Margaret Burtaine,
        soprano; Elizabeth Warner, piano.

W74.   *Visored* (1 min.; Highgate Press)
        Song for soprano and piano; Text by Walt Whitman.

   Performance:

   W74a.   1949 (January 12): Hartford, Connecticut; Institute of Contemporary
           American Music, University of Hartford; Margaret Burtaine,
           soprano; Elizabeth Warner, piano.

W75.   *Wake the Serpent Not* (1 min., 30 sec.; Highgate Press)
        Song for soprano and piano; Text by Percy Bysshe Shelley.

   Performances:

   W75a.   1949 (January 12): Hartford, Connecticut; Institute of Contemporary
           American Music, University of Hartford; Margaret Burtaine,
           soprano; Elizabeth Warner, piano.

   W75b.   1981 (May 3): Kenosha, Wisconsin; University of Wisconsin at
           Parkside; Martha Dodds, soprano; Barbara English Maris, piano.

W76.   *Young Love* (1 min.; G. Schirmer; RRTC)
        Song for soprano and piano; Text by William Blake.
        Also published with W60 and W64 by Schirmer as Three Songs,
        1944.

   Performance:

   W76a.   1980 (December 1): New York; Manhattan School of Music; Group
           for Contemporary Music.

1929

W77.   *Dance Sonata for Piano* (13 min.; Highgate Press; 1976)
        Slow dance -- Blues -- Andante -- Allegro.

   Premiere:

   W77a.   1946 (February 15): New York; WNYC; Gregory Tucker, piano.

W78. *Fantasia for Organ* (7 min.; C. F. Peters, 1963)
    Previous publisher: Circle Blue Print Co., 1952.

Performances:

W78a. 1958 (May 25): New York; Church of the Incantation; Leonard
    Raver, organ.

W78b. 1958 (July 31): New York; St. Paul's Chapel, Columbia University;
    Leonard Raver, organ.

W78c. 1962 (July 18): New York; Ralph Kneeream, organ.

W78d. 1983 (May 1): Kenosha, Wisconsin; University of Wisconsin at
    Parkside; Glenda Mossman, organ.

W79. *Fantasia Brevis, for Flute and Piano* (6 min.; Highgate Press, 1974)
    Previous publisher: American Composers Alliance, 1952.

Performances:

W79a. 1975 (Spring Semester): Bennington, Vermont; Bennington College;
    Sue Ann Kahn, flute; Lionel Nowak, piano.

W79b. 1983 (May 1): Kenosha, Wisconsin; University of Wisconsin at
    Parkside; Marjorie Roth, flute; James McKeever, piano.

W80. *A Farm Picture* (1 min.; Associated Music Publishers, 1944)
    Song for soprano and piano; Text by Walt Whitman.

Performance:

W80a. 1949 (January 12): Hartford, Connecticut; Institute of Contemporary
    American Music, University of Hartford; Margaret Burtaine,
    soprano; Elizabeth Warner, piano.

W81.   *For Like a Chariot's Wheel* (1 min.; Highgate Press)
         Soprano and piano; Anonymous text.

   Performance:

   W81a.   1953 (August 25): Bennington, Vermont; Bennington College; Ethel
           Luening, soprano; Lionel Nowak, piano.

W82.   *Goodnight* (1 min.; Highgate Press)
         Song for soprano and piano; Text by Percy Bysshe Shelley.

   Performance:

   W82a.   1981 (May 3): Kenosha, Wisconsin; University of Wisconsin at
           Parkside; Martha Dodds, soprano; Barbara English Maris, piano.

W83.   Here the Frailest Leaves of Me (1 min.; Highgate Press)
         Song for soprano and piano; Text by Walt Whitman.
         Previous publisher: Associated Music Publishers, 1944.

   Performances:

   W83a.   1935 (December 1): New York; Town Hall; Music Guild Lecture
           Recital; Ethel Luening, soprano; Otto Luening, piano.

   W83b.   1949 (January 12): Hartford, Connecticut; Institute of Contemporary
           American Music, University of Hartford; Margaret Burtaine,
           soprano; Elizabeth Warner, piano.

W84.   *I Faint, I Perish* (1 min.; Highgate Press)
         Song for soprano and piano; Text by Percy Bysshe Shelley.

1930

W85.   *Evangeline* (2 hr., 30 min.; Associated Music ; C. F. Peters, 1974)
         Opera; libretto by the composer on Henry W. Longfellow's
         Evangeline story. Originally commissioned by American Opera
         Company with a Guggenheim Fellowship.
         Composed 1930-1932, 1947.

Premiere:

W85a.   1948 (May 5-7, May 10-12): New York; Columbia University;
         Teresa Stich-Randall, soprano; Otto Luening directing.

Other selected performances:

W85b.   1955 (October 28): St. Martinville, Louisiana; Acadian Bicentennial
         Celebration; Otto Luening directing.

W85c.   1985 (February): Queens, New York; Queensborough Community
         College; After Dinner Opera Company.

W85d.   1985 (February 11): New York; Lincoln Center, Bruno Walter
         Auditorium, New York Public Library; After Dinner Opera
         Company; Richard Flusser, conductor.

W85e.   1986 (May 2-3): Brunswick, Maine; Bowdoin College; Bonnie
         Scarpelli, soprano; Oratorio Chorale; Bowdoin College Chorale;
         Robert Greenlee, conductor.

Excerpts:

W85f.   1932 (December 29): Chicago; Arts Club of Chicago; Ethel Luening,
         soprano; Otto Luening, piano.

W85g.   1934 (November): Bennington, Vermont; Bennington College; Ethel
         Luening, soprano; Otto Luening, piano.

W85h.   1958 (February 9): New York; Carl Fischer Hall; Angela Giordano,
         soprano; Everrett Anderson, baritone; Antonio Lora, piano.

W85i.   1958 (February 17): New York; WNYC American Festival of Music, Carl Fischer Hall; Angela Giordano, soprano; Joseph Lambaise, tenor; Everrett Anderson, baritone; Antonio Lora, piano.

W85j.   1978 (March 15): Danbury, Connecticut; Arts Festival; Western Connecticut State College; Entitled "20th Century American Pioneers"; Don Craig, conductor.

W85k.   "Arietta": 1933 (January 12): San Francisco; Fairmont Hotel; Ethel Luening, soprano; Otto Luening, piano.

W85l.   "Indian Legend": 1950 (January 22): New York; NAACC; Ruth Krug, soprano.

W86.   *Short Fantasy for Violin and Horn* (2 min.; Highgate Press, 1971)

Performance:

W86a.   1987 (September 6); Brewster, New York; Old Southeast Church; Doansburgh Chamber Ensemble; Kenneth Hawes, horn; Robert Zubrycki, violin.

1931

W87.   *Behold the Tabernacle of God* (3 min.; American Composers Alliance)
       Mixed chorus, SATB, soprano solo.

1932

W88.   *Anthem* (4 min.)
       Mixed chorus, SATB, with organ.

W89.   *The Dawn* (1 min., 30 sec.; Highgate Press)
         Soprano and piano; Anon. text.

Performances:

W89a.   1933 (January 12): San Francisco; Fairmont Hotel; Ethel Luening,
         soprano; Otto Luening, piano.

W89b.   1949 (January 12): Hartford, Connecticut; Institute of Contemporary
         American Music, University of Hartford; Margaret Burtaine,
         soprano; Elizabeth Warner, piano.

W89c.   1970 (February 14): New York; Century Association; Stephanie
         Turash, soprano.

W90.   *Fantasia For Piano.* (4 min.)

W91.   *Five Intermezzi* (6 min.; American Composers Alliance; Highgate Press)
         Piano; 1932-1936.
         Intermezzo I-II -- Birds -- Swans -- Stars.

W92.   *When in the Languor of Evening* (5 min.; American Composers
         Alliance)
         Soprano solo, SATB chorus, string/woodwind quartet, piano; Text
         by J. Murrary Gibbon.

1933

W93.   *Mañana* (5 min.; Arrow Music Press, 1941; RRTC)
         Violin and piano.

Performance:

W93a.   1957 (February 17): New York; Museum of the City of New York;
         Florence Nicolaides, violin; Kitta Brown, piano.

1935

W94.   *Phantasy (Fantasy) for Piano* (6 min.; Galaxy, 1958)

W95.   *Six Preludes for Piano* (14 min.; Highgate Press)
        Composed 1935-1951.

Performance:

W95a.   1955 (January 19): New York; Two Preludes were performed at the
        New School of Social Research; Don Shapiro, piano.

W96.   *Two Symphonic Interludes* (No.1: 3 1/2 min.; Edgar Stillman-Kelley
        Society, 1937; No. 2: 8 min.; C. F. Peters, 1964)

Premiere:

W96a.   1936 (April 11): New York; Carnegie Hall; New York Philharmonic;
        Hans Lange, conductor.

Performances:

W96b.   1937 (March 11-12): Chicago; Chicago Symphony Orchestra; Hans
        Lange, conductor.

W96c.   1939 (February): St. Louis, Missouri; St. Louis Symphony; Vladimir
        Golschmann, conductor.

W96d.   1963 (October 22-23): Erie, Penn.; Erie Philharmonic Society; Otto
        Luening, conductor.

W96e.   Symphonic Interlude no. 1: 1959 (May 10): Knoxville, Tennessee;
        University of Tennessee; Knoxville Symphony Orchestra/University
        Training Orchestra.

W96f.   Symphonic Interlude no. 2: 1980 (August 13): Lenox, Massachusetts;
        Berkshire Music Center Orchestra; Gunther Schuller, conductor.

1936

W97.   *Andante for Piano* (4 min.; Highgate Press)

W98.   *At the Last* (1 min., 30 sec.; Highgate Press)
        Soprano and piano; Text by Walt Whitman.

W99.   *Eight Preludes for Piano* (8 min.; New Music Edition, 1942; T. Presser, 1974)
        In *New Music Quarterly*, v. 15, no. 3.

   Performances:

   W99a.   1944 (February 13): New York; New York Public Library; Lydia Hoffman Behrendt, piano.

   W99b.   1949 (January 12): Hartford, Connecticut; Institute of Contemporary American Music, University of Hartford; Madelyn Robb, piano.

W100.   *Fantasia Brevis for Violin, Viola, Cello* (4 min.; Highgate Press; Joshua, 1976)
        Previous publisher: American Composers Alliance, 1952.

W101.   *Fantasia Brevis for Clarinet and Piano* (6 min.; New Music Edition, 1937; T. Presser, 1973)

   Premiere:

   W101a.   1936 (September 12-13): Saratoga Springs, New York; Yaddo Music Festival.

   Performances:

   W101b.   1936 (November): Bennington, Vermont; Robert McBride, clarinet; Otto Luening, piano.

W101c.   1976 (February 19): Baton Rouge; Louisiana State University; Harold Ayme, clarinet; Nancy Saxon, piano.

W101d.   1979 (April 1): Kenosha, Wisconsin; University of Wisconsin at Parkside; Timothy Bell, clarinet; August Wegner, piano.

W102.   *Forever Lost* (Highgate Press)
Song; for soprano and piano; Text by Genevieve Taggard.

W103.   *Hast Never Come to Thee* (1 min.; Highgate Press)
Soprano and flute; Text by Walt Whitman.

W104.   *Only Themselves Understand Themselves* (1 min.; New Music Edition, 1935; T. Presser)
Soprano, mezzo-soprano, tenor or baritone and piano; Text by Walt Whitman.
In *New Music Quarterly*, v. 8, no. 4 (July 1935)

Performance:

W104a.   1944 (February 13): New York; New York Public Library; Maria Maximovitch, soprano; Hellmut Baerwald, piano.

W105.   *Suite for Soprano and Flute* (8 min.; American Composers Alliance; Highgate Press, 1966)
Without words; 1936-1937.
Night Piece -- Dawn Piece -- Morning Song -- Evening Song

Performances:

W105a.   1937: Bennington, Vermont; Ethel Luening, soprano; Otto Luening, flute.

W105b.   1970 (February 14): New York; The Century Association; Stephanie Turash, soprano.

W105c.   1980 (November 20): New York; Carnegie Recital Hall; International Society for Contemporary Music; Sue Ann Kahn, flute; Judith Bettina, soprano.

W106.   *Swing, Swing and Swoon* (1 min.; Highgate Press)
Soprano and piano; Text by Genevieve Taggard.

1937

W107.   *Happy Sinner* (1 min., 30 sec.; RRTC)
For soprano, flute and piano; Text by Irving Fineman.

Performance:

W107a.   1937 (March 22): New York; Town Hall; Ethel Luening, soprano; Otto Luening, flute; Willard Rhodes, piano.

W108.   *Prelude to a Hymn Tune by William Billings* (10 min.; Edition Musicus ; C. F. Peters, 1943)
For orchestra. Tune is Billings' *Hymn to Music*.

Premiere:

W108a.   1937 (February 1): New York; Town Hall; New York Philharmonic Chamber Orchestra; Otto Luening, conductor.

Performances:

W108b.   1937 (September 18): Saratoga Springs, New York; Yaddo Music Festival; Yaddo Orchestra; Otto Luening, conductor.

W108c.   1960 (February 21): New York; American Museum of Natural History; City Symphony Orchestra; Franz Bibo, director.

W109.   *Short Ballad* (2 min.; American Composers Alliance)
Retitled: *Elegy for the Lonesome Ones*
For two clarinets and strings.

W110.   *Short Sonata for Flute and Piano No. 1* (8 min.; Highgate Press)
Or for flute and harpsichord.
Previous publisher: American Composers Alliance, 1952.

Performances:

W110a.   1949 (January 12): Hartford, Connecticut; Institute of
Contemporary American Music, University of Hartford; Otto
Luening, flute; Maxim Shapiro, piano.

W110b.   1949 (January 23): New York; John Wummer, flute; Edmund
Haines, piano.

W110c.   1952 (February 18): New York; WNYC; Mildred Wummer, flute.

W111.   *Suite for String Orchestra* (10 min.; Boosey & Hawkes, 1942)

Premiere:

W111a.   1937 (September 12): Saratoga Springs, New York; Yaddo Music
Festival; New York Philharmonic; F. Charles Adler, conductor.

Performances:

W111b.   1941 (January 22): Rochester, New York; Rochester Civic
Orchestra; Howard Hanson, conductor.

Radio performances:

W111c.   "Dance" from this suite: 1952 (January 13): CBS Radio; Alfred
Antonini and the Alfred Antonini String Orchestra.

W111d.   "Air" from this suite: 1952 (February 24): CBS Radio; Alfred
Antonini and the Alfred Antonini String Orchestra.

1938

W112.   *Short Fantasy for Violin and Piano* (1 min., 30 sec.; Highgate Press)
Previous publisher: American Composers Alliance, 1952.

W113.   *Fuguing Tune for Woodwind Quintet* (5 min.; Associated Music
        Publishers, 1944, 1982; RRTC)
        For flute, oboe, clarinet, bassoon, horn.

W114.   *Eight Inventions for Piano* (14 min. total; Inventions 1 and 2 published
        by Mercury, 1943; 3-8 by Joshua Corp., 1976)

   Performance:

   W114a.   "Two Inventions" (No. 1-2): 1949 (January 12): Hartford,
            Connecticut; Institute of Contemporary American Music,
            University of Hartford; Madelyn Robb, piano.

1939

W115.   *Symphonic Fantasia No. 2* (15 min.; American Composers Alliance)
        For orchestra, with harp, piano; 1939-1949.

   Performances:

   W115a.   1954 (October 26): New York; Carnegie Hall; New York
            Philharmonic; Leopold Stokowski, conductor.

   W115b.   1957 (October 18): New York; During the "Music in the Making"
            series, Cooper Union; David Broekman, conductor.

1940

W116.   *The Bass with the Delicate Air* (6 min.; Highgate Press, 1974)
For flute, oboe, clarinet, bassoon.
Previous publisher: American Composers Alliance, 1958.

Performance:

W116a.   1983 (May 1): Kenosha, Wisconsin; University of Wisconsin at
Parkside; Marjorie Roth, flute; William Wielgus, oboe; Timothy
Bell, clarinet; Daryl Durran, bassoon.

W117.   *Blood Wedding*
Incidental music for 3 act play adapted by Francis Fergusson; for
violin, piano, and voices; Text by Federico Garcia-Lorca.

Premiere:

W117a.   1940 (December 1): Bennington, Vermont; Music/Drama
Departments of Bennington College.

W118.   *Christ is Arisen* (2 min., 30 sec.; Joshua Corp., 1981)
Mixed chorus, SSAATB, with piano, organ string quartet or winds
ad lib.

Performance:

W118a.   1987 (March 7): New York; Gregg Smith Singers; Gregg Smith,
conductor.

W119.   *Short Sonata for Piano No. 1* (8 min., 10 sec.; Joshua Corp., 1976)

W120. *Variations for Harpsichord or Piano* (9 min.; American Composers Alliance; Bradley)

Performances:

W120a. 1953 (March 22): New York; New York Historical Society; Yella Pessl, harpsichord.

W120b. 1953 (November 13): New York; New School of Social Research; Don Shapiro, piano.

W120c. 1955 (January 19): New York; New School of Social Research; Don Shapiro, piano.

W120d. 1956 (August 14): Tel-Aviv, Israel; Z.O.A. House; Don Shapiro, piano.

1941

W121. *Canonical Study* (7 min.)
For piano.

W122. *Canons for Harpsichord* (5 min.; Bradley Publications, 1980)
Previous publisher: Galaxy, 1960.

W123. *Easy Canons for Piano* (9 min.)

1942

W124. *Aria for Cello and Piano* (8 min.; 1942-1943; Highgate Press)

W125.   *Dickinson Song Cycle* (10 min.; Highgate Press, 1983)
          Nine songs for soprano and piano (1942-1951).
          No. 1. Our share of the night to bear -- No. 2. The Show is not the
          Show -- No. 3. Hope is the Thing with Feathers -- No. 4. If I Can
          Stop One Heart from Breaking -- No. 5. Experiment to me -- No.
          6. I Felt a Cleavage in my mind -- No. 7. Few Get Enough -- No.
          8. Soul, Wilt Thou Toss Again? -- No. 9. When I hoped I Feared.

Premiere:

W125a.   1951 (August 21): Bennington, Vermont; Bennington Composers
          Conference; Stephanie Turash.

First public performance:

W125b.   1951 (December 11): New York; Carnegie Recital Hall; Stephanie
          Turash.

Other performances:

W125c.   1958 (May 6): San Francisco, California; The Little Theatre,
          Palace of the Legion of Honor; Phalen Tassie, soprano; LeRoy
          Miller, piano.

W125d.   No. 4. "If I Can Stop One Heart from Breaking": 1944 (February
          13): New York; New York Public Library; Maria Maximovitch;
          Hellmut Baerwald, piano.

W125e.   No. 4. "If I Can Stop One Heart from Breaking": 1980 (December
          9): Washington, D.C.; Library of Congress; Carolyn Haefner,
          soprano; Shirley Anne Seguin, piano.

W125f.   No. 5. "Experiment to me": 1980 (December 9): Washington, D.C.;
          Library of Congress; Carolyn Haefner, soprano; Shirley Anne
          Seguin, piano.

W125g.   No. 6. "I Felt a Cleavage in my Mind": 1980 (December 9):
          Washington, D.C.; Library of Congress; Carolyn Haefner, soprano;
          Shirley Anne Seguin, piano.

W125h.　No. 6. "I Felt a Cleavage in my Mind": 1986 (November 6): Memphis; Memphis State University; Jo Ann Lacquet Sims, mezzo-soprano; Samuel Porter, piano.

W125i.　No. 6. "I Felt a Cleavage in my Mind": 1986 (November 13): Urbana, Illinois; University of Illinois; Jo Ann Lacquet Sims, mezzo-soprano; Samuel Porter, piano.

W126.　*Fantasia for Harpsichord or Piano* (4 min., 30 sec.; Bradley Publications, 1980)

W127.　*Ich denke Dein* (2 min.)
Women's chorus, SSAA, a cappella; text by the composer.

W128.　*Variations on Bach's Chorale Prelude Liebster Jesu wir sind hier* (8 min.; Joshua Corporation, 1976)
For cello and piano; dedicated to George Finckel.
Previous publisher: American Composers Alliance, 1952.

Premiere:

W128a.　1942: Bennington, Vermont; George Finckel, cello; Otto Luening, piano.

Performance:

W128b.　1981 (November 11): Milwaukee, Wisconsin; Michael Masters, cello; Marc Taslitt, piano.

1943

W129.   *Sonata for Violin and Piano No. 3* (15 min.; New Valley Music Press, 1959)
Also called Andante and Variations.
Previous publisher: American Composers Alliance, 1950.

Premiere:

W129a.   1951 (February 6): New York; Carnegie Hall; Maurice Wilk, violin; Leopold Mittman, piano.

Performances:

W129b.   1953 (November 1): New York; Museum of the City of New York; Florence Nicolaides, violin; Kitta Brown, piano.

W129c.   1971 (March 28): Storrs, Connecticut; Group for Contemporary Music.

1944

W130.   *Alleluia* (Westminster College Press; T. Presser, 1949)
Mixed chorus; dedicated to Edgard Varèse.

Performances:

W130a.   1947 (April 20): New York; New Music Society, Choral Group; Edgard Varèse, conductor.

W130b.   1952 (April 27): New York; For the Columbia Festival; broadcast on CBS Radio; Trinity Church Choir; Andrew Tietjen, conductor.

W130c.   1955 (May 6): New York; Trinity Church Choir; on CBS's "Church of the Air".

W130d.   1955 (November 13): New York; Trinity Church Choir; on CBS's "Church of the Air".

W130e. 1956 (April 27): Normal, Illinois; Illinois State University; University Choir; Emma R. Knudson, director.

W130f. 1976 (February 19): Baton Rouge, Louisiana; Louisiana State University; LSU A Cappella Choir; Victor Klimash, conductor.

1945

W131. *Canon in the Octave* (3 min.)
       For piano.

1946

W132. *Ten Pieces for Five Fingers for Piano* (6 min.; Bradley Publications, 1980)
       Children's pieces for piano.

W133. *Pilgrim's Hymn for Chamber Orchestra* (4 min.; T. Presser; RRTC)

Premiere:

W133a. 1946 (September 14): Saratoga Springs, New York; Yaddo Festival; Otto Luening, conductor.

Performances:

W133b. 1952 (October 12): New York; Local 802 Orchestra; David Broekman, conductor.

W133c. 1955 (May 25): Huntington Station, New York; Walt Whitman School.

W134.   *Pilgrim's Hymn for Orchestra* (4 min.; T. Presser; RRTC)
        Revision of W133.

Premiere:

W134a.   1949 (January 23): New York; Philharmonic Symphony of New
         York; Leopold Stokowski, conductor. (1st performance of new
         version for large orchestra)

W135.   *Prelude for Chamber Orchestra* (4 min.; Highgate Press)

Premiere:

W135a.   1946 (September 14): Saratoga Springs, New York; Yaddo
         Festival; Otto Luening, conductor.

W136.   *Suite for Cello and Piano* (16 min.; Highgate Press, 1972)
        For cello or viola and piano.
        Previous publisher: American Composers Alliance, 1951.

Premiere:

W136a.   1946 (ca.): Bennington, Vermont; George Finckel, cello; Otto
         Luening, piano.

Performances:

W136b.   1952 (January 13): New York; Town Hall; George Finckel, cello;
         Otto Luening, piano.

W136c.   1979 (April 1): Kenosha, Wisconsin; University of Wisconsin at
         Parkside; Harry Sturm, cello; Carol Bell, piano.

W136d.   1987 (November 4): Washington, D. C.; Kennedy Center; Joel
         Krosnick, cello; Gilbert Kalish, piano.

1947

W137.   *Pilgrim's Hymn* (T. Presser, 1958; RRTC)
        Chorus, for children's voices, with solo soprano/alto with piano or
        organ; Text by Howard Moss.
        Commissioned by East Woods School, Oyster Bay, Long Island,
        New York.

W138.   *Suite for Flute Solo No. 1* (5 min.; Highgate Press, 1969)

Performance:

   W138a.   1964 (November 8): Madison, Wisconsin; University of Wisconsin
            at Madison; Otto Luening lecture; Robert F. Cole, flute.

1949

W139.   *Divine Image* (3 min.; Edward B. Marks, 1951; Hudson Bay Music
        Company)
        Soprano and piano; words by William Blake.

Performances:

   W139a.   1953 (August 5): New York; McMillin Theater, Columbia
            University; Everett Anderson, baritone; Otto Luening, piano.

   W139b.   1970 (February 14): New York; Century Association; Stephanie
            Turash, soprano.

W140.   *Love's Secret* (3 min.; Edward B. Marks, 1951; Hudson Bay Music
        Company)
        Soprano and piano; Words by William Blake.

Performances:

   W140a.   1949 (January 12): Hartford, Connecticut; Institute of
            Contemporary American Music, University of Hartford; Margaret
            Burtaine, soprano; Elizabeth Warner, piano.

W140b.   1953 (August 5): New York; McMillin Theater, Columbia University; Everett Anderson, baritone; Otto Luening, piano.

W140c.   1957 (April 29): New York; Town Hall; Everett Anderson, baritone; Arpad Sandor, piano.

W140d.   1970 (February 14): New York; Century Association; Stephanie Turash, soprano.

The Maidens of Shang-Ti
See *Vocalise* (W201)

1950

W141.   *Easy March for Wind Instruments and Piano* (2 min.; Juilliard Repertory Library; RRTC)
For recorder, flute, oboe, and piano.

1951

W142.   *The Harp the Monarch Minstrel Swept* (3 min.; Highgate Press)
Soprano and piano; Text by Lord Byron.

Premiere:

W142a.   1951 (April 3): New York; Town Hall; Margaret Turnley, soprano.

Performance:

W142b.   1981 (May 3): Kenosha, Wisconsin; University of Wisconsin at Parkside; Martha Dodds, soprano; Barbara English Maris, piano.

W143.   *Kentucky Concerto* (20 min.; American Composers Alliance, 1952;
          Highgate Press, 1955)
               Original title: "Louisville Concerto"
               For orchestra. Commissioned by the Louisville Orchestra.
               Louisville -- Lexington -- Kentucky Rondo.
               "Kentucky Rondo" (ca. 6 min.; Highgate Press, 1955, 1970)

Premiere:

W143a.   1952 (March 5): Louisville, Kentucky; Louisville Philharmonic
          Symphony; Otto Luening, conductor.

Performances:

W143b.   1953 (January 28): Washington, D. C.; U. S. Air Force Symphony;
          Dai-Keong Lee, conductor.

W143c.   1953 (March 1): New York; Cooper Union; Symphony of the Air;
          David Broekman, conductor.

W143d.   1953 (March 26): Montpelier, Vermont; Vermont Symphony; Alan
          Carter, conductor.

W143e.   1953 (April 12): Springfield, Vermont; Vermont Symphony; Alan
          Carter, conductor.

W143f.   1953 (April 19): Middlebury, Vermont; Vermont Symphony; Alan
          Carter, conductor.

W143g.   1953 (April 20): Norwich, Vermont; Vermont Symphony; Alan
          Carter, conductor.

W143h.   1953 (May 1): New York; Local 802 Orchestra; David Broekman,
          conductor; "Music in the Making Series."

W143i.   1955 (March 17): Bennington, Vermont; Bennington College.

W143j.   1956 (March 11 and 13): Honolulu; Honolulu Symphony; George
          Barati, conductor.

W143k.   1959 (May 24): Washington, D. C.; National Gallery Orchestra;
          Richard Bales, conductor.

W143l.   1959 (October 25): Washington, D. C.; National Gallery Orchestra; Richard Bales, conductor.

Other Performances:

W143m.   "Kentucky Rondo": 1957 (September 8): New York; WNYC Radio.

W143n.   "Kentucky Rondo": 1965 (February 6): Westchester Symphony Orchestra; Newell Jenkins, conductor.

W143o.   "Kentucky Rondo": 1985 (October 19): Burlington, Vermont; Vermont State Symphony; Otto Luening, conductor.

W144.   *Legend for Oboe and Strings* (12 min.; Highgate Press, 1952, 1975)

Premiere:

W144a.   1951 (July 1): New York; Radio Station WNYC; Robert Bloom, oboe; New Chamber Music Society; Paul Wolfe, conductor.

Other selected performances:

W144b.   1951 (August 24): Bennington, Vermont; Bennington Composers Conference, Robert Bloom, oboe; an ensemble conducted by Otto Luening.

W144c.   1952 (July 4-5): Ipswich, Massachusetts; Robert Bloom, oboe; Vermont State Symphony Orchestra; Alan Carter, conductor.

W144d.   1986 (February 28): New York; McMillin Theater, Columbia University; Lisa Kozenko, oboe; National Orchestra of New York; Efrain Guigui, conductor.

W145.   *Three Nocturnes for Oboe and Piano* (ca. 8 min.; Joshua Corp., 1976)
Nights in the Garden of Chopin -- Nights in the Garden of
Paganini -- Nights in the Garden of a Nightclub.

Premiere:

W145a.   1951 (August 15): Bennington, Vermont; Bennington Composers
Conference; Robert Bloom, oboe; Otto Luening, piano.

W146.   *She Walks in Beauty* (Highgate Press)
Song for soprano; Text by Lord Byron.

Premiere:

W146a.   1951 (April 3): New York; Town Hall; Margaret Turnley, soprano.

Performance:

W146b.   1981 (May 3): Kenosha, Wisconsin; University of Wisconsin at
Parkside; Martha Dodds, soprano; Barbara English Maris, piano.

W147.   *The Tiger's Ghost* (4 min.; American Composers Alliance)
Chorus (TTBB); Text by May Swenson.
Commissioned by Leonard de Paur.

Performances:

W147a.   1955: Tour of the De Paur Infantry Chorus; Leonard de Paur,
conductor.

W147b.   1966: Tour of the De Paur Infantry Chorus; Leonard de Paur,
conductor.

W147c.   1967 (April 22): New York; Town Hall; Colgate University Glee
Club; Gilbert Brumgardt, conductor.

1952

W148. *Fantasy in Space* (4 min.; Highgate Press)
       For flute on tape.

   Premiere:

   W148a. 1952 (October 28): New York; Museum of Modern Art; Otto
           Luening, flute.

   Performances:

   W148b. 1952 (December 4): New York; NBC-TV Network.

   W148c. 1953 (March 22): Urbana-Champaign, Illinois; University of
           Illinois.

   W148d. 1953 (March 24): New York; Barnard College.

   W148e. 1953 (April 9): New York; New York Academy of Science.

   W148f. 1953 (June 12 and 17): Paris, France; Centre d'Etudes
           Radiophoniques.

   W148g. 1966 (October 17): Kalamazoo, Michigan; Kalamazoo College.

   W148h. 1970 (May 13): Baltimore; Peabody Conservatory of Music.

   W148i. 1971 (July 13): Baltimore; Peabody Conservatory of Music.

   W148j. 1979 (April 1): Kenosha, Wisconsin; University of Wisconsin at
           Parkside.

W149. *Invention in Twelve Tones* (5 min.; Highgate Press)
       For flute on tape.

   Premiere:

   W149a. 1952 (October 28): New York; Museum of Modern Art; Otto
           Luening, flute.

Performances:

W149b.   1953 (March 24): New York; Barnard College.

W149c.   1953 (April 9): New York; New York Academy of Science.

W149d.   1953 (June 12 and 17): Paris, France; Centre d'Etudes
Radiophoniques.

W149e.   1971 (July 13): Baltimore; Peabody Conservatory of Music.

W150.   *Low Speed* (5 min.; Highgate Press)
For flute on tape.

Premiere:

W150a.   1952 (October 28): New York; Museum of Modern Art; Otto
Luening, flute.

Performances:

W150b.   1953 (March 22): Urbana-Champaign, Illinois; University of
Illinois.

W150c.   1953 (March 24): New York; Barnard College.

W150d.   1953 (April 9): New York; New York Academy of Science.

W150e.   1953 (June 12 and 17): Paris, France; Centre d'Etudes
Radiophoniques.

W150f.   1971 (July 13): Baltimore; Peabody Conservatory of Music.

W150g.   1979 (April 1): Kenosha, Wisconsin; University of Wisconsin at
Parkside.

W150h.   1985 (June 16): Electro-Acoustic Music Association of Great
Britain (EMAS); Almeida Festival; Stephen Montague, technical
supervisor.

W151.   *Sonata for Bassoon and Piano* (9 min.; Highgate Press, 1970)
Previous publisher: Independent Music Publishers, 1952.

Performances:

W151a.   1963: New York; Carnegie Hall; William Scribner, bassoon.

W151b.   1971 (November): Bennington, Vermont; Maurice Pachman, bassoon; Lionel Nowak, piano.

W151c.   1972 (March 1): Devon, England; Maurice Pachman, bassoon; Elliott Schwartz, piano.

W151d.   1972 (March 6): Sussex, England; Maurice Pachman, bassoon; Elliott Schwartz, piano.

W151e.   1981 (May 3): Kenosha, Wisconsin; University of Wisconsin at Parkside; Daryl Durran, bassoon; August Wegner, piano.

W151f.   1981 (September 30): Brunswick, Maine; Bowdoin College; Steve Gammon, bassoon; Elliott Schwartz, piano.

W151g.   1985 (April 15): New York; New School for Social Research; Robert Thompson, bassoon; Jeffrey Peterson, piano.

W152.   *Trio for Flute, Violin and Piano* (15 min.; Highgate Press, 1974)
Previous publisher: American Composers Alliance, 1952.
Dedicated to Douglas and Emily Moore.
Commissioned by the League of Composers.

Performances:

W152a.   1956 (March 18): New York; At Kaufmann Concert Hall, in the 'Music in Our Time' Series; Otto Luening, flute; Max Pollikoff, violin; Douglas Nordli, piano.

W152b.   1961 (November 30): Hartford, Connecticut; The Musical Club of Hartford; Nancy Turetsky, flute; Ruth Ray, violin; Sarah Swett, piano.

W152c.   1965 (July 13): Munich; Uta Koppe, [flute]; Hirolo Abe, [violin]; Maki Ko Abe, [piano].

1953

W153.   *Incantation* (2 min., 30 sec.; Highgate Press)
Tape music; in collaboration with Vladimir Ussachevsky; for Leopold Stokowski's "Twentieth Century Concert Hall."

Premiere:

W153a.   1953 (October 25): New York; "Twentieth Century Concert Hall," CBS.

Performances:

W153b.   1955 (March 13): New York; NBC Studios; "Today" program.

W153c.   1956 (March 5): New York; CBS Television Studio I.

W154.   *Sonata for Trombone and Piano* (11 min.; Highgate Press, 1953)
Previous publisher: American Composers Alliance, 1953.

Performances:

W154a.   1953 (April 12): New York; YMHA, (Bennington Composers Conference); Elliott Phillips, trombone; Otto Luening, piano.

W154b.   1954 (October 7): Urbana-Champaign; School of Music, University of Illinois; Lloyd Farrar, trombone; Gordon Binkerd, piano.

W154c.   1970 (March 16): Storrs, Connecticut; University of Connecticut; Arnold Fromme, Trombone; Zita Carno, piano.

W154d.   1976 (February 19): Baton Rouge, Louisiana; Larry Campbell, trombone; Myrtis Riley, piano.

W154e.   1977 (April 2): Seattle, Washington; Meany Theatre, University of Washington; Stuart Dempster, trombone; Kevin Aanerud, piano.

W154f. 1984 (September): Bennington, Vermont; David Titcomb, trombone; Elizabeth Wright, piano.

W155. *Suite for Bass and Piano* (12 min.; Highgate Press)
For double bass and piano.
Previous publisher: American Composers Alliance, 1953.

Premiere:

W155a. 1957 (January 22): New York; Carnegie Hall; Robert Gladstone, double bass; Alvin Brehm, piano.

Performance:

W155b. 1957 (April 24): Austin, Texas; University of Texas; Tommy Coleman, double bass; Paul Pisk, piano.

W156. *Suite for Flute Solo No. 2* (7 min.; Belwin Mills; Colfranc Music, 1964; RRTC)
Previous publisher: F. Colombo, 1964.

Performance:

W156a. 1965 (May 24): Rome; American Academy in Rome; Severino Gazzelloni, flute.

1954

W157. *Of Identity* (10 min.)
Ballet, with Vladimir Ussachevsky; commissioned by American Mime Theater.
Previously published by American Composers Alliance.

Private Performance (Rehearsal):

W157a. 1954 (August 16): Westport, Connecticut; American Mime Theatre.

Premiere:

W157b.   1955 (February 9): Brooklyn, New York; Brooklyn Academy of Music; American Mime Theatre; Paul Curtis, choreographer.

W158.   *A Poem in Cycles and Bells for Tape Recorder and Orchestra* (14 min.; C. F. Peters)
> In collaboration with Vladimir Ussachevsky; commissioned by the Los Angeles Philharmonic.

Premiere:

W158a.   1954 (November 18-19): Los Angeles; Los Angeles Philharmonic; Alfred Wallenstein, conductor.

Performance:

W158b.   1957 (May 12): Portland, Oregon; Portland Junior Symphony Orchestra; Jacob Avshalomov, conductor.

W159.   *Rhapsodic Variations for Tape Recorder and Orchestra* (17 min.; C. F. Peters)
> In collaboration with Vladimir Ussachevsky; commissioned by the Louisville Orchestra.
> Alternative title: *Concerto for Solo Tapesicord with Symphonic Accompaniment.*

Premiere:

W159a.   1954 (March 20): Louisville, Kentucky; Louisville Orchestra; Robert Whitney, conductor.

Performances:

W159b.   1955 (December 3): New York; McMillin Theater, Columbia University; Columbia University Orchestra; Howard Shanet, conductor.

W159c.   1958?: Brussels, Belgium; "Decade of New American Music," Concert I.N.R.--18 Place E. Flagey; George Byrd, conductor.

W159d. 1961 (December 12): Amsterdam; Netherlands Philharmonic Orchestra; Henri Arends, conductor.

W159e. 1962 (May 4): Rochester, New York; Rochester Philharmonic; Howard Hanson, conductor.

W159f. 1970 (March 1): Jacksonville, Florida; Jacksonville University Orchestra; William J. McNeiland, conductor.

W159g. 1987 (February 2): New York; Festival of 20th-Century Music; Manhattan Philharmonia; Paul Dunkel, conductor.

W159h. 1987 (September 25): Louisville, Kentucky; Louisville Orchestra; Lawrence Leighton Smith, conductor.

W160. *Wisconsin Suite* (8 min.; Joshua Corp., 1977)
        Childhood tunes remembered; for orchestra.
        Previous publisher: American Composers Alliance, 1954.

Premiere:

W160a. 1954 (March 28): New York; David Broekman, conductor.

Performances:

W160b. 1976 (June 15): Washington, D. C.; Kennedy Center; Wisconsin Youth Symphony.

W160c. 1985 (October 19): Burlington, Vermont; Vermont State Symphony; Otto Luening, conductor.

W160d. 1986 (February 28): New York; McMillin Theater, Columbia University; National Orchestra of New York; Otto Luening, conductor.

1955

W161.   *Carlsbad Caverns* (3 min.)
             In collaboration with Vladimir Ussachevsky; sequence from "Wide,
             Wide World" of NBC.
             Previously published by American Composers Alliance.

   Performance:

   W161a.   1956 (May 12): New York; CBS Television.

W162.   *Sonata for Piano* (20 min; American Composers Alliance, 1975; Bardic
             Edition, 1988)
             In Memoriam Ferruccio Busoni; completed 1966.

   Premiere:

   W162a.   1975 (November 18): New York; Fifth Avenue Presbyterian
             Church; Ursula Oppens, piano.

   Performances:

   W162b.   1976 (February 8): New York; National Arts Club; Frederick
             Rzewski, piano.

   W162c.   1976 (February 19): Baton Rouge, Louisiana; Daniel Sher, piano.

1956

W163.   *Serenade for Flute and Strings* (10 min.; Highgate Press)

   Performance:

   W163a.   1956 (October 19): New York; Cooper Union; D. Antoinette
             Handy, flute; David Broekman, conductor.

W164.   *Suite from King Lear* (4 min., 30 sec.)
             In collaboration with Vladimir Ussachevsky; commissioned by
             Orson Welles and the New York City Center.
             Previously published by American Composers Alliance.

   Premiere:

W164a.   1956 (January 12): New York; City Center; produced by Orson
             Welles. (Premiere of the Welles Production)

   Performance:

W164b.   1960 (August 12): Stratford, Ontario; International Conference of
             Composers.

W165.   *Theatre Piece No. 2* (35 min.; Rights Reverted to the composer)
             For tape, piano, soprano, narrator, percussion and wind
             instruments.
             Commissioned by Doris Humphrey.
             Revised in 1965 under title: *Opening* (10 min.)

   Premiere:

W165a.   1956 (April 20-22): New York; Juilliard Concert Hall;
             choreography by Doris Humphrey; Jose Limon and Dance
             Company; an ensemble conducted by Otto Luening.

   Performances:

W165b.   1956 (August 18): New London, Connecticut; Connecticut College
             Festival of the Dance; choreography by Doris Humphrey; Jose
             Limon and Dance Company; Simon Sadoff, musical director.

W165c.   1967 (February 9): New York; Guggenheim Museum;
             Contemporary Music Society, sponsor; Carolyn Carlson, dancer
             and choreographer.

W165d.   1972 (August 31): Washington, D. C.; Kennedy Center.

Otto Luening

1957

W166.   *Gay Picture* (Merion Music, 1958)
            For piano; also published in American Music by Distinguished
            Composers, edited by Isadore Freed, Bryn Mawr, PA, T. Presser,
            1964.

W167.   *Suite for Violin Solo*

            Performance/premiere:

    W167a.   1957 (August 24): Bennington, Vermont; Bennington Composers
            Conference; Max Pollikoff, violin.

1958

W168.   *Back to Methuselah* (10 min.)
            Tape music.
            In collaboration with Vladimir Ussachevsky; Text by George
            Bernard Shaw.
            Previously published by American Composers Alliance.

    Performance:

    W168a.   1958 (March 5): New York; Margaret Webster's Theater Guild.

W169.   *Dynamophonic Interlude* (12 min.)
            Tape music.
            Alternative title: *Dynamophonic Suite*.

    Performance:

    W169a.   1958: Rome; Presented at the American Academy of Rome.

W170.   *Fantasia for String Quartet and Orchestra* (10 min.; American
          Composers Alliance)
                For string quartet and orchestra.

    Premiere:

    W170a.   1959 (April 18): New York; McMillin Theater, Columbia
              University; Columbia University Orchestra; Howard Shanet,
              conductor.

    Performance:

    W170b.   1967 (April 22): New York; Columbia University Orchestra; Max
              Schlefer, conductor.

W171.   *Lyric Scene for Flute and Strings* (7 min.; C. F. Peters, 1958)
                In memory of Ferruccio Busoni.

    Premiere:

    W171a.   1964 (October 25): Arlington, Virginia; Arlington Civic Symphony;
              Joan Moore, flute; Karl Rucht, conductor.

    Performances:

    W171b.   1972 (August 23): Johnson, Vermont; Johnson State College
              Composers Conference; Karl Kraber, flute; Alan Carter,
              conductor.

    W171c.   1976 (March 29): New York; Alice Tully Hall; Harvey Sollberger,
              flute; Group for Contemporary Music.

    W171d.   1986 (February 28): New York; McMillin Theater, Columbia
              University; Laurel Ann Maurer, flute; National Orchestra of New
              York; Efrain Guigui, conductor.

W172.   *Short Sonata for Piano No. 2* (5 min., 55 sec.; Joshua Corporation,
          1976)

W173.   *Short Sonata for Piano No. 3* (7 min., 15 sec; Joshua Corporation, 1976)
Dedicated to Jacques Barzun.

W174.   *Sonata for Bass Solo* (8 min.; Highgate Press, 1966)
For double bass.

Performance:

W174a.   1979 (April 1): Kenosha, Wisconsin; University of Wisconsin at
Parkside; Karel Netolicka, double bass.

W175.   *Sonata for Cello Solo No. 2 composed in Two Dayturnes* (7 min.; New
Valley Music Press, 1976)
Previous publisher: American Composers Alliance, 1958; Galaxy,
1958.

Premiere:

W175a.   1958 (February 2): New York; Kaufmann Concert Hall; Charles
McCracken, cello.

W176.   *Sonata for Viola Solo* (9 min.; Highgate Press, 1958)
Previous publisher: American Composers Alliance, 1958.

Performances:

W176a.   1957 (July 28): East Hampton, Long Island, New York; Walter
Trampler, viola.

W176b.   1975 (March): Bennington, Vermont; Jacob Glick, viola.

W177.   *Sonata for Violin Solo No. 1* (11 min.; C. F. Peters, 1974)
Written for Max Pollikoff.

Premiere:

W177a.   1960 (April 30): New York; Kaufmann Concert Hall; Max
Pollikoff, violin.

W178.   *Song, Poem and Dance for Flute and Strings* (10 min.; American
          Composers Alliance; Highgate Press)

    Premiere:

  W178a.   1958 (ca): Rome; American Academy in Rome; Severino
         Gazzelloni, flute; RAI String Quartet.

    Performance:

  W178b.   1959 (March 25): New York; Kaufmann Concert Hall; Julius
         Baker, flute; Gerald Tarack, Alan Martin, violins; Carl Eberl,
         viola; Joseph Tekula, violoncello; Julius Levine, bass.

W179.   *Ulysses in Nighttown* (2 min.)
         Electronic music, in collaboration with Vladimir Ussachevsky.
         Music for the Burgess Meredith adaptation of the James Joyce
         novel.

    Premiere:

  W179a.   1958 (June 5): New York; Rooftop Theatre; directed by Burgess
         Meredith; featured Zero Mostel.

1960

W180.   *Concerted Piece for Tape Recorder and Orchestra* (9 min.; C. F. Peters)
         In collaboration with Vladimir Ussachevsky; commissioned by the
         New York Philharmonic.

    Premiere:

  W180a.   1960 (March 31): New York; New York Philharmonic; Leonard
         Bernstein, conductor.

Performances:

W180b.   1960 (November 11): St. Louis; St. Louis Symphony; Edouard Van Remoortel, conductor.

W180c.   1962 (February 17): Minneapolis; Minneapolis Symphony; Stanislaw Skrowaczewski, conductor.

W180d.   1962 (November 24): Mexico City; National Symphony Orchestra of Mexico; Jose Serebrier, conductor.

W180e.   1964 (February 7): New York; Carnegie Hall; American Symphony Orchestra; Leopold Stokowski, director/narrator.

W180f.   1965 (October 17): Madison, Wisconsin; Madison Symphony; Roland Johnson, conductor.

W180g.   1967 (March 11): Corpus Christi, Texas; Del Mar College; Corpus Christi Symphony in a Young People's Concert; Maurice Peress, conductor.

W180h.   1971 (October 5): Oklahoma City; Oklahoma City Symphony Orchestra; Guy F. Harrison, conductor.

W180i.   1971 (November 17): Seattle, Washington; Seattle Philharmonic.

W181.   *Electronic Fanfare* (10 min.)
For percussion, recorder, and synthesized sounds; in collaboration with Halim El-Dabh.

Premiere:

W181a.   1962 (June 23): Spoleto, Italy; Festival Dei Due Mondi.

W182.   *Three Fantasias for Solo Guitar* (6 min.; Associated Music Publishers, 1984)
Also published by Galaxy, 1963.

W183.   *Gargoyles for Violin Solo and Synthesized Sound* (9 min.; C. F. Peters, 1965)

Premiere:

W183a.   1962 (May 9-10): New York; McMillin Theater, Columbia University; Max Pollikoff, violin.

Performances:

W183b.   1962 (February 10): Rome; American Academy in Rome.

W183c.   1962 (February 12-13): Norton, Massachusetts; Wheaton College; Max Pollikoff, violin.

W183d.   1962 (June 17): New York; Cafe Figaro; Max Pollikoff, violin.

W183e.   1964 (February 7): New York; Town Hall; Arlie Furman, violin.

W183f.   1970 (February 27): Corpus Christi, Texas; Del Mar College; Achille Di Russo, violin.

W183g.   1972 (March 2): Edmonton, Alberta; University of Alberta; Jerry Ozipko, violin.

W183h.   1974 (July): Rochester, New York; Eastman School of Music; Virginia Kellogg, violin.

W183i.   1981 (November 11): Milwaukee, Wisconsin; Ali Forough, violin.

1961

W184.   *A Day in the Country* (7 min., 30 sec.)
Violin and tape; Sometimes called *Duo Concertante*.

Premiere:

W184a.   1962 (April 30): New York; Kaufmann Concert Hall; Max Pollikoff, violin; Otto Luening, tape.

W185.   *Study in Synthesized Sound* (5 min.)
              Electronic music; realized at the Columbia-Princeton Electronic
              Music Center.

W186.   *Suite for Flute Solo No. 3* (6 min.; Joshua Corporation, 1977)

         Premiere:

   W186a.   1965: New York; Music in Our Time Series; Harvey Sollberger,
             flute.

1962

W187.   *Diffusion of Bells*
              For tape; in collaboration with Halim El-Dabh.

W188.   *Three Duets for Two Flutes* (6 min.; New Valley Music Press, 1976)
              Previous publisher: American Composers Alliance, 1965.

         Performance:

   W188a.   1964 (January 13): New York; McMillin Theater, Columbia
             University; Harvey and Sophie Sollberger, flutists; for the Group
             for Contemporary Music.

W189.   *Rondo for Accordion* (3 min.; Pietro Deiro, 1962)
              Commissioned by the American Accordion Society.

         Premiere:

   W189a.   1962 (May 6): New York; Town Hall; Carmen Carrozza,
             accordion.

         Performance:

   W189b.   1984 (December 6): New York; William Schimmel, accordion.

W190.   *Rondo for Accordion*
         Arranged for accordion and chamber orchestra by William
         Schimmel.

Performance:

W190a.   1981 (December 4): New York; William Schimmel accordion;
         North/South Consonance; Max Lifchitz, conductor.

W191.   *Sonority Canon for Two to Thirty-Seven Flutes* (6 min.; Highgate Press,
         1973)

Performances:

W191a.   1962 (May 15): New York; Columbia University; Harvey
         Sollberger, Paul Dinkel, John Heiss, Sophie Schultz, flutists.

W191b.   1963 (May 6-8): New York; McMillin Theater, Columbia
         University; Harvey Sollberger, Paul Dinkel, John Heiss, Sophie
         Schultz, flutists.

W191c.   1964 (November 8): Madison, Wisconsin; University of Wisconsin
         Student Flute Ensemble; Robert F. Cole, conductor.

W191d.   1971 (January 12): Storrs, Connecticut; University of Connecticut
         at Storrs; Nadine Markarian, Donna Ulrich Hutchinson, flutes.

W191e.   1975 (May): Bennington, Vermont; Bennington College; an
         ensemble of flutists, including Henry Brant, Sue Ann Kahn, and
         others.

W191f.   1985 (August 22): Denver; National Flute Association Convention;
         William Montgomery, conductor.

W191g.   1987 (August 22): St. Louis; former students of Joseph Mariano;
         John Heiss, conductor.

W192.   *Synthesis for Orchestra and Electronic Sound* (8 min.; C. F. Peters, 1969)
> For orchestra and tape; commissioned by BMI for it's 20th anniversary.

Premiere:

W192a.   1963 (October 22-23): Erie, Pennsylvania; Erie Philharmonic Society; Otto Luening, conductor.

Performances:

W192b.   1965 (October 10): Milwaukee, Wisconsin; Milwaukee Symphony; John Brown, conductor.

W192c.   1966 (December 15-16): Dallas; Dallas Symphony Orchestra; Charles Blackman, conductor.

W192d.   1967 (March 3): Fresno, California; Fresno Philharmonic Orchestra; Thomas Griswold, conductor.

W192e.   1971 (October 30-31): St. Johnsbury, Vermont; Vermont State Symphony; Alan Carter, conductor.

W193.   *Trio for Flute, Cello and Piano* (10 min.; C. F. Peters, 1973)
Commissioned by the Group for Contemporary Music.
Also published by Galaxy, 1966.

Premiere:

W193a.   1962 (October 22): New York; Group for Contemporary Music, Columbia University; Joel Krosnick, violoncello; Harvey Sollberger, flute; Charles Wuorinen, piano.

Performances:

W193b.   1970 (January 12): New York; Columbia University; Fred Sherry, violoncello; Harvey Sollberger, flute; Charles Wuorinen, piano.

W193c.　1986 (May 3): Washington, D. C.; Inter-American Music Festival, Organization of American States, Hall of the Americas; North/South Consonance Ensemble.

1963

W194.　*Duo for Violin and Viola* (8 min.; Joshua, 1976)
　　　　Previous publishers: American Composers Alliance, Galaxy, 1964.

Premiere:

W194a.　1964 (March 8): New York; Max Pollikoff, violin; Jacob Glick, viola.

Performances:

W194b.　1975 (Spring Semester): Bennington, Vermont; Bennington College; Mitchell Moskowitz, Jacob Glick, violins; during a lecture by the composer.

W194c.　1981 (September 30): Brunswick, Maine; Bowdoin College; Malcolm Goldstein, violin; Erika Cleveland, viola.

W195.　*Elegy for Violin* (5 min.; C. F. Peters, 1965)
　　　　For Maurice Wilk.

Premiere:

W195a.　1964 (February 7): New York; Arlie Furman, violin.

Performances:

W195b.　1973: Lubbock, Texas; Texas Tech. University; Shirley Cobb, violin.

W195c.　1981 (September 30): Brunswick, Maine; Bowdoin College; Malcolm Goldstein, violin.

W195d. 1983 (October 27): New York; Carnegie Recital Hall; Dinos Constantinides, violin.

W196. *Suite for Flute Solo No. 4* (8 min.; Joshua Corp., 1977)

Premiere:

W196a. 1967 (February 27): New York; Town Hall; Otto Luening, flute.

Performances:

W196b. 1981 (November 11): Milwaukee, Wisconsin; Janet Millard, flute.

W197. *Suite for High and Low Instruments* (5 min.; Joshua; Highgate Press, 1966)
Any combination; Commissioned by Chapin School, New York City.

Premiere:

W197a. 1964 (May 7): New York; Chapin School; Beryl Benacerraf, Lois Schaefer, flutes; Joan Speers, cello.

Performance:

W197b. 1975 (December 8): New York; Hunter College.

1964

W198. *Entrance and Exit Music* (8 min.; C. F. Peters, 1966)
For 3 trumpets, 3 trombones, cymbal.

Premiere:

W198a. 1964: New York; Barnard College Convocation to commemorate 75th Anniversary of Barnard College.

Performance:

W198b.   1970 (April 13): New York; At the Convocation to Honor Pablo Casals, at Columbia University; The Brass Ensemble of the Manhattan School of Music.

W199.   *Lines from a Song for Occupations* (7 min.; C. F. Peters, 1966) For chorus, SATB, a cappella; Text by Walt Whitman.

Premiere:

W199a.   1964: New York; Barnard College Convocation to commemorate 75th Anniversary of Barnard College.

Performance:

W199b.   1976 (February 19): Baton Rouge, Louisiana; Louisiana State University; LSU A Cappella Choir; Victor Klimash, conductor.

W199c.   1978 (February 26): New York; Carnegie Recital Hall; New Calliope Singers; Peter Schubert, conductor.

1965

W200.   *Fanfare for a Fellow Composer* (6 min.; C. F. Peters, 1973) Retitled: *Fanfare for a Festive Occasion.* In honor of Seth Bingham. For brass and percussion (3 trumpets, 3 horns, 3 trombones, bells, cymbals, timpani).

Premiere:

W200a.   1965 (May 9): New York; Juilliard, Manhattan, and Mannes School players.

Performances:

W200b.   1972 (April 6): New York; Columbia University.

W200c.   1979 (April 1): Kenosha, Wisconsin; Students of University of Wisconsin at Parkside; Thomas Dvorak, conductor.

Otto Luening

W201.   *Vocalise* (3 min.; Highgate Press, 1966)
            For chorus, SSAA, A Cappella.
            Composed for Jacob Avshalomov.
            Formerly The Maidens of Shang-Ti (SSA), composed in 1949 (3
            min.; American Composers Alliance)

1966

W202.   *Broekman Fantasia for String Orhcestra* (Highgate Press)

    Premiere:

    W202a.   1979: Munich Radio Broadcast; Munich Philharmonic; Jose
                Serebrier, conductor.

W203.   *Fantasia for Cello Solo* (5 min.; New Valley Music Press)
            Previous publisher: Joshua, 1976.

    Performance:

    W203a.   1987 (November 4): Washington, D. C.; Kennedy Center; Joel
                Krosnick, cello.

W204.   *Short Sonata for Flute and Piano No. 3* (5 min.; New Valley Music
            Press, 1976)
            Dedicated to Harvey Sollberger.
            Original title: *Two Pieces*.

    Premiere:

    W204a.   1977 (November 21): New York; Manhattan School of Music;
                Group for Contemporary Music.

    Performance:

    W204b.   1985 (April 15): New York; New York University; American New
                Music Consortium; Sue Ann Kahn, flute; Andrew Willis, piano.

W205.   *Trio for Three Flutists* (13 min.; Highgate Press, 1967)
         For 3 flutes, alternating 2 piccolos and 1 alto flute.

Premiere:

W205a.   1966 (December 18): New York; New York Flute Club; Harvey
         and Sophie Sollberger, Otto Luening, flutes.

1967

W206.   *Bells of Bellagio* (C. F. Peters, 1973)
         For piano, four or six hands.
         Hail -- Farewell.

Premiere:

W206a.   1967: Bellagio, Italy; Catherine and Otto Luening, and Janet
         Paine, pianos.

Performance:

W206b.   1982 (April 2): Kenosha, Wisconsin; University of Wisconsin at
         Parkside; Carol Bell, August Wegner, pianos; assisted by Frances
         Bedford, piano.

W207.   *Fourteen Easy Duets for Recorders* (12 min.; C. F. Peters, 1974)

W208.   *Short Sonata for Piano No. 4* (8 min.; Joshua Corporation, 1976)

1968

W209. *Meditation for Violin Solo* (3 min.; C. F. Peters, 1973)

> **Performance:**

> W209a. 1976 (February 27): New York; Theodore Roosevelt Birthplace; Alison Nowak, violin.

> W209b. 1983 (October 27): New York; Carnegie Recital Hall; Dinos Constantinides, violin.

W210. *Six Proverbs* (Highgate Press)
> For mezzo-soprano and piano.

> **Premiere:**

> W210a. 1968 (August 12): New York; Lincoln Center; Joan Kersenbrock, soprano.

W211. *Sonata for Violin Solo No. 2* (12 min.; C. F. Peters, 1974)
> Composed for Max Pollikoff.

> **Premiere:**

> W211a. 1970 (May 21): New York; Gallery of Music in Our Time; YMHA; Max Pollikoff, violin.

> **Performance:**

> W211b. 1970 (August 19): Bennington, Vermont; Bennington Composers' Conference; Max Pollikoff, violin.

1969

W212.   *Incredible Voyage*
            Electronic music; with Vladimir Ussachevsky; sound track for
            television film; assisted by Alice Shields and Pril Smiley.

   Premiere:

   W212a.   1969 (October 13): CBS TV's Twenty-First Century; Narrated by
               Walter Cronkite.

W213.   *Moonflight* (3 min.; Highgate Press)
            For flute on tape; Otto Luening, flute.

W214.   *Suite for Flute Solo No. 5* (5 min.; Joshua Corporation,1977)

W215.   *Symphonic Fantasia no. 3* (3 min.; American Composers Alliance)
            1969-1982; for orchestra.

   Premiere:

   W215a.   1982 (January 26): New York; Alice Tully Hall; Juilliard
               Philharmonia; Jose Serebrier, conductor.

W216.   *Symphonic Fantasia no. 4* (9 min.; American Composers Alliance)
            1969-1982; for orchestra.

   Premiere:

   W216a.   1984 (May 14): New York; Alice Tully Hall; American Composers
               Orchestra; Leonard Slatkin, conductor.

Otto Luening

W217. *Trio for Trumpet, Horn and Trombone* (C. F. Peters, 1974)

Performance:

W217a.   1972 (February 10): New York; Carnegie Hall; ISCM Concert.

1970

W218. *Introduction and Allegro for Trumpet and Piano* (3 min.; C. F. Peters, 1972)

Premiere:

W218a.   1972 (March 13): New York; Manhattan School of Music; Ronald Anderson, trumpet; Robert Miller, piano.

Performance:

W218b.   1982 (April 2): Kenosha, Wisconsin; University of Wisconsin at Parkside; Scott Mather, trumpet; August Wegner, piano.

W219. *Psalm 146* (3 min.; C. F. Peters, 1971)
For chorus, SATB, piano (organ) optional.

Performances:

W219a.   1976 (February 19): Baton Rouge; Louisiana State University; Louisiana State University Choir; Victor Klimash, conductor.

W219b.   1987 (March 7): New York; Gregg Smith Singers; Gregg Smith, conductor.

W220. *Sonata for Violin Solo No. 3* (13 min.; C. F. Peters, 1973)
Composed for Max Pollikoff.

Premiere:

W220a.   1971 (March 7): New York; YMHA; Max Pollikoff, violin.

Performances:

W220b.   1971 (August 15): Bennington, Vermont; Bennington Composers Conference; Max Pollikoff, violin.

W220c.   1984 (November 7): Ellensburg, Washington; Hertz Hall, Central Washington University; Wendy J. Richards, violin.

1971

W221.   *Fugue for Organ* (World Library Publications)
For Fred Tulan.

Premiere:

W221a.   1971 (November 28): Washington, D. C.; National Cathedral; Fred Tulan, organ.

Performances:

W221b.   1971 (May 9): San Francisco; Fred Tulan, organ.

W221c.   1972 (August 27): Salt Lake City, Utah; Fred Tulan, organ.

W222.   *Short Sonata for Flute Piano No. 2* (6 min.; New Valley Music Press, 1976)

W223.   *Eight Tone Poems for Two Violas* (Joshua, 1973)

Premiere:

W223a.   1972 (January 25): Albany, New York; Walter Trampler and Karen Phillips, violas.

Performance:

W223b.   1974 (January 14): New York; Manhattan School of Music; Group for Contemporary Music.

1973

W224. *Variations on Fugue and Chorale Fantasy* (22 min.; World Library
        Publications, 1975)
            For organ and electronic tape; electronic mutations of the Ruffati
            pipe organ, St. Mary's Cathedral, San Francisco.
            Based on *Fugue for Organ* (W221) and *Chorale Fantasy for Organ*
            (W43).
            Alternative title: *Electronic Doubles of Chorale Fantasy and
            Fugue.*

    Premiere:

    W224a. 1974 (July 19): Berkeley, California; Hertz Hall; University of
            California at Berkeley; Fred Tulan, organ.

W225. *Sonority Forms No. 1* (American Composers Alliance)
            For orchestra.

    Premiere:

    W225a. 1973 (October 14): North Bennington, Vermont; Sage City
            Symphony; Otto Luening, conductor.

1974

W226. *Mexican Serenades* (10 min.; Highgate Press, 1974)
            Winds, percussion, contrabass. Commissioned by the University of
            Mexico.
            Morning Serenade -- Evening Serenade.

W227. *Four Cartoons* (5 min.; Highgate Press)
       For Flute, Clarinet and Bassoon; Short Suite is a version for string
       trio.

   Performance:

   W227a. 1975 (Spring Semester): "Fugue for Flute, Clarinet and Bassoon"
           (a movement); Bennington, Vermont; Bennington College; Sue
           Ann Kahn, flute; Gunnar Schonbeck, clarinet; Maurice Pachman,
           bassoon.

   W227b. 1981 (September): "Trio for flute, clarinet, bassoon"; Bennington,
           Vermont; Sue Ann Kahn, flute; Gunnar Schonbeck, clarinet;
           Maurice Pachman, bassoon; Faculty Concert.

1975

W228. *Symphonic Interlude No. 3* (Joshua Corporation, 1976)
       For orchestra.

   Premiere:

   W228a. 1980 (August 13): Lenox, Massachusetts; Berkshire Music Center
           Orchestra; Gunther Schuller, conductor.

   Performance:

   W228b. 1982 (January 26): New York; Juilliard Philharmonia; Jose
           Serebrier, conductor.

W229. *Triadic Canons* (American Composers Alliance)
       Canons for two violins and flute.

   Performance:

   W229a. 1976 (February 27): New York; Theodore Roosevelt Birthplace;
           Olga Gussow, Alison Nowak, violins; Otto Luening, flute.

W230.   A *Wisconsin Symphony* (45 min.; American Composers Alliance)
             For orchestra; commissioned by Milwaukee Symphony and
             National Endowment for the Arts.

Premiere:

W230a.   1976 (January 4): Milwaukee; Milwaukee Symphony; Kenneth
             Schermerhorn, conductor.

Performance:

W230b.   1986 (January 17-18): Albany, New York; Albany Symphony
             Orchestra; Julius Hegyi, conductor.

1976

W231.   *Suite for Two Flutes and Piano with Cello Ad Lib.* (14 min.; Joshua
             Corporation, 1976)
             Written for Greenwood Music Camp.

Premiere:

W231a.   1978: Cummington, Massachusetts; Greenwood Music Camp.

1979

W232.   *Ten Canons for Two Flutes* (14 min.; American Composers Alliance)

Premiere:

W232a.   1983 (May 24): New York; Manhattan School of Music; Harvey
             Sollberger, Rachel Rudich, flutes.

W233.   *Potawatomi Legends No. 2 : Fantasias on Indian Motives for Flute Solo*
             (11 min.; American Composers Alliance)

W234.   *Short Sonata for Piano no. 5* (5 min., 55 sec.; Joshua Corporation, 1981)

   Premiere:

   W234a.   1980 (November 20): New York; Carnegie Recital Hall.

W235.   *Short Sonata for Piano no. 6* (6 min., 30 sec.; Joshua Corporation, 1981)

   Premiere:

   W235a.   1980 (November 20): New York; Carnegie Recital Hall.

W236.   *Short Sonata for Piano no. 7* (6 min., 40 sec.; Joshua Corporation, 1981)

   Premiere:

   W236a.   1980 (November 20): New York; Carnegie Recital Hall.

W237.   *Short Symphony* (American Composers Alliance)
           Revision of Symphonietta (1933)

   Premiere:

   W237a.   1982 (February 28): Milwaukee, Wisconsin; Milwaukee Symphony;
           Lukas Foss, conductor.

W238.   *Symphonic Fantasia no. 5* (American Composers Alliance)
           1979-1985.

   Premiere:

   W238a.   1989 (March 30, 31-April 1): Milwaukee, Wisconsin; Milwaukee
           Symphony; Lukas Foss, conductor.

93

1980

W239. *Little Vagabond* (American Composers Alliance)
For soprano and piano; Text by William Blake.

W240. *Potawatomi Legends for Chamber Orchestra* (American Composers
Alliance; [1980?])
Commissioned by the University of Wisconsin at Parkside.

Premiere:

W240a. 1980 (April 13): Kenosha, Wisconsin; University of Wisconsin at
Parkside; Members of the Milwaukee Symphony; Otto Luening,
conductor.

Performances:

W240b. 1984 (October 24): Miami, Florida; International Festival of the
Americas; University of Miami faculty; Otto Luening, conductor.

W240c. 1984 (December 2): Baltimore; Res Musica; Otto Luening,
conductor.

W241. *Silent, Silent Night* (American Composers Alliance)
For soprano and piano; Text by William Blake.

1981

W242. *Fantasia for Violin, Cello and Piano* (10 min.; American Composers
Alliance)

Premiere:

W242a. 1982 (February 24): New York; Rogeri Trio.

1982

W243.   *Fantasia for Clarinet* (8 min.; Soundspell Productions, 1989)
Previously published by American Composers Alliance.

Premiere:

W243a.   1982: Max Kupferman, clarinet.

Performance:

W243b.   1986 (June 3): New York; Whitney Museum; International Society
for Contemporary Music.

W244.   *Fantasia for Violin* (9 min.; American Composers Alliance)

Premiere:

W244a.   1982: New York; New School for Social Research; Max Pollikoff,
violin.

W245.   *No Jerusalem But This* (American Composers Alliance)
Cantata for solo voices, mixed chorus, and 15 instruments; Text by
Samuel Menashe.

Premiere:

W245a.   1982: Saranac Lake, New York; Gregg Smith Singers ; Gregg
Smith, conductor.

W246.   *Sonority Forms No. 1* (American Composers Alliance)
1982-1983; for piano; Commissioned by Music School at Rivers in
Weston, Massachusetts.

Premiere:

W246a.   1983 (May 8): Boston; Music School at Rivers; Tammy Anderson,
piano.

1983

W247.   *Lines from The First Book of Urizen and Vala, or a Dream of Nine Nights* (15 min.; C. F. Peters, 1989)
For solo voices and chorus, SATB a capella; Text by William Blake.
Commissioned by the Muse of Eloquence, Inc., for The New Calliope Singers.

Premiere:

W247a.   1984 (May 4): New York; Margery Daley, soprano; Lori Henig, alto; David Frye, tenor; Paul Rowe, baritone; New Calliope Singers; Peter Schubert, conductor.

W248.   *Serenade* (American Composers Alliance)
For violin, cello, piano.

W249.   *Sonority Forms No. 2* (American Composers Alliance)
For orchestra; Commissioned by the Sage City Symphony.

Premiere:

W249a.   1983 (June 4): Bennington, Vermont; Sage City Symphony; Otto Luening, conductor.

1984

W250.   *Ah! Sunflower* (American Composers Alliance)
For soprano and piano; Text by William Blake.

Premiere:

W250a.   1986 (September 30): New York; Merkin Concert Hall; Danielle Woerner, soprano; Robert Schwartz, piano.

W251.   *Fantasia and Dance in memoriam Max Pollikoff* (Soundspell
         Productions, 1989)
              For violin. Other title: *Fantasia and Dance for Violin Solo*

Premiere:

W251a.   1984 (October 31): Bennington, Vermont; Bennington College;
          Joseph Schor, violin.

Performance:

W251b.   1985 (ca. May 22): New York; Carnegie Recital Hall; Mary
          Findley, violin.

W252.   *Laughing Song* (American Composers Alliance)
              For tenor, baritone, and baritone/countertenor; Text by William
              Blake.

W253.   *The Lily* (American Composers Alliance)
              For soprano and piano; Text by William Blake.

Premiere:

W253a.   1986 (September 30): New York; Merkin Concert Hall; Danielle
          Woerner, soprano; Robert Schwartz, piano.

W254.   *Sonority Forms No. 2* (American Composers Alliance)
              For piano, right hand; "The Right Hand Path"

Premiere:

W254a.   1984 (November): Bennington, Vermont; Bennington College;
          Lionel Nowak, piano.

1985

W255.　*Three Canons for Two Flutes* (5 min.; Highgate Press, 1986)
　　　　Canon no. 3 dedicated to Sue Ann Kahn.

　　Premiere:

　　W255a.　1985 (February 24): New York; New York Flute Club; Sue Ann
　　　　　　Kahn and John Wion, flutes.

W256.　*Duo for Flute and Viola* (American Composers Alliance)

W257.　*Opera Fantasia* (15 min.; C. F. Peters, 1987)
　　　　For violin and piano; Commissioned by the McKim Fund of the
　　　　Library of Congress.

　　Premiere:

　　W257a.　1985 (May 30-31): Charleston, South Carolina; Spoleto Festival;
　　　　　　Joshua Bell, violin; Kenneth Cooper, piano.

　　Performances:

　　W257b.　1985 (June 4): Charleston, South Carolina; National Music Council
　　　　　　Meeting; Joshua Bell, violin; Kenneth Cooper, piano.

　　W257c.　1986 (April 10): New York; Composer's Forum Fiftieth
　　　　　　Anniversary Gala Retrospective; Carnegie Recital Hall; Benjamin
　　　　　　Hudson, violin; Gwendolyn Mok, piano.

W258.　*Serenade and Dialogue* (5 min., 30 sec.; C. F. Peters)
　　　　For flute and piano.
　　　　Previously published by American Composers Alliance

　　Premiere:

　　W258a.　1985 (September 19): Poughkeepsie, New York; Vassar College;
　　　　　　John Solum, flute; Irma Vallecillo, piano.

W259.   *Symphonic Fantasia no. 6* (American Composers Alliance)

   Premiere:

   W259a.   1986 (February 28): New York; McMillin Theater, Columbia
             University; National Orchestra of New York; Efrain Guigui,
             conductor.

W260.   *Symphonic Interlude no. 4* (American Composers Alliance)

W261.   *Tango* (Quadrivium Press)
         For piano.

   Premiere:

   W261a.   Radio Tour Through Europe; Ivar Mikhashoff, piano.

1986

W262.   *Symphonic Fantasia no. 7* (American Composers Alliance)
         Commissioned by the Centennial Celebration of Horace Mann
         School Orchestra.

   Premiere:

   W262a.   1987 (February 20): New York; Horace Mann School Orchestra;
             Henry Bloch, conductor.

W263.   *Symphonic Fantasia no. 8* (American Composers Alliance)
         Commissioned by the Centennial Celebration of Horace Mann
         School Orchestra.

   Premiere:

   W263a.   1987 (February 20): New York; Horace Mann School Orchestra;
             Henry Bloch, conductor.

Otto Luening

W264.   *Symphonic Interlude No. 5* (C. F. Peters)

W265.   *Suite for Baroque Flute* (Bardic Edition, 1988)
         Other title: *Three Fantasias for Baroque Flute*
         Commissioned by John Solum.

   Premiere:

   W265a.   1987 (November 13): Poughkeepsie, New York; Vassar College.

1987

W266.   *Song Without Words*
         For piano; earlier title: *Short Piece no. 8.*

   Premiere:

   W266a.   1987 (April 24): Buffalo, New York; North American New Music
            Festival; Ivar Mikhashoff, piano.

   Performance:

   W266b.   1987 (November 29): New York; Cathedral of St. John the Divine;
            American Composers Alliance 50th Anniversary; Robert Helps,
            piano.

W267.   *Suite for Horn* (American Composers Alliance)
         Other title: *Morning Song and Evening Song.*

   Premiere:

   W267a.   1987 (May 31): New York; Bird Coler Memorial Hospital; Tracy
            Turner, horn.

1988

W268. *Divertimento for Brass* (American Composers Alliance)
       For two trumpets, horn, trombone, and tuba.

   Performance:

   W268a. 1988 (August 27): Troy, New York; Rensselaer Institute; Catskill
           Quintet.

   W268b. 1988 (September 3): Oneonta, New York; SUNY at Oneonta;
           Catskill Quintet.

W269. *Divertimento for Oboe and String Trio* (American Composers Alliance)
       Premiered as a tribute to Robert Bloom.

   Premiere:

   W269a. 1988: New York; Alice Tully Hall; Harry Sargous, oboe; Syoko
           Aki, violin; Linda Moss, viola; Timothy Eddy, cello.

   Performance:

   W269b. 1988 (August 6): Bennington, Vermont; Bennington College;
           Chamber Music Conference and Composer's Forum of the East;
           Paticia Stenberg, oboe; Joel German, violin; Mary James, viola ;
           Kermit Moore, cello.

W270. *Green Mountain Evening* (American Composers Alliance)
       For flute, oboe, clarinet, two cellos, and piano.

   Premiere:

   W270a. 1988 (August 6): Bennington, Vermont; Bennington College;
           Chamber Music Conference and Composer's Forum of the East;
           Bonnie Levy, flute; Edward Brown, oboe; Norman Abrams,
           clarinet; Donald Farley, Ingrid Porter, cello; Marjorie Fryxell,
           piano.

Otto Luening

1989

W271.   *Symphonic Fantasia no. 9* (American Composers Alliance)

W272.   *Suite for Flute and Soprano.* (American Composers Alliance)
          Canonic variations for flute -- Declamation for soprano -- Duet for
          flute and soprano, "Hast Never Come to Thee an Hour." Text by
          Walt Whitman.

Codes:

   RRTC   Rights Reverted to the Composer

Discography
(D1-D59)

D1.   *Carlsbad Caverns* (In collaboration with Vladimir Ussachevsky) (W161)

    D1a.   RCA Victor LPM 1280. (1956)
           Sequence from "Wide, Wide World" television series
           David Broekman and his Orchestra.
           Out of print.

D2.   *Concerted Piece for Tape Recorder and Orchestra* (In collaboration with Vladimir Ussachevsky) (W180)

    D2a.   Composers Recordings CRI 227 (1968)
           Oslo Philharmonic Orchestra; Jose Serebrier, conductor.
           Album title: Music for Electronic & Older Instruments.

    Dawn Piece (See D49)
           From *Suite for soprano and flute*

D3.   *Dickinson Song Cycle: If I Can Stop One Heart From Breaking* (W125. No. 4.)

    D3a.   Music Library MLR 7117 (1967)
           Phalen Tassie, soprano; LeRoy Miller, piano.

D4.   *Divine Image* (W139)

    D4a.   Desto DST 411-2 mono. (1964)
        Mildred Miller, mezzo-soprano; Edwin Biltcliffe, piano.
        Album title: *Songs of American Composers.*

    D4b.   Desto DST 6411-12 (1964)
        Mildred Miller, mezzo-soprano; Edwin Biltcliffe, piano.
        Album title: *Songs of American Composers.*
        With: *Love's Secret.*

    D4c.   ST/AND SLP 411 (1964)
        Mildred Miller, mezzo-soprano; Edwin Biltcliffe, piano.
        Album title: *Songs of American Composers.*
        With: *Love's Secret.*

D5.   *Evangeline* (Excerpts) (W85)

    D5a.   Indiana University
        Non-commercial tape (1981?)

    Evening Song (See D49)
        From *Suite for soprano and flute*

D6.   *Fantasia for Organ* (W78)

    D6a.   Composers Recordings CRI 219 (1968)
        Ralph Kneeream, organ.
        With: *Synthesis for Orchestra and Electronic Sound.*

D7.   *Fantasy in Space* (W148)

   D7a.   CMS X46466 [197-?]
          Cassette
          Album title: *Tape music, an historic concert.*
          Title on container: *Classics of electronic music ... Museum of Modern Art, October 28, 1952.*
          With: *Incantation for Tape Recorder; Invention in Twelve Tones; Legend for Oboe and Strings; Low Speed; Lyric Scene for Flute and Strings; Moonflight.*

   D7b.   Desto DC 6466 (1968)
          Electronic sound.
          Album title: *Tape music, an historic concert.*
          With: *Incantation for Tape Recorder; Invention in Twelve Tones; Legend for Oboe and Strings; Low Speed; Lyric Scene for Flute and Strings; Moonflight.*

   D7c.   Folkways 6160. (1958)
          mono.
          Album title: *"Sounds of New Music."*

   D7d.   Highgate 123 (1977)
          Issued with *Electronic Tape Music, 1952,* as a 7" disc.
          See B7.
          With: *Incantation for Tape Recorder.*

   D7e.   Innovation Records. (1955)
          GB 1 (Gene Buck Enterprises)
          Out of print.
          March, 1955.
          Album title: *"Top Tape Recorder Music."*
          With: *Incantation for Tape Recorder; Invention in Twelve Tones; Low Speed.*

   D7f.   Silver Burdett.
          In series *Making Music Your Own.*
          Album 6, record no. 2, in series of Twelve Recorded Lessons for the First Six Grades

D8.   *Farm Picture* (W80)

> D8a.   New Music Quarterly Recordings NM1211B (1936)
> Ethel Luening, soprano; Otto Luening, piano.
> Album title: *Four Songs for Soprano.*
> With: *Here the Frailest Leaves of Me; Hast Never Come to Thee;
> Only Themselves Understand Themselves.*

D9.   *Four Cartoons (Short Suite for Woodwind Trio)* (W227)

> D9a.   Golden Crest Recordings CRS 4140 (1975)
> Sue Ann Kahn, flute; Gunnar Schonbeck, clarinet; Maurice
> Pachman, bassoon (Bennington Woodwind Trio)

D10.   *Fugue and Chorale Fantasy with Electronic Doubles* (W224)

> D10a. Composers Recordings CRI 334 (1975)
> Alec Wyton, organ; with electronic tape.
> With: *Sonata In Memoriam Ferruccio Busoni.*

D11.   *Gargoyles for Violin and Synthesized Sound* (W183)

> D11a.   Columbia ML 5966, MS 6566 (1964)
> Max Pollikoff, violin.

D12.   *Hast Never Come To Thee* (W103)

> D12a.   New Music Quarterly Recordings NM1211B (1936)
> Ethel Luening, soprano; Otto Luening, flute.
> Album title: *Four Songs for Soprano.*
> With: *Farm Picture; Here the Frailest Leaves of Me; Only
> Themselves Understand Themselves.*

D13. *Here the Frailest Leaves of Me* (W83)

    D13a. New Music Quarterly Recordings NM1211B (1936)
Ethel Luening, soprano; Otto Luening, piano.
Album title: *Four Songs for Soprano.*
With: *Farm Picture; Hast Never Come to Thee; Only Themselves Understand Themselves.*

    In the Beginning
See *Theatre Piece no. 2. In the Beginning* (W165)

D14. *Incantation for Tape Recorder* (In collaboration with Vladimir Ussachesvky) (W153)

    D14a. CMS X46466 [197-?]
Cassette
Album title: *Tape music, an historic concert.*
Title on container: *Classics of electronic music ... Museum of Modern Art, October 28, 1952.*
With: *Fantasy in Space; Invention in Twelve Tones; Legend for Oboe and Strings; Low Speed; Lyric Scene for Flute and Strings; Moonflight.*

    D14b. Desto DC 6466 (1968)
Album title: *Tape music, an historic concert.*
With: *Fantasy in Space; Invention in Twelve Tones; Legend for Oboe and Strings; Low Speed; Lyric Scene for Flute and Strings; Moonflight.*

    D14c. Highgate 123 (1977)
Issued with *Electronic Tape Music, 1952,* as a 7" disc.
See B7.
With: *Fantasy in Space.*

    D14d. Innovation Records. (1955)
GB 1 (Gene Buck Enterprises)
Out of print.
March, 1955.
Album title: *"Top Tape Recorder Music."*
With: *Fantasy in Space; Invention in Twelve Tones; Low Speed.*

D15.   *Invention in Twelve Tones* (W149)

    D15a.   CMS X46466 [197-?]
          Cassette
          Album title: *Tape music, an historic concert.*
          Title on container: *Classics of electronic music ... Museum of Modern Art, October 28, 1952.*
          With: *Fantasy in Space; Incantation for Tape Recorder; Legend for Oboe and Strings; Low Speed; Lyric Scene for Flute and Strings; Moonflight.*

    D15b.   Desto DC 6466 (1968)
          Otto Luening, flute; with tape recorder.
          Album title: *Tape music, an historic concert.*
          With: *Fantasy in Space; Incantation for Tape Recorder; Legend for Oboe and Strings; Low Speed; Lyric Scene for Flute and Strings; Moonflight.*

    D15c.   Innovation Records. (1955)
          GB 1 (Gene Buck Enterprises)
          Out of print.
          March, 1955.
          Album title: *"Top Tape Recorder Music."*
          With: *Fantasy in Space; Incantation for Tape Recorder; Low Speed.*

D16.   *Kentucky Rondo* (W143. No. 3.)

    D16a.   Composers Recordings CRI 103 (1956)
          Vienna Orchestra; Charles Adler, conductor.
          With: *Symphonic Fantasia no. 1.*

    D16b.   Composers Recordings ACS 6011 (1985)
          Vienna Orchestra; Charles Adler, conductor.
          Cassette, Anthology series
          Album title: *Music of Otto Luening.*
          With: *Legend for Oboe and Strings; Poem in Cycles and Bells; Symphonic Fantasia no. 1; Sonata In Memoriam Ferruccio Busoni.*

D17. *Legend for Oboe and Strings* (W144)

    D17a. Composers Recordings CRI 501 (1984)
          James Ostryniec, oboe; David Rossi, bass viol; Alard Quartet.

    D17b. Composers Recordings ACS 6011 (1985)
          James Ostryniec, oboe; David Rossi, bass viol; Alard Quartet.
          Cassette, Anthology series
          Album title: *Music of Otto Luening.*
          With: *Kentucky Rondo; Poem in Cycles and Bells; Sonata In Memoriam Ferruccio Busoni; Symphonic Fantasia no. 1.*

    D17c. CMS X46466 [197-?]
          Cassette
          Album title: *Tape music, an historic concert.*
          Title on container: *Classics of electronic music ... Museum of Modern Art, October 28, 1952.*
          With: *Fantasy in Space; Incantation for Tape Recorder; Invention in Twelve Tones; Low Speed; Lyric Scene for Flute and Strings; Moonflight.*

    D17d. Desto DC 6466 (1968)
          Erik Larsen, oboe; Oslo Philharmonic Orchestra; Jose Serebrier, conductor.
          Album title: *Tape music, an historic concert.*
          With: *Fantasy in Space; Incantation for Tape Recorder; Invention in Twelve Tones; Low Speed; Lyric Scene for Flute and Strings; Moonflight.*

D18. *Lines from a Song for Occupations* (W199)

    D18a. Finnadar 90850 (1987)
          New Calliope Singers, Peter Schubert, conductor.
          Album title: *10th Anniversary Anthology of New Choral Chamber Music.*

Otto Luening

D19. *Love's Secret* (W140)

    D19a. Desto DST 6411-12 (1964)
        Mildred Miller, mezzo-soprano; Edwin Biltcliffe, piano.
        Album title: *Songs of American Composers.*
        With: *Divine Image.*

    D19b. ST/AND SLP 411 (1964)
        Mildred Miller, mezzo-soprano; Edwin Biltcliffe, piano.
        Album title: *Songs of American Composers.*
        With: *Divine Image.*

D20. *Low Speed* (W150)

    D20a. CMS X46466 [197-?]
        Cassette
        Album title: *Tape music, an historic concert.*
        Title on container: *Classics of electronic music ... Museum of Modern Art, October 28, 1952.*
        With: *Fantasy in Space; Incantation for Tape Recorder; Invention in Twelve Tones; Legend for Oboe and Strings; Lyric Scene for Flute and Strings; Moonflight.*

    D20b. Desto DC 6466 (1968)
        Otto Luening, flute; with tape recorder.
        Album title: *Tape music, an historic concert.*
        With: *Fantasy in Space; Incantation for Tape Recorder; Invention in Twelve Tones; Legend for Oboe and Strings; Lyric Scene for Flute and Strings; Moonflight.*

    D20c. Innovation Records. (1955)
        GB 1 (Gene Buck Enterprises)
        Out of print.
        March, 1955.
        Album title: *"Top Tape Recorder Music."*
        With: *Fantasy in Space; Incantation for Tape Recorder; Invention in Twelve Tones.*

D21. *Lyric Scene for Flute and Strings* (W171)

   D21a. CMS X46466 [197-?]
   Cassette
   Album title: *Tape music, an historic concert.*
   Title on container: *Classics of electronic music ... Museum of Modern Art, October 28, 1952.*
   With: *Fantasy in Space; Incantation for Tape Recorder; Invention in Twelve Tones; Legend for Oboe and Strings; Low Speed; Moonflight.*

   D21b. Desto DC 6466 (1968)
   Per Oien, flute; Oslo Philharmonic Orchestra; Jose Serebrier, conductor.
   Album title: *Tape music, an historic concert.*
   With: *Fantasy in Space; Incantation for Tape Recorder; Invention in Twelve Tones; Legend for Oboe and Strings; Low Speed; Moonflight.*

D22. *Mexican Serenades* (W226)

   D22a. New England Conservatory Contemporary Music Ensemble; Gunther Schuller. conductor; recorded at Jordan Hall, New England Conservatory, February 28, 1976. Non-commercial.

D23. *Moonflight* (W213)

   D23a. CMS X46466 [197-?]
   Cassette
   Album title: *Tape music, an historic concert.*
   Title on container: *Classics of electronic music ... Museum of Modern Art, October 28, 1952.*
   With: *Fantasy in Space; Incantation for Tape Recorder; Invention in Twelve Tones; Legend for Oboe and Strings; Low Speed; Lyric Scene for Flute and Strings.*

D23b.   Desto DC 6466 (1968)
        Otto Luening, flute; with tape recorder.
        Album title: *Tape music, an historic concert.*
        With: *Fantasy in Space; Incantation for Tape Recorder; Invention in Twelve Tones; Legend for Oboe and Strings; Low Speed; Lyric Scene for Flute and Strings.*

Morning Song (See D49)
        From *Suite for Soprano and Flute*

Night Piece (See D49)
        From *Suite for Soprano and Flute*

D24.   *Only Themselves Understand Themselves* (W104)

D24a.   New Music Quarterly Recordings NM1211B (1936)
        Ethel Luening, soprano; Otto Luening, piano.
        Album title: *Four Songs for Soprano.*
        With: *Farm Picture; Hast Never Come to Thee; Here the Frailest Leaves of Me.*

D25.   *Poem in Cycles and Bells for Tape Recorder and Orchestra* (with Vladimir Ussachevsky) (W158)

D25a.   Composers Recordings CRI 112 (1957)
        Royal Danish Radio Orchestra; Otto Luening, conductor; Vladimir Ussachevsky, technical director.
        With: *Suite from King Lear.*

D25b.   Composers Recordings ACS 6011 (1985)
        Royal Danish Radio Orchestra; Otto Luening, conductor; Vladimir Ussachevsky, technical director.
        Cassette, Anthology series
        Album title: *Music of Otto Luening.*
        With: *Kentucky Rondo; Legend for Oboe and Strings; Sonata In Memoriam Ferruccio Busoni; Symphonic Fantasia no. 1.*

D26. *Prelude to a Hymn Tune by William Billings* (W108)

    D26a.   Desto DST 6429 (1967)
                Vienna Orchestra; Dean Dixon, conductor.
                With: *Symphonic Interlude no. 1-2.*

    D26b.   American Recording Society ARS 8 B (1953)
                 American Recording Society Orchestra; Dean Dixon, conductor.
                 With: *Symphonic Interlude no. 1-2.*

    D26c.   Yaddo 9B; 78 rpm. (1937)
                No performers given.

D27. *Preludes for Piano, no. 2-8* (W99)

    D27a.   Yaddo 26B; 78 rpm. (1937)
                Edwin Gerschefski, piano.

    D27b.   Yaddo 123A-B; 78 rpm. (1937)
                 Edwin Gerschefski, piano.

D28. *Rhapsodic Variations for Tape Recorder and Orchestra* (In collaboration with Vladimir Ussachevsky) (W159)

    D28a.   Louisville LOU 545-5 (1955, released 1959)
                Louisville Orchestra; Robert Whitney, conductor.

D29. *Rondo for Accordion* (W189)

    D29a.   Finnadar 902341 (1984)
                William Schimmel, accordion.
                Album title: *Accordion revisited.*

D30. *Short Sonata for Flute and Harpsichord, No. 1* (W110)

    D30a.   Yaddo M-7; 78 rpm. (1938)
                Otto Luening, flute; Ralph Kirkpatrick, harpsichord.

D31. *Short Sonata for Flute and Piano, No. 3* (W204)

> D31a. CRI SD 531 (1986)
> Sue Ann Kahn, flute; Andrew Willis, piano.

D32. *Short Sonata for Piano No. 1* (W119)

> D32a. Serenus SRS 12091 (1980)
> Dwight Peltzer, piano
> With: *Short Sonata for Piano No. 2-3, 5-7.*

D33. *Short Sonata for Piano No. 2* (W172)

> D33a. Serenus SRS 12091 (1980)
> Dwight Peltzer, piano
> With: *Short Sonata for Piano No. 1, 3, 5-7.*

D34. *Short Sonata for Piano No. 3* (W173)

> D34a. Serenus SRS 12091 (1980)
> Dwight Peltzer, piano
> With: *Short Sonata for Piano No. 1-2, 5-7.*

D35. *Short Sonata for Piano No. 5* (W234)

> D35a. Serenus SRS 12091 (1980)
> Dwight Peltzer, piano
> With: *Short Sonata for Piano No. 1-3, 6-7.*

D36. *Short Sonata for Piano No. 6* (W235)

> D36a. Serenus SRS 12091 (1980)
> Dwight Peltzer, piano
> With: *Short Sonata for Piano No. 1-3, 5, 7.*

D37. *Short Sonata for Piano No. 7* (W236)

    D37a. Serenus SRS 12091 (1980)
    Dwight Peltzer, piano
    With: *Short Sonata for Piano No. 1-3, 5-6.*

D38. *Sonata In Memoriam Ferruccio Busoni* (W162)

    D38a. Composers Recordings CRI 334 (1975)
    Ursula Oppens, piano.
    With: *Fugue and Chorale Fantasy with Electronic Doubles.*

    D38b. Composers Recordings ACS 6011 (1985)
    Cassette, Anthology series
    Album title: *Music of Otto Luening.*
    Ursula Oppens, piano.
    With: *Kentucky Rondo; Legend for Oboe and Strings; Poem in Cycles and Bells; Symphonic Fantasia no. 1.*

D39. *Sonata for Trombone and Piano* (W154)

    D39a. Crystal Records S388 (1982)
    Ronald Borror, trombone; Edmund Niemann, piano.

    D39b. University of Washington avs 8424-8425 (1977)
    Non-commercial tape
    Stuart Dempster, trombone; Kevin Aanerud, piano.

D40. *Sonata for Violin and Piano no. 3* (W129)

    D40a. Remington Records 199-211. (1956)
    Out of print.
    Saschko Garilov, violin; K. P. Pietsch, piano.

Otto Luening

D41. *Sonata for Violin Solo no. 3* (W220)

D41a. Composers Recordings CRI 303 (1973)
Max Pollikoff, violin.
With: *String quartet no. 2; String quartet no. 3; Trio for Flute, Cello, and Piano.*

D42. *String quartet no. 2* (W53)

D42a. Composers Recordings CRI 303 (1973)
Sinnhoffer Quartet.
With: *Sonata for Violin Solo no. 3; String quartet no. 3; Trio for Flute, Cello, and Piano.*

D43. *String quartet no. 3* (W72)

D43a. Composers Recordings CRI 303 (1973)
Sinnhoffer Quartet.
With: *Sonata for Violin Solo no. 3; String quartet no. 2; Trio for Flute, Cello, and Piano.*

D43b. Yaddo 12A-B; 78 rpm. (1937)
No performers given.

D44. *Suite for Flute Solo no. 1 : Monologue* (1st movement) (W138)

D44a. New Music Quarterly Recordings 1000 C-D (1949)
Rene LeRoy, flute
10 in. disc

D45. *Suite for Flute Solo no. 2* (W156)

D45a. Composers Recordings CD 561 (1988)
Compact disc
Members of the New York Flute Club.
Gerardo Levy, flute.
Album Title: *A Tribute to Luening.*
With: *Three Canons for Two Flutes; Trio for Three Flutists.*

D46. *Suite for Flute Solo no. 3* (W186)

    D46a. Composers Recordings **CRI 400** (1979)
            Harvey Sollberger, flute.
            Album title: *Flute possibilities.*
            With: *Suite for Flute Solo no. 4; Suite for Flute Solo no. 5.*

D47. *Suite for Flute Solo no. 4* (W196)

    D47a. Composers Recordings CRI 400 (1979)
            Harvey Sollberger, flute.
            Album title: *Flute possibilities.*
            With: *Suite for Flute Solo no. 3; Suite for Flute Solo no. 5.*

D48. *Suite for Flute Solo no. 5* (W214)

    D48a. Composers Recordings CRI 400 (1979)
            Harvey Sollberger, flute.
             Album title: *Flute possibilities.*
            With: *Suite for Flute Solo no. 3; Suite for Flute Solo no. 4.*

D49. *Suite for Soprano and Flute* (W105)

    D49a. New Music Quarterly Recordings NM 1513 78 rpm. (1939)
            Out of print.
            Ethel Luening, soprano; Otto Luening, flute.
            Night Piece -- Dawn Piece -- Morning Song -- Evening Song.

D50. *Suite from King Lear* (W164)
    D50a. Composers Recordings CRI 112. (1957)
            In collaboration with Vladimir Ussachevsky.
            Royal Danish Radio Orchestra; Otto Luening, conductor.
            With: *Poem in Cycles and Bells.*

D51. *Symphonic Fantasia no. 1* (W56)

  D51a. Composers Recordings CRI 103 (1956)
  Vienna Orchestra; Charles Adler, conductor.
  With: *Kentucky Rondo.*

  D51b. Composers Recordings ACS 6011 (1985)
  Vienna Orchestra; Charles Adler, conductor.
  Cassette
  With: *Kentucky Rondo; Legend for Oboe and Strings; Poem in Cycles and Bells; Sonata In Memoriam Ferruccio Busoni.*

D52. *Symphonic Interlude no. 1* (W96. No. 1)

  D52a. Desto DST 6429 (1967)
  Vienna Orchestra; Dean Dixon, conductor.
  With: *Prelude to a Hymn Tune; Symphonic Interlude no. 2.*

  D52b. American Recording Society ARS 8 B (1953)
  American Recording Society Orchestra; Dean Dixon, conductor.
  With: *Prelude to a Hymn Tune; Symphonic Interlude no. 2.*

D53. *Symphonic Interlude no. 2* (W96. No. 2)

  D53a. Desto DST 6429 (1967)
  Vienna Orchestra; Dean Dixon, conductor.
  With: *Prelude to a Hymn Tune; Symphonic Interlude no. 1.*

  D53b. American Recording Society ARS 8 B (1953)
  American Recording Society Orchestra; Dean Dixon, conductor.
  With: *Prelude to a Hymn Tune; Symphonic Interlude no. 1.*

D54. *Synthesis for Orchestra and Electronic Sound* (W189)

  D54a. Composers Recordings CRI 219. (1968)
  Hessian Radio Symphony; David Van Vactor, conductor.
  With: *Fantasia for Organ.*

D55. *Theatre Piece no. 2. In the Beginning* (W165)

    D55a. Composers Recordings CRI 268 (1972)
           Electronic Sound.

    D55b. Composers Recordings ACS 6010 (1985)
           Recorded at the Columbia-Princeton Electronic Music Center.
           Cassette
           Album Title: *Electronic music: the pioneers.*

D56. *Three Canons for Two Flutes* (W255)

    D56a. Composers Recordings CD 561 (1988)
           Compact disc
           Members of the New York Flute Club.
           Sue Ann Kahn, John Wion, flutes.
           Album Title: *A Tribute to Luening.*
           With: *Suite for Flute Solo no. 2; Trio for Three Flutists.*

D57. *Three Inventions for Piano* (W114)

    D57a. Yaddo III-4; 78 rpm. (1940)
           Lionel Nowak, piano.

D58. *Trio for Flute, Cello, and Piano* (W193)

    D58a. Composers Recordings CRI 303 (1973)
           Harvey Sollberger, flute; Fred Sherry, cello; Charles Wuorinen,
           piano.
           With: *Sonata for Violin Solo no. 3; String quartet no. 2; String
           quartet no. 3.*

Otto Luening

D59. *Trio for Three Flutists* (W205)

    D59a. Composers Recordings CD 561 (1988)
          Compact disc
          Members of the New York Flute Club.
          Eleanor Lawrence, Paige Brook, Florence Nelson, flutes.
          Album Title: *A Tribute to Luening.*
          With: *Suite for Flute Solo no. 2; Three Canons for Two Flutes.*

Bibliography by Luening
(B1-B34)

B1.   "Brief[en] an den Herausgeber." In *Komponisten über Komponisten*. Edited by Uwe Kraemer. Wilhelmshaven: Heinrichshofen's Verlag, 1972.

        In German. Letters to the editor, dated 12 October 1971, with impressions of Carl Orff (p. 147), Schoenberg (p. 160), and Karlheinz Stockhausen (p. 176-177), similar in content to **B12**.

B2.   "Composer and Community." *Music Journal* 7 (November-December 1949): 9.

        Luening comments on composer-community relationships, and the need for contemporary music in the repertoire to achieve balance. These comments were taken from an address given at the Hartt Institute.

B3.   "The Composer Speaks." *Music Clubs Magazine* 39 (November 1959): 11.

        Luening comments on his recent experiences which indicated there is "cultural erosion." Two specific situations cited were the loss of the Columbia Broadcasting System Symphony and the National Broadcasting Corporation Symphony, "without a murmur or a protest."

B4.   "Creativity in the 80's." Brookdale Institute on Aging and Adult Human Development, December, 1984.

B5.   "Discussion of American Music Continues : Correspondents Take Up Question of the Composer and the Press." *New York Times*, 31 December 1939, Section 9, p. 8.

        In a letter to the editor captioned "From Another American Composer," Otto Luening, then at Bennington College, replies to an article by Olin Downes. He comments on the lack of performance reviews of the works of several American composers.

B6.   "Douglas Moore." *Modern Music* 20 (May-June 1943): 248-253.

A biography of Douglas Moore and description of several of his compositions. Includes a classified list of works.

B7.   *Electronic Tape Music, 1952: The First Compositions* (with Vladimir Ussachevsky). New York: Highgate Press, 1977.

This includes an essay on "Electronic Music -- the First Pieces," analyses of *Fantasy in Space* (W148), *Low Speed* (W150) and *Invention in Twelve Tones* (W149), and a postlude, "The Old and the New are the Same." Facsimiles of several works by Luening, and in collaboration with Vladimir Ussachevsky are also included, as are articles by the latter.

B8.   "Electronische Musik" ("Electronic Music.") In *50 Jahre im Horfunk: Beitrage* and Berichte (50 years of Broadcast Music: Contributions and Reports), edited by Kurt Blaukopf, 50-55. Vienna and Munich: Jugend und Volk, 1973.

In German. On the evolution of electronic music in the United States, beginning with Alexander Melville Bell. Covers developments with Vladimir Ussachevsky in 1952, the historic concert of 28 October 1952, including Otto Luening's *Fantasy in Space* (W148). Also discusses the founding of the Columbia-Princeton Electronic Music Center and other composers allied with it, including Milton Babbitt, Edgard Varèse, and Mario Davidovsky.

B9.   "Electronic Music." Jerusalem: Center for Experimental Music, Hebrew University of Jerusalem, 1984.

B10.   "Experimentelle Musik in den Vereinigten Staaten." *Neue Zurcher Zeitung* 30 April 1967.

In German. A history of electronic music from Benjamin Franklin and William Billings, through Henry Cowell, Edgard Varèse, and the Columbia-Princeton Electronic Music Center. Includes commentaries on the premieres of *Rhapsodic Variations for Tape Recorder and Orchestra* (W159), *Fantasy in Space* (W148), *Invention in Twelve Tones* (W149), and *Low Speed* (W150).

B11.   "Foreword" to *Genesis of a Music* by Harry Partch. Madison: University of Wisconsin Press, 1949.

A three page introduction to Partch's contributions in writing as well as those in musical notation.

B12.   "Karlheinz Stockhausen." *Juilliard Review* 6 (Winter 1958-1959): 10-11.
       A brief biography of Stockhausen with a portrait. Luening counters the
three B's idea with the "three S's: Sound, Silence and Stockhausen." The
chronological development of the Cologne Group, 1949-1954, is given.

B13.   "Monos, Hombres y Maquinas" ("Monkeys, Men, and Machines") *Talea
       (National* University of Mexico), No. 1 (September-December 1975): 70-73.
       In Spanish. Discusses the definition of music, use of tape recorders or
synthetic sounds, the RCA synthesizer, and the investigation of the science
of sound. A brief biography appears on p. 135.

B14.   "Music." *Proceedings of the American Philosophical Society* 83 (September
       1940): 569-572.
       In an address read April 19, 1940, during the Symposium on
Characteristics of American Culture and Its Place in General Culture,
Luening discusses various types of American composers, projects and
funding sources, and enumerates several contributions of American
musicians.

B15.   *Music Materials and the Public Library: A Report to the Director of the
       Public Library Inquiry.* New York: Social Science Research Council, 1949.
       This study "centers attention on the essential characters and users of
a medium of mass communication." Luening presents a summary of musical
activities in the United States, and defines suggestions for better music
library service. Various libraries (e.g., New York Public, and Library of
Congress) are examined. It concludes with "The Role of the Public Library
in Contemporary Music Culture."

B16.   "Musical Finds in the Southwest." *Modern Music* 13 (May-June 1936): 18-22.
       Luening discusses various influences upon music in Arizona, including
the Spanish, Mexicans, Indians, cowboys, miners, and Mormons. He also
shares some of his experiences from the University of Arizona, Tucson.

B17.   "Musicology and the composer." *Current Musicology* 15 (1973): 92-94.
       Otto Luening explores various definitions of musicology and its
influence upon the composer. His research in acoustics has helped him as
a composer. Includes comments on library cataloging systems and patron
service.

123

B18.   "Die Musikpflege in den Vereinigten Staaten" ("The Cultivation of Music in the United States") *Melos: Zeitschrift fur Musik* 8, no. 10 (October 1929): 431-437.

In German. Discusses church music, choral music and their decline in early twentieth century America, the important role of the radio and phonograph, various orchestras and orchestral composers' works performed in the United States, and opera in the U.S. The pattern roughly follows the cities in which Luening resided or performed.

B19.   "New Sound Techniques in Music." *Art and Artist*. Berkeley and Los Angeles: University of California Press, 1956.

Following a brief biographical sketch of the composer, Luening describes musique concrete, the history of sound techniques, and such influential people as Ferruccio Busoni, Arnold Schoenberg, Pierre Schaeffer, and Edgard Varèse. There are also descriptions of the first public concert of tape music, October 28, 1952, including *Low Speed* (W150), *Invention in Twelve Tones* (W149), and *Fantasy in Space* (W148), and later concerts of historic nature, such as the premiere of *Rhapsodic Variations for Tape Recorder and Orchestra* (W159), on March 20, 1954. Includes a list of recent compositions of 1953-1955.

B20.   "Notes from My Diary." *American Composers Alliance Bulletin* 11, no. 2-4 (1963): 16-17.

Miscellaneous notes on the development of the American Composers Alliance.

B21.   *The Odyssey of an American Composer: the Autobiography of Otto Luening*. New York: Charles Scribner's Sons, 1980.

This semi-informal autobiography includes passages from the composer's family life in Wisconsin, his early education in Germany, and Zurich, explorations in Chicago, Tucson, and Vermont, and his innovations in electronic music at Columbia. **See also: B272, B396, B406, B454, B460.**

B22.   "Origins". In *The Development and Practice of Electronic Music*, edited by Jon H. Appleton and Ronald C. Perera, 1-21. Englewood Cliffs, N. J.: Prentice-Hall, 1975.

Following a brief biography of Luening is an essay by Luening on the origins of electronic music. Included are a description of the term, and such influential people in its development as Harry Partch, Thaddeus Cahill, Edgard Varèse, Henry Cowell, Pierre Schaeffer, Luening, and Vladimir Ussachevsky. There are quotes from Ferruccio Busoni and Varèse. **See also: B55.**

B23.   "R & D & Music." *BMI*, no. 4 (1982): 42-43.
        Brief history of research and development in music during the twentieth century, showing the "dramatic" increase in music education from 1949 to 1980, and the increased funding for research, some of which the author hopes "will trickle down to composers."

B24.   Rev. of *Muisica ex Machina*, by Frederick Prieberg. *The Juilliard Review* 7, no. 3 (Fall 1960): 24-25.
        "Mr. Prieberg's book is an impressive accomplishment in every way." Commenting that it is comprehensive and impressive from a scholarly perspective, Luening notes "the rich content of this work covers the Futurist movement in a most comprehensive and stimulating way." **See also: B488.**

B25.   "Roger Goeb." *American Composers Alliance Bulletin* 2, no. 2 (June 1952): 2-5.
        Biography of Roger Goeb with chronological list of works. Includes quotes from the *New York Times*, New York Herald-Tribune, and the *New York World Telegram*.

B26a.   "Some Random Remarks About Electronic Music." In *Contemporary Composers on Contemporary Music*, edited by Elliot Schwartz and Barney Childs, 251-260. New York: Holt, Rinehart and Winston, 1967.

B26b.   "Some Random Remarks About Electronic Music." *Journal of Music Theory* 8 (1964): 89-98.
        In an effort to "highlight events from the past that have a bearing on the present or point to the future," Luening covers the history of electronic music, the influences of Ferruccio Busoni, Pierre Schaeffer, Edgard Varèse, Leon Theremin, and Vladimir Ussachevsky. Included is a description of his work, *Dynamophonic Interlude* (W169), presented in 1958 at the American Academy in Rome. A reprint appeared in *Contemporary Composers on Contemporary Music* **See: B26a.**

B27.   "Stravinsky: a Composers' Memorial." *Perspectives of New Music* 9 (1971): 131-133.
        Several composers gave their appraisal of Stravinsky, shortly after his death. "Stravinsky's position in twentieth-century music is unique. There is no one like him and no matter in which direction the future turns, his position as a landmark is assured." Luening briefly tells of his contact with the music and person of Stravinsky.

B28.   "Try It ... You'll Like It?" *New York Times*, 15 October 1972, Section 2, p. 18.
         This is a satirical reply to "Are Today's Composers Adrift in a Void?" by Harris Green, which had appeared in a previous edition of the *New York Times*.

B29a.   "An Unfinished History of Electronic Music." *Music Educators Journal* 55 (November, 1968): 43+.

B29b.   "An Unfinished History of Electronic Music." In *The Liberation of Sound: An Introduction to Electronic Music*, edited by Herbert Russcol, 266-269. Englewood Cliffs, N. J.: Prentice-Hall, 1972.
         The composer begins by giving his philosophy of electronic music, and highlighting such influential people as Thaddeus Cahill, Ferruccio Busoni, Edgard Varèse, and Pierre Schaeffer. He also discusses the historic concerts with Vladimir Ussachevsky, their appearances on the Today program, and other collaborated compositions with Ussachevsky. Includes portrait of composer. **See also: B520.**

B30.   "Wallingford Riegger, 1885-1960." *New York Times*, 9 April 1961, Section 2, p. 13.
         This obituary gives a brief biography of Riegger and his musical influence.

B31.   "Widening Horizons for Music." *The Story of Our Time, Encyclopedia Yearbook*, 1954.
         Article about tape music.

B32.   "A Winding Path to Emily Dickinson." *Parnassus Poetry in Review* 10 (Sept. 1983): 225-250.
         Luening reminisces about his early life and the influence of parents, of literature, and of nineteenth and twentieth century composers of song upon himself (e.g. Richard Strauss, Max Reger). This is a capsule autobiography of vocal music its influences. Includes a printed copy of *Nine Songs (Dickinson Song Cycle)* (W125) published in 1983 by Galaxy-Highgate.

B33.   "The Young Composer Looks at Copyright." *National Music Council Bulletin* 17:9 (May 1957)
         Analyzes the position of the young composer, long-term versus short-term music, and suggestions for copyright law reforms.

B34. Rev. of *A Bibliography of Electronic Music*, by Lowell Cross. *NOTES* 25 (March 1969): 502-503.

In this review, Luening hopes that a second edition with several additional titles will be forthcoming. **See: B163.**

Bibliography about Luening
(B35-B621)

B35.　"14 Win Admission to Arts Institute." *New York Times*, 8 February 1952, p. 18.

Composer Douglas Moore announced the naming of fourteen people to the National Institute of Arts and Letters, one of whom was Otto Luening.

B36.　"67 Stars Highlighted Philharmonic Concert, Get Standing Ovation." *Erie Daily Times*, 23 October 1963.

This concert celebrated the 50th anniversary of the Erie Philharmonic Orchestra, with Otto Luening conducting two of his works. The premiere of *Synthesis for Orchestra and Electronic Sound* (W192), was noted for lacking a pure melodic line. However "one cannot deny that the field of electronic sound offers a great challenge to the modern-day composer, and this eight-minute work may open new avenues to the music of the future." *Symphonic Interludes No. 1-2* (W96) "proved to be modern in vein but quite listenable."

B37.　"76 Bicentennial Report." *BMI* (Spring 1976): 32-35.

Reviews the premiere performance of *Wisconsin Symphony* (W230), premiered in January 4, 1976, by the Milwaukee Symphony Orchestra, Kenneth Schermerhorn conducting. Includes quotes from the *Milwaukee Journal* and *Milwaukee Sentinel*.

B38.　"$175,000 Rockefeller Fund Gift for Electronic Music." *Musical Courier* 159 (February 1959): 42.

This grant would aid in "establishing the first American center devoted to composition and research in electronic music." Located at Columbia University, it would be jointly administered by Otto Luening and Vladimir Ussachevsky of Columbia, with Roger Sessions and Milton Babbitt from Princeton.

B39.   "$4.1 Million to Go to 342 Scholars." *New York Times*, 14 April 1974, p. 27.
        Luening is a recipient of an award from the John Simon Guggenheim
        Memorial Foundation.

B40.   *Acadian Bicentennial Celebration*. St. Martinville, Louisiana: The Acadian
        Bicentennial Association, 1955.
        Describes activities and people involved in the Acadian Bicentennial
        Celebration. Otto Luening, of Barnard College/Columbia University was
        scheduled to present a special program on Sunday, October 30, 1955, playing
        recordings of songs collected both here and in Grand Pre, commenting on
        them. Also included is a brief description of Luening.

B41.   Achter, Barbara Ann Zuck. "Americanism and American Art Music,
        1939-1945." Diss. University of Michigan, 1978.
        "Otto Luening, a composer one would not associate readily with
        folklorism, grew excited about the traditional music he found in Arizona."
        (p. 299) Achter then quotes Luening, referring to "Musical Finds in the
        Southwest," *Modern Music*, 13 (May-June 1936): 18. **See: B16.**

B42.   Allen, John. "Music Lectures Bat .500." *Middlebury Campus*, 27 April 1967,
        p. 6, 9.
        Review of lecture by Otto Luening at Middlebury on March 15, 1967.

B43.   Alston, Vernon. "Electronic Music Composer Luening Featured in Sparkling
        LSU Concert." *State-Times* (Baton Rouge), 20 February 1976.
        Review of the lecture/performance of Otto Luening on February 19,
        1976, at Louisiana State University, Baton Rouge. Luening spoke about the
        beginnings of electronic music, with comments particularly about his *Theatre
        Piece No. 2* (W165). The concert's "sensational finale" included four choral
        works performed by the LSU A Capella choir.

B44.   Altman, Leonard. "The Music of the Future; Conference of Composers at
        Stratford, Ontario." *American Record Guide* 27 (1960): 192-195, 256-258.
        Brief mention of Luening at a conference he attended.

B45.   "American Composer Update." *Pan Pipes of Sigma Alpha Iota* 76 (Winter
        1984): 35.
        Lists premieres, performances, publications, and other news of 1983.
        Noteworthy among these were the premieres of *Ten Canons for Two Flutes*
        (W232), several concerts dedicated to Luening, publications in *Parnassus
        Poetry in Review, Sonus*, and publications in Hebrew University of

Jerusalem, plus new recordings of *Sonata for Trombone and Piano* (W154) and *Legend for Oboe and Strings* (W144). **See: B31, B9, D39a, D17a.**

B46. "American Composer Update." *Pan Pipes of Sigma Alpha Iota* 78 (Winter 1986): 30-31.
Lists premieres, performances, publications, and other news of 1984 and 1985. Noteworthy among these were the premieres of *Fantasia and Dance in Memoriam Max Pollikoff* (W251), *Opera Fantasia* (W257) for violin and piano, and the performance of *Evangeline* (W85) in Maine. In December of 1984, Otto Luening was a featured speaker on a program of the Brookdale Institute on Aging and Adult Human Development entitled "Creativity in the 80s." **See: B4.**

B47. "American Composer Update." *Pan Pipes of Sigma Alpha Iota* 79 (Winter 1987): 32.
Lists premieres, performances, publications, and other news of 1985 and 1986. Noteworthy among these were the premieres of *Symphonic Fantasia No. 6* (W259), and two songs with texts by William Blake, *Ah! Sunflower* (W250), and *The Lily* (W253). The New Calliope Singers made a recording of his *Lines from a Song for Occupations* (W199), and the New York Flute Club created an 85th birthday record. **See: D18a, D45a, D56a, D59a.**

B48. "American Composer Update." *Pan Pipes of Sigma Alpha Iota* 80 (Winter 1988): 32-33.
Lists premieres, performances, publications, and other news of 1987. Noteworthy among these were the premieres of *Symphonic Fantasias No. 7 and 8* (W262-W263) and *Three Fantasias for Unaccompanied Baroque Flute* (W265), also known as *Suite for Baroque Flute*. *Sonority Canon* (W191) was performed at the National Flute Association convention.

B49. "American Music Festivals." *National Music Council Bulletin* 12 (May 1952): 17.
The Columbia University Contemporary American Music Festival occurred in April of 1952, including music of Luening; a nationwide broadcast was made possible through a CBS hook-up.
The Thirteenth Annual Music Festival of Station WNYC from February 12-22, 1952, included 75 programs, with American compositions, including those of Luening.
The University of Texas had its 1st annual Symposium of American Music, March 20-22, 1952.

B50.   "American Vocal Music of Today and Yesterday (Recordings) *American Record Guide* 31 (May 1965): 808-809+.

   Listed are *The Divine Image* (W139) and *Love's Secret* (W140). **See D14, D19.**

B51.   Anderson, Dwight. "Orchestra Starts Final Concerts." *Courier-Journal* (Louisville), 6 March 1952.

   Review of premiere of *Louisville Concerto* (W143). "The new work is made of American homespun, nostalgic, but aimless. It is much too long for its content, and would profit by ruthless cutting. It seemed to be played much too slow, but since the conductor was in charge one must assume that last night's tempi were what he wanted."

B52.   Anderson, E. Ruth. "Luening, Otto." In *Contemporary American Composers: A Biographical Dictionary*, 330-331. 2nd. ed. Boston: G. K. Hall, 1982.

   The biographical information includes awards and honors, with a selective works list. Contributed by the composer.

B53.   "An Annotated Sampler of Electronic Music Recordings." *Music Educators Journal* 55 (November 1968): 177-179.

   Recordings of several composers are reviewed, including Luening's *Synthesis for Orchestra and Electronic Sound* (W192) (CRI 219 USD), *A Poem in Cycles and Bells for Tape Recorder and Orchestra* (W158) (CRI 112), and *Rhapsodic Variations for Tape Recorder and Orchestra* (W159) (Lou 545-5). **See: D25a, D28a, D54a.**

B54.   Apel, Paul H. *Music of the Americas, North and South*. New York: Vantage Press, 1958.

   A very brief biographical sketch with some of the major works listed.

B55.   Appleton, Jon H., and Ronald C. Perera, editors. *The Development and Practice of Electronic Music*. Englewood Cliffs, N. J.: Prentice-Hall, 1975.

   The first article in this set of essays is "Origins" by Otto Luening. **(See: B22)** Elsewhere in the text are brief descriptions of *Deserts* by Varèse, and *Rhapsodic Variations for Tape Recorder and Orchestra* (W159) and *A Poem in Cycles and Bells for Tape Recorder and Orchestra* (W158), both collaborations of Luening and Ussachevsky.

B56.   Archibald, Bruce. "Reviews of Records (Otto Luening: Chamber Music)" *Musical Quarterly* 60 (1974): 321-326.

   Reviews *Chamber Music* (CRI SD 303), including *String Quartet(s) no. 2* (W53) and *no. 3* (W72), *Trio for Flute, Cello and Piano* (W193), and

Sonata for Violin Solo No. 3 (W220). "As a pioneer in electronic music in America Otto Luening tends to be thought of only in that context; overlooked is his vast catalogue of purely instrumental or vocal works." **See D41a, D42a, D43a, D58a.**

B57.   Arnold, Robert, and James Johnson. "Thirteenth Annual Spring Festival Concert." *American Organist* (Staten Island, N.Y.) 48 (July 1965): 7.
   Fanfare for a Fellow Composer (W200), was premiered in a program honoring the long career of Dr. Seth Bingham as a composer and teacher.

B58.   "Arts and Letters Group Names Writer President." *New York Times*, 20 January 1956, p. 7.
   The National Institute of Arts and Letters elected its council, including essayist Malcolm Cowley as President and composer Otto Luening as its treasurer.

B59.   Atkinson, Brooks. "Orson Welles' 'King Lear.'" *New York Times*, 13 January 1956, p. 17.
   Review of *Suite from King Lear* (W164), as performed January 12, 1956. The tape music was composed by Ussachevsky and Luening.

B60.   "Atkinson, Brooks. "Shavian Prose: 'Back to Methuselah' is at Ambassador." *New York Times*, 27 March 1958, p. 41.
   Review article. Arnold Moss condensed *Back to Methuselah* (W168) from 90,000 to 30,000 words. The drama was "disappointingly prosy." Luening and Ussachevsky created the electronic effects. **See: B423.**

B61.   "Awards--The 1970 Year." *Pan Pipes of Sigma Alpha Iota* 63, no. 2 (1971): 8-11.
   Luening is awarded the American Composers Alliance Laurel Leaf Award for 1970. While at Columbia University, "his teaching has touched over 200 composers." He was also the recipient of a Citation from the Eastman School of Music in 1970.

B62.   Babbitt, Milton. "An Introduction to the R.C.A. Synthesizer." *Journal of Music Theory* 8 (1964): 251-265.
   A colleague of Luening describes the synthesizer used at the Columbia-Princeton Electronic Music Center.

B63.   Bailey, Barbara Elliott. "A Historic and Stylistic Study of American Solo Piano Music published from 1956 to 1976." Diss. Northwestern University, 1980.

Luening is one of 25 composers whom Bailey believes to have composed works important in the musical academic world. In comparing various four-movement sonatas, she writes: "The first movement of Otto Luening's *Sonata in Memoriam Ferruccio Busoni* (W162), called 'Introduction', resembles a French overture. A ternary movement, 'Dramatic Scene' follows. A 'Minuet' ends the sectional 'Burlesque' and is followed by the fourth movement titled 'Fantasia.'"

B64.   Barlow, S. L. M. "In the Theatre." *Modern Music* 23 (Summer 1946): 222-223.

Otto Luening conducted the premiere of *The Medium*, a chamber opera by Gian-Carlo Menotti.

B65.   Baruch, David J. "Music in Our Time." *Musical America* 80:36 (June 1960)

Premiere review of *Sonata for Solo Violin* (W177), most likely the first sonata. "Luening's Sonata, in seven short movements, was well written but routine in musical interest."

B66.   Barzun, Jacques. ["Letter"] *New York Herald Tribune*, 28 May 1961, Section 4, p. 11.

This clarified an alleged "misquote" by saying "if they (Columbia audience) wished to understand what they were about to hear they must lend their minds to it." This article, and those of Paul Henry Lang were a series of exchanges about the May 9-10 concerts, which included *Gargoyles* (W183). **See: B355-B357.**

This is also described by Otto Luening in "Origins." **See: B22.**

B67.   Beauchamp, James. "Electronic Music: Apparatus and Technology." In *Dictionary of Contemporary Music*, edited by John Vinton. New York: Dutton, 1974.

Briefly mentions the RCA Synthesizer.

B68.   Beckwith, John, and Udo Kasemets. *The Modern Composer and His World*. Toronto: University of Toronto Press, 1961.

A report from the International Conference of Composers, Stratford, Ontario, Canada, August, 1960. A panel including Canadian physicist Hugh LeCaine, Josef Tal of Israel, and Vladimir Ussachevsky discussed "Synthetic Means."

Ussachevsky spoke of electronic music in the Columbia-Princeton Electronic Music Center, his colleague Otto Luening, and compositional techniques used in two works they jointly composed: *Rhapsodic Variations for Tape Recorder and Orchestra* (W159) and *A Poem in Cycles and Bells for Tape Recorder and Orchestra* (W158).

The ensuing discussion included comments by Edgard Varèse, Luciano Berio, and Otto Luening. Concert no. 3 of the conference included *Suite from King Lear* (W164) by Luening and Ussachevsky.

B69. Beeson, Jack. "Luening, Otto (Clarence)." *The New Grove Dictionary of Music and Musicians*. London: Macmillan, 1980.

A succinct biography, with a classified list of selected works.

B70. Beeson, Jack. "Otto Luening." *American Composers Alliance Bulletin* 3, no. 3 (Autumn 1953): 2-8.

This biographical article includes a list of works and emphasizes the diversity found in the music of Otto Luening. "Repertoire of Otto Luening Compositions" is a classified list of works, with a facsimile of the *Louisville Concerto* (W143).

B71. Berger, Melvin. *Masters of Modern Music*. New York: Lothrop, Lee, & Shepard, 1970.

In a book written for young people, several contemporary composers are discussed, including Vladimir Ussachevsky. Describes *Rhapsodic Variations for Tape Recorder and Orchestra* (W159) (Luening-Ussachevsky)

B72. Berges, Ruth. "News of the NOA." *Opera News* 23 (26 January 1958): 14-15.

The fourth meeting of the National Opera Association was held at the Manhattan School of Music on Dec. 29-30, 1958. The article includes a portrait of Otto Luening, who discussed his opera *Evangeline* (W85) during the convention.

B73. Bernheimer, Martin. "Columbia Princeton Center Presents Electronic Music." *New York Herald Tribune*, 10 May 1961, p. 19.

A review of the May 9, 1961 concert which included music of Mario Davidovsky, Halim El-Dabh, Milton Babbitt, Vladimir Ussachevsky, and Otto Luening. Reviewed only first portion of the concert, excluding Luening, Charles Wuorinen, and Bülent Arel.

B74. "Bernstein Discusses Unusual Instruments." *Musical America* 80 (April 1960): 24.

On March 26, 1960, at Carnegie Hall, Leonard Bernstein conducted the New York Philharmonic in a Young People's Concert: "Unusual Instruments of Present, Past and Future." It included the premiere of *Concerted Piece for Tape Recorder and Orchestra* (W180) by Luening and Ussachevsky, the latter in charge of the tape recorder.

B75. *Bio-Bibliographical Index of Musicians in the United States of America Since Colonial Times = Indice Bio-Bibliografico de musicos de los Estados Unidos de America desde la epoca de la colonia.* By District of Columbia Historical Survey. 2nd ed. Washington, D. C. : Music Section, Pan American Union, 1956.

Four entries of commentary on Luening are listed in this index, sponsored by the Works Projects Administration.

B76. Bisha, Calvin W. "The Philosophy Behind the Orchestra's Commissions." *Louisville Times*, 13 April 1954.

A letter to the editor which takes issue with the comments of Sidney Harth (**See: B265**). "The issuance of a commission to Otto Luening and Vladimir Ussachevsky is more than defensible .... These gentlemen are recognized composers with many performances of their works to their credit." Bisha was Principal Bass of the Louisville Orchestra. The concert was the premiere of *Rhapsodic Variations for Tape Recorder and Orchestra* (W159).

B77. Blair, William G. "Columbia Graduates Told U. S. Aid Cuts Are 'Gross Error'" *New York Times*, 14 May 1981, Section 2, p. 3.

Otto Luening, a composer, musicologist, and professor emeritus of Columbia University, receives an honorary Doctor of Letters for having "combined love and respect for tradition with imaginative and unconventional exploration into new territories."

B78. Bloom, Julius. *The Year in American Music, 1946-1947.* New York: Allen, Towne & Heath, 1947.

Covers events such as the Yaddo Festival of September, 1946, when two unnamed compositions were performed (p. 21); the New Music Society performed *Alleluia* (W130) in April, 1947. And Otto Luening was in a program "Meet the American Composer," in which he introduced Herbert Haufrecht (p. 257)

B79.   Bohm, Jerome D. "Maurice Wilk, Good Violin." *New York Herald Tribune*, 7 February 1951, p. 17.

In the premiere of Luening's *Sonata for Violin and Piano No. 3* (W129), called *Andante and Variations*, Maurice Wilk performed a work "unproblematically diatonic and unaffectedly tuneful. The theme is an agreeably lyrical one, and the variations are expertly devised, some of them in American folk style, others exuding a faint whiff of Brahms, so fleeting that one senses that the composer was himself aware of the path he was treading and quickly forsook it. A greater variety of mood would have been achieved had the composer made completer use of the violin's wide range and exploited more fully its capacity for expressing other attributes than unrelieved lyricism."

B80.   Bort, James. "Violinist Stern Sparkles in Philharmonic Concert." *Fresno Bee*, 4 March 1967, p. 6-B.

A favorable review of the Fresno Philharmonic concert of March 3, 1967, with "something for everyone." Thomas Griswold conducted *Synthesis for Orchestra and Electronic Sound* (W192). "Both in the orchestral writing and in the scoring of the electronic sequences, there is an impelling and dynamic forward thrust that stimulates even if it does not always please the ear."

B81.   Boyd, Joe. "Symphony, Machinery Team Up." *Milwaukee Sentinel*, 11 October 1965, part 2, p. 1, 9.

Synthesis for Orchestra and Electronic Sound (W192) was the "high point" of a concert, October 10, 1965. Includes description of the piece and comments by the composer about electronic music.

B82.   Breuer, Robert. "A New Dimension in Music." *Showcase (Music Clubs Magazine)* 40, no. 5 (1961): 8-11.

Asks the question, "What is going on in music?" Discusses the evolution of electronic music, descriptions by Fred Prieberg in *Musica ex Machina* (**B488**), and Luening's essay "New Sound Techniques in Music" (**B19**) Includes comments by Luening and Ussachevsky on the future of electronic music. Photograph of the two composers and an excerpt from the score of *Rhapsodic Variations for Tape Recorder and Orchestra* (W159) precedes the article.

B83.   Browning, James. "25 Years of the American Music Center." *Composer* (London) no. 21 (Autumn 1966): 3-4.

A brief history of the American Music Center, founded in 1940 by a group of "far-sighted composers." Otto Luening was the chairman; other composers were Marion Bauer, Aaron Copland, Howard Hanson, Quincy Porter, and Harrison Kerr.

B84. Brozen, Michael. "Music in Our Time." *Musical America* 81 (June 1961): 67.
      This is a critical review of the premiere of *Duo Concertante* (W184) for violin and tape recorder, performed by Max Pollikoff, April 30, 1961, and subtitled "A Day in the Country." "It takes more than just sound recorded on tape to make a piece either modern or music." The composition is described as an unedited record of an auction, with a folksy set of variations played by the violinist.

B85. Burbank, Richard. *Twentieth Century Music*. New York: Facts on File, 1984.
      Sixteen events are described in this chronological dictionary of twentieth century music, including 13 premieres of works by Luening, most notably *Evangeline* (W85) and *Rhapsodic Variations for Tape Recorder and Orchestra* (W159). Also the opening and early history of the Columbia-Princeton Electronic Music center is discussed.

B86. Burke, Harry. "Russian Paintings set to Music; St. Louis Symphony plays Mussorgsky's Tone Translation of Hartmann's Art." *St. Louis Globe-Democrat*, 6 February 1939, part 3, p. 1.
      Favorable review of *Two Symphonic Interludes* (W96), performed February 5 by the St. Louis Symphony. The first interlude is in a spirit of driving energy, while the second is a languorous, introspective work.

B87. Butterworth, Neil. "Luening, Otto." In *A Dictionary of American Composers*. New York: Garland, 1984.
      A biographical article highlighting the composer's career, major compositions, and collaboration with Vladimir Ussachevsky.

B88. Butterworth, Neil. *The Music of Aaron Copland*. [New York?]: Toccata Press, 1985.
      This describes an all-Copland concert, May 5, 1926, with artists Ethel and Otto Luening and Robert McBride, "the two instrumentalists themselves composers of note in later years."

B89. Cage, John. *Notations*. New York: Something Else Press, 1969.
      Facsimile and description of Luening's *Rorschach Symphonic Sonata*.

B90. Calta, Louis. "Welles Returns as 'Lear' Tonight." *New York Times*, 12 January 1956, p. 23.

Description of the Shakespearian production with Orson Welles. The electronic sound score is by Otto Luening and Vladimir Ussachevsky.

B91. Cantrell, Scott. "Orchestra's Performance Compared to Major Leagues." *Times-Union* (Albany, N. Y.), 19 January 1986, Section B, p. 7.

The Albany Symphony Orchestra was considered to be in "finest form" on January 17, 1986, in a performance of Luening's *Wisconsin Suite* (W160). The reviewer described the piece as alternating between modality, tart polytonality, Ivesian haze; but the audience "evidently enjoyed it."

B92. Carter, Elliott. "American Music in the New York Scene." *Modern Music* 17 (January-February 1940): 93-101.

Ralph Kirkpatrick announced a program of twentieth century music for harpsichord, arousing interest. Luening's *Short Sonata for Flute and Piano no. 1* (W110), the flute accompanied by harpsichord, was the "best conceived work for the instruments; it had a delicate, wistful simplicity."

B93. Carter, Elliott. "Forecast and Review: Late Winter, New York, 1937." *Modern Music* 14 (March-April 1937): 147-154.

Prelude to a Hymn Tune by William Billings (W108), a set of variations grows successively more dissonant and then returned to somewhat simpler harmonies. "This proved to be somewhat crippling, for Luening, at his best in dissonant contrapuntal anguish, could not sustain the interest in more consonant parts."

B94. "A Catalogue of Works by American Composers on LP Records." *American Composers Alliance Bulletin* 4, no. 3 (1955): 18-20.

Lists the ARS recordings of *Two Symphonic Interludes* (W96) and *Prelude to a Hymn by William Billings* (W108). **See: D52b, D53b, D26b.**

B95. Chapin, Louis. "The Future Started Here." *BMI* (Summer 1970): 23-30.

Ten innovators are examined, including Luening, Vladimir Ussachevsky, Milton Babbitt, Edgard Varèse, Karlheinz Stockhausen, and Luciano Berio. There is brief discussion of the collaborated works of Luening and Ussachevsky, *Rhapsodic Variations for Tape Recorder and Orchestra* (W159), *Concerted Piece for Tape Recorder and Orchestra* (W180), *A Poem in Cycles and Bells for Tape Recorder and Orchestra* (W158), and *Suite from King Lear* (W164). Also discussed are some works solely by Luening: *Synthesis for Orchestra and Electronic Sound* (W192), *Moonflight* (W213), and *Sonority Canon for Two to Thirty-Seven Flutes* (W191).

B96. "Chapters Active in American Music Interests." *Pan Pipes of Sigma Alpha Iota* 46 (January 1954): 68-70.
   A concert of contemporary American music was presented on March 4, 1953, at Bethany College, Lindsborg, Kansas. Included a performance of *If That High World* (W61). **See also: B150.**

B97. Chase, Gilbert. "United States." In *Dictionary of Contemporary Music*, edited by John Vinton. New York: Dutton, 1974.
   Mentions the pioneering efforts in electronic music of Otto Luening and Vladimir Ussachevsky.

B98. *Chicago Symphony Orchestra Program Notes.* 46th Season, 1936-1937, p. 325-326.
   This gives a description of *Two Symphonic Interludes* (W96), performed by the Chicago Symphony and Hans Lange. Includes biographical comments by Otto Luening.

B99. Chion, Michel. "Luening, Otto." In *Larousse de la Musique*. Paris: Larousse, 1982.
   This brief biography, in French, emphasizes the film music of Luening. It includes references to two other articles by Chion, "Electronique (Musique)", and "Electroacoustique (Musique)".

B100. "Choirs, U of I Symphony in ISNU Festival." *The Pantagraph* (Bloomington, Ill.), 26 April 1956, p. 11
   Announces concerts of the Festival of American Music at Illinois State University, Normal, Illinois, including Luening's *Alleluia* (W130) on April 27, 1956.

B101. Chute, J. "Hey Fred! Otto's Really Made It!." *Milwaukee Journal*, 27 May 1984.
   An interview with composer Otto Luening.

B102. Claghorn, Charles Eugene. "Otto Luening." In *Biographical Dictionary of American Music*, 282. West Nyack, N. Y.: Parker, 1973.
   This is a brief biography.

B103. "Classical: New York." *Music Journal* 36 (September 1978): 32-33.
   "Otto Luening waited 55 years for the premiere of his *Music for Orchestra* (W51). It proved to be traditional, tunes and all, in an Ivesian, American style. It was interesting, seminally, as is beginning Schoenberg."

B104. "Classified Chronological Catalog of Works by United States Composer Otto Luening." *Inter-American Music Bulletin* 25 (September 1961): 28-39.

B105. Cohn, Arthur. "Electronic Music." *American Record Guide* 30 (June 1964): 924-925, 940.

A review of the disc Columbia ML-5966 (mono.), MS-6566 (stereo.). Includes a photograph of Columbia-Princeton Electronic Music Center, and portraits of Otto Luening, Vladimir Ussachevsky, and Milton Babbitt. *Gargoyles for Violin Solo and Synthesized Sound* (W183) is reviewed and described as a solo violin pitted against and adjoined to synthesized sound. "Using variation form, the design is cogently delineated and beautifully projected." **See: D11a**.

B106. Cohn, Arthur. "New York." *Musical Courier* 163 (June 1961): 18-19.

Included is a review of the May 9, 1961 performance of *Gargoyles for Violin Solo and Synthesized Sound* (W183), at the Columbia-Princeton Electronic Music Center. This was "the 'Haydn' work of the evening (even a resemblance to (Bach's) third *Brandenburg Concerto* was noted by a number of listener's)." Cohn ponders that the strength of electronic music discovery may lie in a "multistructure and hybrid of the instrumental and the machine."

B107. Cohn, Arthur. "New York Philharmonic." *Musical Courier* 161 (May 1960): 17-18.

The premiere of *Concerted Piece for Tape Recorder and Orchestra* (W180) on 2 April 1960, was an "exciting program." The composition was a "sensible musical effort," utilizing both new techniques and vivid new timbres, with the contrast being "exhilarating," a work worthy of further performances.

B108. "Columbia, Princeton get Rockefeller Grant." *Musical America* 79 (February 1959): 213.

A brief announcement of the $175,000 grant from the Rockefeller Foundation for the "purpose of establishing the first center devoted to composition and research in electronic music." It would be jointly administered by Luening and Ussachevsky.

B109. "Composer Luening to Perform." *Kenosha News*, 26 April 1983.

Announces a fifth consecutive year in which Luening is the visiting composer. The concert on Sunday, May 1, 1983, would include *Fantasia for Organ* (W78), *Fantasia Brevis for Flute and Piano* (W79), and *Bass with the*

Delicate Air (W116). Article emphasizes achievements since 1959. Includes photograph.

B110. "Composer Returns Home." *Milwaukee Sentinel,* 12 November 1981.

Review of concert November 11, 1981 in Milwaukee. *Variations on Bach's Chorale Prelude Liebster Jesu wir sind hier* (W128) exhibited a spirit similar to Hindemith's *Gebrauchmusik*. A "fluent reading" of *Suite for Flute Solo No. 4* (W193) showed Luening's "eclecticism lurching, in the space of a single work, from an almost bucolic simplicity to highfalutin melodic leaps and a merry windup suggesting a circus band." *Soundless Song* (W52) was eloquently sung," *Gargoyles for Violin Solo and Synthesized Sound* (W183) exhibited a violinist's virtuosity, and *Sextet* (W32) "revealed a young composer at peace with a melodious world."

B111. "Composer's Corner." *Musical America* 75 (July 1955): 29.

Barnard College received a $9955 grant from the Rockefeller Foundation, enabling Otto Luening and Vladimir Ussachevsky to survey, catalog, and evaluate recent developments in electronic music which affect composition. The two composers also left for six weeks in Europe to examine trends and techniques used by various radio stations.

B112. "Composer's Corner." *Musical America* 77 (February 1957): 202.

Robert Gladstone premiered the *Suite for Bass and Piano* (W155), on January 22, 1957, at Carnegie Hall. "The limitation of the solo double bass stimulated Mr. Luening to find some interesting solutions to this challenging problem. It was a spicy work written on simple effective lines, fully exploiting the G string's characteristic lyric flavor."

B113. "Composers Create Weird Effects for 'Tape Recorder Rhapsody.'" *Courier-Journal* (Louisville), 19 March 1954.

Otto Luening and Vladimir Ussachevsky gave a demonstration of the sound of *Rhapsodic Variations for Tape Recorder and Orchestra* (W159) at the Louisville Free Public Library, March 18, 1954, in preparation for the work's premiere on Saturday, March 20. The noise suggested a "wind tunnel, stomach rumblings, wild animals on Mars, and Hiroshima during the atom-bomb raid." Photograph of Luening and Ussachevsky with the tape recorder, and comments by Luening.

B114. "Composers' Forum." *Music & Artists* 1, no. 2 (1968): 49-56.

Luening, Morton Gould, and Ned Rorem engage in a free discussion on music. Otto Luening speaks much to electronic music.

B115. "Composers Group at Recital Hall." *New York Herald Tribune*, 23 January 1957, p. 14.

Review of the *Suite for Bass and Piano* (W155), performed 22 Jan. 1957 by Gladstone. The suite was "concise rhythmic and developed to the saturation point." **See also: B211.**

B116. "Composers Perform 7 Numbers. *Austin American*, 25 April 1957, p. 3.

Review of a performance of April 24, 1957, including Luening's *Suite for Bass and Piano* (W155), with Tommy Coleman, double bass accompanied by Paul Pisk on piano. This "short and deceptive simple piece lies well for the unusual solo instrument, states its thoughts bluntly and is a welcome addition to the scanty literature for this instrument."

B117. "Composers Group Plays New Works." *New York Times*, 23 January 1957, p. 25.

On January 22, 1957, the *Suite for Bass and Piano* (W155) was premiered. Luening's composition showed "a real professional at work, who said what he had to say neatly and succinctly."

B118. "The Composers Organize: A Proclamation." *Modern Music* 15 (January-February 1938): 92-95.

Luening is named as one of the co-founders of the American Composers' Alliance.

B119. "Concert Blended With a Rehearsal." *New York Times*, 13 October 1952, p. 25.

Subtitled "Three Composers Appear in Unusual Program Present by Cooper Union Forum." On October 12, 1952, Roger Goeb, John Cage and Otto Luening were present for a performance of *Pilgrim's Hymn for Chamber Orchestra* (W133). Subsequent forums would be called "Music in the Making."

B120. "Concert Hall." *American Composers Alliance Bulletin* 2, no. 1 (1952): 15.

Includes announcements of 1951 and 1952 performances of the *Dickinson Song Cycle* (W125) and *Suite for Cello and Piano* (W136). Includes excerpts from reviews from the *New York Herald Tribune* on the both works, with comments from the *New York Times* on the 2nd work.

B121. "Concert Hall." *American Composers Alliance Bulletin* 2, no. 4 (1952-1953): 22.

Includes announcement of performance of *Pilgrim's Hymn for Chamber Orchestra* (W133), with excerpts of reviews from the October 13,

1952 editions of the *New York World-Telegram and Sun*, and the *New York Herald Tribune*. Other works performed during 1952 are listed.

B122. "Concert Hall." *American Composers Alliance Bulletin* 3, no. 1 (Spring 1953): 26.

Louisville Concerto (W143), performed March 1, 1953, was reviewed by Peggy Glanville-Hicks of the *New York Herald Tribune* (March 2, 1953), evoking "a deal of dissention in the talk period for its somewhat undigested vernacular elements." **See also: B233.**

John Haskins reviews an earlier performance by the Air Force Symphony Orchestra, in the January 29, 1953, edition of the *Washington Times Herald*. Other works performed included *Low Speed* (W150) and *Fantasy in Space* (W148), on March 22 at the University of Illinois, and March 24 at Barnard College, New York.

B123. "Concert Hall." *American Composers Alliance Bulletin* 3, no. 2 (Summer 1953): 24.

Lists performances of six works, four being performed in foreign countries, including *Sonata for Violin and Piano No. 3* (W129) in Germany, with *Fantasy in Space* (W148), *Invention in Twelve Tones* (W149), and *Low Speed* (W150) in France.

B124. "Concert Hall." *American Composers Alliance Bulletin* 3, no. 4 (Winter 1953-1954): 14-15.

Lists performances of 1953, including Ethel Luening's performance of *Auguries of Innocence (To See the World in a Grain of Sand)* (W64) and *For Like a Chariot's Wheel* (W81). Includes excerpts from the *New York Herald Tribune* review of *Two Preludes for Piano* (W99a-b).

B125. "Concert Hall." *American Composers Alliance Bulletin* 4, no. 1 (1954): 23.

Two 1954 performances of *Wisconsin Suite* (W160) announced.

B126. "Concert Hall." *American Composers Alliance Bulletin* 5, no. 3 (1956): 19.

Lists selected performances of 1955 and 1956.

B127. "Concert Hall." *American Composers Alliance Bulletin* 6, no. 1 (Autumn 1956): 19.

Announces the premiere of *Theatre Piece No. 2* (W165), April 6-8, 1956, with choreography by Doris Humphrey.

Also *Alleluia* (W130), performed by the University Choir, Illinois State University, Normal, Illinois, April 27, 1956, Emma R. Knudson, director.

B128. "Concert Hall." *American Composers Alliance Bulletin* 7, no. 1 (Fall 1957): 22.

The *Suite for Bass and Piano* (W155) was performed on April 24, 1957. in Austin, Texas. Includes comments from the *Austin American* (April 25, 1957). **See also: B116.**

The collaborated composition, *A Poem in Cycles and Bells for Tape Recorder and Orchestra* (W158) (with Ussachevsky), was performed on May 12, 1957, in Portland, Oregon, by the Portland Junior Symphony Orchestra, with Jacob Avshalomov conducting. Includes comments from the *Oregon Journal* (May 13, 1957): "In an evening filled with musical novelty, Ussachevsky-Luening's 'Poem in Cycles and Bells,' tape recorder solo with orchestra, easily walked off with the novelty honors."

B129. "Concert Hall." *American Composers Alliance Bulletin* 7, no. 2 (1958): 24.

Includes two performance announcements of 1957: *Symphonic Fantasia no. 2* (W115) premiered October 18, 1957, with David Broekman conducting. *Rhapsodic Variations for Tape Recorder and Orchestra* (W159) was performed in the series "Decade of New American Music," in Brussels, Belgium, with George Byrd conducting.

B130. "Concert Hall." *American Composers Alliance Bulletin* 7, no. 3 (1958): 23.

Earth's Answer (W71, No. 2) was performed November 21, 1958, at Vassar College, Poughkeepsie, New York, with Marvin Hayes, bass-baritone, and Lalan Parrott, piano.

B131. "Concert Hall." *American Composers Alliance Bulletin* 7, no. 4 (1958): 26.

Lists performances and excerpts of reviews. Included are three 1958 performances with excerpts from *Evangeline* (W85). The *Sonata for Cello Solo No. 2* composed in Two Dayturnes (W175) was premiered February 2, 1958, with comments by Allen Hughes in the February 3, 1958 issue of the *New York Herald Tribune*. Also included comments by Ezra Laderman, from the March 1958 *Musical America*. **See also: B292, B352.**

B132. "Concert Hall." *American Composers Alliance Bulletin* 8, no. 1 (1958): 27.

Lists performances of the *Dickinson Song Cycle* (W125) and *Fantasia* (W78) for organ.

B133. "Concert Hall." *American Composers Alliance Bulletin* 8, no. 2 (1959): 24.

Fantasia (W78) for organ was performed July 31, 1958, by Leonard Raver, organ.

B134. "Concert Hall." *American Composers Alliance Bulletin* 8, no. 3 (1959): 23.
A performance of two pieces for tape recorder on December 5, 1958, is listed.

B135. "Concert Hall." *American Composers Alliance Bulletin* 8, no. 4 (1959): 28.
Lists two premieres: *Song, Poem and Dance for Flute and Strings* (W178), performed March 25, 1959, by Julius Baker, flute; includes excerpts of a review by Ross Parmenter in the *New York Times* (March 26, 1959). *Fantasia for String Quartet and Orchestra* (W170) premiered April 18, 1959. See: B464.

B136. "Concert Hall." *American Composers Alliance Bulletin* 9, no. 1 (1959): 23.
Includes in the list a 1959 performance of *Kentucky Concerto* (W143).

B137. "Concert Hall." *American Composers Alliance Bulletin* 9, no. 2 (1960): 22.
Includes in the list one 1959 performance of *Kentucky Concerto* (W143).

B138. "Concert Hall." *American Composers Alliance Bulletin* 9, no. 4 (1961): 24.
Includes in the list a performance of *Sonata for violin solo no. 1* (W177), Max Pollikoff performing at the Kaufmann Concert Hall, April 30, 1960. Includes excerpt from a review by Lester Trimble in the *New York Herald Tribune* (May 2, 1960). See: B578.

B139. "Concert Hall." *American Composers Alliance Bulletin* 10, no. 1 (1961): 21, 28.
Concerted Piece for Tape Recorder and Orchestra (W180), was performed, March 31, April 1 and 3, 1960, by the New York Philharmonic, Leonard Bernstein, conductor. Includes excerpts from reviews by Jay S. Harrison in the *New York Herald Tribune* (April 2, 1960), and Rafael Kammerer in *Musical America* (May 1960). The keyboard section listed *Chorale Fantasy for Organ* (W43), performed April 21, 1960, by Ralph Kneeream, organ. See also: B262, B315.

B140. "Concert Hall." *American Composers Alliance Bulletin* 10 (September 1962): 35.
A *Day in the Country (Duo Concertante)* (W184) was premiered April 30, 1962. Includes excerpts of the review by Allen Hughes (*New York Times*, May 1, 1962) See also: B294.

B141.   "Concert Hall." *American Composers Alliance Bulletin* 11, no. 2-4 (December 1963): 37.

List performances of 1962 and 1963, including Carmen Carrozza performing the *Rondo for Accordion* (W189) on May 6, 1962, with excerpts from the review of May 7, 1962 by Howard Klein in the *New York Times*. **See: B327.**

B142.   "Concert Hall." *American Composers Alliance Bulletin* 12, no. 1 (Spring 1964): 20.

Announces premiere and review of *Synthesis for Orchestra and Electronic Sound* (W192) with reviews from the *Erie Daily Times* of October 23, 1963. **See: B36.**

B143.   "Concert Hall." *American Composers Alliance Bulletin* 13, no. 1 (1965): 28.
Announces premiere of *Duo for Violin and Viola* (W194) in 1964.

B144.   "Concert Heralds Autumns Coming : Audience Response." *The Daily Oklahoman*, 6 October 1971.

The opening concert of the 1971-72 season of the Oklahoma City Symphony Orchestra, included a performance of *Concerted Piece for Tape Recorder and Orchestra* (W180). The reviewer was critical, stating he did not "personally care for this type of writing but there were many in attendance who obviously enjoyed the uninspired bit of nonsense."

B145.   "Concert Music." *BMI* (July 1965): 16.

Otto Luening's 65th birthday was celebrated in both Wisconsin and in Munich. The Wisconsin legislature passed a joint resolution honoring its native son composer.

B146.   "Concert of Novelties." *New York Times*, 19 March 1956, p. 27.

In the seventh program of Max Pollikoff's 'Music in Our Time' series, on 18 March 1956, tape recorder music was a "most striking novelty." It included Ussachevsky's *Piece for Tape Recorder*, Luening's *Trio for Flute, Violin, and Piano* (W152), and works by Mel Powell and Lester Trimble.

B147.   "Concert on Long Island : Five Modern Works Presented in Easthampton Home." *New York Times*, 29 July 1957, p. 16.

Included Luening's *Sonata for Viola Solo* (W176), performed in a beach house with about 150 hearing this and works by Charles Wuorinen, Carl Ruggles, Teo Macero, and Robert Starer. **See also: B429.**

B148. "Conductor Whitney Wins Music Award of $1,000." *Courier-Journal* (Louisville), 27 February 1951.

Otto Luening would present Robert Whitney, conductor of the Louisville Orchestra, the 1951 Ditson Award on February 28. A photograph of the ceremony appeared in the *Courier-Journal* the day after it occurred.

B149. "Contemporary American Music at Columbia." *New York Times*, 23 April 1950, Section 2, p. 7.

Recounts history of Annual Festival of Contemporary American Music, with 1950 being the first year without an opera. Gian-Carlo Menotti's *The Medium* was performed in 1946, Virgil Thomson's *The Mother of Us All* in 1947, and Otto Luening's *Evangeline* (W85) in 1948.

B150. "Contemp. American Musicale Coming." *Bethany Messenger*, New Series, 42, no. 11 (24 February 1953).

The weekly paper of Bethany College gives a preview of a concert set for March 4, 1953, in Lindsborg, Kansas. The S.A.I. Chorus would be performing *If That High World* (W61). **See also: B96.**

B151. "Cooper Union Plans to Retain Concerts." *New York Times*, 3 December 1958, p. 44.

Cooper Union Forum would continue "Music in the Making," performing works of living composers. Otto Luening would serve as musical director.

B152. Copland, Aaron. "Active Market in New Music Records." *Modern Music* 13 (January-February 1936): 45-47.

Copland analyzes market trends in contemporary music, and in particular the *New Music Quarterly Recordings*, under the leadership of Henry Cowell. It includes a record review of *Four Songs* by Otto Luening. These songs are *Farm Picture* (W80), *Here the Frailest Leaves of Me* (W83), *Only Themselves Understand Themselves* (W104), and *Hast Never Come to Me* (W103) **See: D8a, D12a, D13a, D24a.**

B153. Copland, Aaron. "Scores and Records." *Modern Music* 15 (November-December 1937): 45-48.

In a review of recently released material, Copland includes Luening's *Fantasia Brevis* (W101) for clarinet and piano.

B154. Copland, Aaron. "Scores and Records." *Modern Music* 15 (March-April 1938): 179-182.

One of the scores reviewed is Luening's *Two Symphonic Interludes* (W96) for orchestra (Affiliated Music Corporation). Luening "is the type of composer who tries his hand at every field and every style in music, with the result that it is hard to catalogue him.... With a greater concentration of his gifts, Luening should take rank among our best men."

B155. "Courante." *American Composers Alliance Bulletin* 11 (June, 1963): 10.

Another new concert series begins with the foundation of the Group for Contemporary Music. The co-founders were Charles Wuorinen, Harvey Sollberger, and Joel Krosnik. Compositions of George Perle, Otto Luening, and Vladimir Ussachevsky were performed.

B156. Cowell, Henry. "American Composition Committee Reviews." *Music Clubs Magazine* 30 (February 1951): 19.

Alleluia (W130), for SATB is "a spirited religious work, moderately conservative, easy to sing, and with genuine dynamic thrust."

B157. Cowell, Henry. "Composing With Tape." *Hi-Fi Music at Home* 2 (January-February 1956): 57-59.

Cowell relays his ideas of tape music, commenting on Luening's use of the flute with tape. The Louisville Symphony, in 1955, issued a recording, *Concerto for Solo Tapesicord with Symphonic Accompaniment (Rhapsodic Variations for Tape Recorder and Orchestra)* (W159), "a very musical work," by Luening and Ussachevsky. A "later work by these two composers, [*A Poem in Cycles and Bells for Tape Recorder and Orchestra* (W158)] commissioned for the Los Angeles Philharmonic for tapesicord and orchestra is still more mature, and one feels that perhaps for the first time the experiment is over and real music is forthcoming."

B158. Cowell, Henry. "Current Chronicle: New York." *Musical Quarterly* 34 (1948): 599-603.

Evangeline (W85) was performed in May, 1948, at Columbia University, the revised version reducing the orchestra to 30 performers. "The vocal writing is excellent in the Italian fashion; the liberal sprinkling of unresolved dissonance never creates a radical modern texture, although the new uses Luening finds for archaic modes made them seem modern." Cowell notes a fine sense of contrast, rhythmic shifts, and vaguely modal music. However, Cowell views the dramatic form of the opera as Luening's weakness, perceiving this more as a "documentary film, appealing more by the reasonableness of its behaviors and by its pathos than be its drama."

B159. Cowell, Henry. "Current Chronicle: New York." *Musical Quarterly* 39 (1953): 254-255.

Works by Luening and Ussachevsky were reviewed here and in a previous issue. Cowell found "the comments after the recent concert very interesting, because they emphatically supported [his] opinion that the American version of Musique Concrete is more musical and shows better organization."

B160. Cowell, Henry. "Current Chronicle: New York." *Musical Quarterly* 41 (1955): 368-373.

This article was written following the first American performance of the Varèse's *Deserts* at Bennington College, on May 17, 1955. Cowell compared the Varèse composition to *Rhapsodic Variations for Tape Recorder and Orchestra* (W159) by Luening and Ussachevsky. "Luening and Ussachevsky, working together, use many human-voice sounds, changed in range and out of original context. Varèse uses none." Cowell had called the Luening work *Concerto for Solo Tapesicord with Symphonic Accompaniment* **(See: B157)** The text of *MQ* has the title *Louisville Concerto*, a work actually composed by Jacques Ibert, which is found on the same disc.

B161. Cowell, Henry. "Current Chronicle: New York." *Musical Quarterly* 42 (1956): 240-244.

Included is a review of the incidental music to *Suite from King Lear* (W164), an Orson Welles production. "Whatever one may think of this as pure music, there is no doubt that it is ideally suited for the theater, and that probably no other sort of music-sound should produce as good a background for the storm scene.... It straddles the arts of pure theatrical sound effect and music in a new manner."

B162. Cox, Ainslee. "New York." *Music Journal* 25 (April 1967): 61.

On February 27, 1967, a concert from the series "Music in Our Time" was held at Town Hall, including a variety of current styles. "Otto Luening's *Suite for Flute Solo no. 4* (W196) seemed understated in such overstated surroundings. Its seven short movements would not be demanding for the fingers or musicianship of many flute students, nor their audiences' appreciation."

B163. Cross, Lowell. "Electronic Music, 1948-1953." *Perspectives of New Music* 7 (1968): 32-65.

"Until he began to work with tape, [Luening's] reputation was based upon flute playing, opera conducting, and a compositional style of conventional means." *Rhapsodic Variations for Tape Recorder and Orchestra*

(W159) is traditional in tonality, form and orchestration--an example of musical conservatism. "Despite the somewhat anomalous results of their conventional approach to new media, the Ussachevsky-Luening collaboration must be judged a successful one." Several chronologies are included. **See also: B34.**

B164. Dalhaus, Carl. "Luening, Otto." In *Brockhaus Riemann Musiklexikon.* Wiesbaden: Brockhaus, 1979.
This biography, in German, highlights the electronic compositions of Luening, his co-founding of the Columbia-Princeton Electronic Music Center, with a brief list of non-electronic works.

B165. "Dance Series Put Off." *New York Times,* 6 April 1956, p. 14.
Due to accidental damage of stage equipment, Jose Limon's premiere of Luening's *Theatre Piece No. 2* (W165) would be postponed until April 20-22, 1956. **See: B400.**

B166. Daniel, Oliver. "Loops and Reels." *Saturday Review,* 12 April 1969, 62.
"Music for Electronic and Older Instruments" (CRI S-227) brings us works that are the perfect introduction for the more conventional listener to the world of electronic music." The disc includes *Concerted Piece for Tape Recorder and Orchestra* (W180). Also included in the article is a photograph of the "two tape Gemini" at the Columbia-Princeton Electronic Music Center. **See: D2a.**

B167. Daniel, Oliver. "The New Festival." *American Composers Alliance Bulletin* 5, no. 1 (1955): 18.
Includes a brief discussion of Otto Luening's various compositional styles, with a brief discography.

B168. Daniel, Oliver. *Otto Luening.* New York: Broadcast Music, 1970.
This BMI pamphlet gives a biography of the composer, with several photographs of Luening, his associates at the Columbia-Princeton Electronic Music Center and elsewhere, facsimiles of scores and programs, and a classified list of compositions.

B169. Daniel, Oliver. *Philipp Jarnach.* New York: Broadcast Music, [196-?]
This small BMI pamphlet has a brief biography of Jarnach, a teacher of Luening's. Includes Otto Luening's comments on Jarnach's influence upon contemporary music, excerpts of which are in Pozzi Escot's article **(B196).** A selective list of works is also included.

B170.   Davies, Hugh. "Electronic Music: History and Development." In *Dictionary of Contemporary Music*, edited by John Vinton. New York: Dutton, 1974.
     Contrasts Karlheinz Stockhausen's *Studies 1-11* with the Luening-Ussachevsky works, such as *Rhapsodic Variations for Tape Recorder and Orchestra* (W159), *A Poem in Cycles and Bells for Tape Recorder and Orchestra* (W158).

B171.   Davies, Hugh. *Repertoire International des Musiques Electroacoustiques = International Electronic Music Catalog*. Paris: Group de Recherches Musicales de l'O.R.T.F.; New York: Independent Electronic Music Center; Cambridge, Mass.: M.I.T. Press, 1968.
     Indexes by composer, country of studio, disc manufacturer, and tape manufacturer. Includes descriptions of *Dynamophonic Interlude* (W169), *Fantasy in Space* (W148), *Low Speed* (W150), and *Rhapsodic Variations for Tape Recorder and Orchestra* (W159).

B172.   Davis, Peter G. "America's Senior Composers--Why was Their Impact Profound?" *New York Times*, 28 September 1980, Section 2, p. 25+.
     Includes caricature of Otto Luening, with Aaron Copland, William Schuman, and Samuel Barber. Compares various composers over 70. "Today's generation of composers under 60 are simply not making an equivalent impact."

B173.   Devries, Rene. "Works by Luening and Oldberg Heard." *Musical Courier*, 20 March 1937, 25.
     Review of March 11-12, 1937 performance of *Two Symphonic Interludes* (W96), are written in a "Peculiarly concise and effective idiom." The first is "ultra-modern," and dissonant contrasted with the second, which is melodic and harmonic. Luening's orchestration is also praised.

B174.   Dickinson, Peter. "The Avant-Garde in New York: Spring 1960." *Musical Times* 101 (June 1960): 377-378.
     A review of *Concerted Piece for Tape Recorder and Orchestra* (W180) (Luening-Ussachevsky), with the New York Philharmonic conducted by Leonard Bernstein, which "seemed at once a poor synthesis or antithesis of live and prefabricated music." The reyiewer felt uncomfortable with abstracted sounds being offset by the orchestra. He further noted that "independently, both men have notable achievements to their credit, but this venture showed itself to be as hazardous as the combination of a symphony orchestra and a jazz band."

B175. Dickinson, Peter. "New York." *Musical Times* 102 (July 1961): 440-441.
In March of 1961, a program at the Columbia-Princeton Electronic Music Center included *Gargoyles for Violin Solo and Synthesized Sound* (W183), in which Luening "used a solo violinist in connection with some tuneful electronic sound which pointed the way towards space-age 'pop' tunes."

B176a. *Directory of New Music.* Sedro Wooley, Wash.: Crystal Musicworks, 1978.

B176b. *Directory of New Music.* Sedro Wooley, Wash.: Crystal Musicworks, 1979.

B176c. *Directory of New Music.* Sedro Wooley, Wash.: Crystal Musicworks, 1980.

B176d. *Directory of New Music.* Sedro Wooley, Wash.: Crystal Musicworks, 1983.
"Composium: annual index of contemporary compositions" includes newly published works, and directory-type information on the composer.
In addition to the biographical/directory-type information are the recent compositions of Luening.

B177. Donner, Jay M. Rev. of *Accordion Revisited. The New Records*, 53 (October 1985): 16.
"The accordion market is [quite] limited, outside of Lawrence Welk and ethnic weddings. Unashamedly, I admit to enjoying this display of eight original works--no transcriptions here--Luening, Cowell, Surinach and the soloist being the major contributors. Friends who happened by as the recording was on the turntable were willing to pay me to turn it off, so be forewarned. Sound and pressing are excellent, and so is Schimmel." **(See: D29a)** Includes Luening's *Rondo for Accordion* (W189).

B178. Donoghue, John D. "Luening Gets Warm Welcome as Vermont Symphony's Guest." *Burlington Free Press*, 21 October 1985, p. 10A.
The first concert of the 51st year of the Vermont Symphony "needed another youngster to add spice to its program" of October 19, 1985. This was to be the 85 year old composer, Otto Luening, who conducted his *Kentucky Rondo* (W143) and *Wisconsin Suite* (W160). A complimentary review of the concert, in which the second work began to "sound like Charles Ives, only neater." The audience was appreciative of the musician who had helped to get this orchestra started, and who had appeared previously as a guest conductor and flute soloist.

B179. Downes, Edward. "Variety at 'Music in Our Time Concert'." *New York Times*, 3 February 1958, p. 26.

Review of the February 2, 1958 concert of "Music in Our Time" by Max Pollikoff. Charles McCracken premiered Luening's *Sonata for Cello No. 2 Composed in Two Day-Turns* (W175), which "contributed variety of tone color to the program" of music by Peggy Glanville-Hicks, Walter Sear, and Hal Overton.

B180. Downes, Edward. "Records: Contemporary Americans." *New York Times*, 13 January 1957, Section 2, p. 15.

In reviewing the then recent releases of Composers Recordings, the author discusses the recording of *Symphonic Fantasia No. 1* (W56) and *Kentucky Rondo* (W143), both on CRI 103. Includes a photo of the conductor, F. Charles Adler. **See: D16a, D51a.**

B181. Downes, Olin. "Luening Conducts Bennington Series." *New York Times*, 2 February 1937, p. 21.

Reviews concerts of February 1, 1937, in Town Hall--performed *Prelude to a Hymn Tune by William Billings* (W108), "an old-fashioned tune is subjected to new-fashioned counterpoint."

B182. Downes, Olin. "Opera by Luening Has Its Premiere." *New York Times*, 6 May 1948, p. 31.

Critical review of the premiere of Luening's opera *Evangeline* (W85), criticizing the composition and libretto, while praising the performance and the conductor. The premiere was May 5, 1948.

B183. Doyle, Mrs. George F. "Letter." *Louisville Times*, 5 April 1954.

Commendation of Sidney Harth's letter (**B265**) concerning the premiere of *Rhapsodic Variations for Tape Recorder and Orchestra* (W159). "The whole thing must be written off as a curious--and expensive--experiment." However, she did support the concerts as a way of hearing new music.

B184. "Dr. Luening to Keynote PBK." *The Colgate Maroon*, 20 October 1966, p. 6.

During the Otto Luening Festival, the composer would spend a week at Colgate University, in conjunction with the Phi Beta Kappa convocation. As part of the PBK Visiting Scholar Program, a concert on Wednesday, October 25, 1966, would feature Luening's works, including *Variations for Harpsichord or Piano* (W120), *Sonata for Bassoon and Piano* (W151), and chamber orchestra music.

B185. Drone, Jeanette. "American Composer Update." *Pan Pipes of Sigma Alpha Iota* 73 (Winter 1981): 35.

A list of the premieres, other performances and publications of music by Otto Luening during the year of 1980. Two new works premiered were *Potawatomi Legends for Chamber Orchestra* (W240) and *Symphonic Interlude No. 3* (W228). Several new recordings were issued.

B186. Drone, Jeanette. "American Composer Update." *Pan Pipes of Sigma Alpha Iota* 75 (Winter 1983): 34.

A list of performances and publications of music by Otto Luening during the year 1982. Noteworthy were premieres of *No Jerusalem But This* (W245), *Fantasia for Violin Solo* (W244). Luening was awarded an Honorary Doctorate from Columbia University.

B187. Drucker, Arno Paul. "A Chronological Survey and Stylistic Analysis of Selected Trios for Piano, Violin, and 'Cello Composed by Native-Born United States Composers During the Period 1920 to 1945." Diss., Peabody Conservatory of Music, 1970.

Describes the *Trio for Violin, Cello and Piano* (W42), opus 7, including over 10 musical examples. Also includes a brief biography and a list of piano trios by American composers.

B188. Duchow, Martin. "International Conference of Composers at Stratford." *Canadian Music Journal* 5 (Autumn 1960): 4-16.

A description of the international conference, including a photograph of Luening, Ussachevsky, and other composers. Of the program on August 12, 1960, the reviewer thought the *Suite from King Lear* (W164) was "not very interesting."

B189. "Electronic Music." *Faculty Notes* (Antioch College) 11 April 1962, p. 5.

Otto Luening would be heard Friday, April 20, 1962. Gives highlights of his career and pioneering into electronic music.

B190. Elsner, Carmen. "Lively Program Opens 40th Symphony Season." *Wisconsin State Journal*, 18 October 1965, Section 2, p. 1.

The Madison Civic Symphony performed *Concerted Piece for Tape Recorder and Orchestra* (W180), when conductor Roland Johnson "threw an excursion into adventure by programming" this work. Reviewer describes the orchestral part as no more dissonant or daring than works heard recently in Wisconsin, but the tape recorder was "another story."

Sounds of bells and voices of various ranges "pealed as they would from a church tower, ... with twisted sounds ..." The work is described as haunting, puzzling, with some humor, and novel.

B191. "Electronic Music." In *Academic American Encyclopedia*, 7:124-126. Danbury, Conn.: Grolier, 1984.

The article comments on the Columbia-Princeton Electronic Music Center, Luening, Ussachevsky, and their electronic compositions.

B192. Ericson, Raymond. "Music: A First for Sonata by Luening." *New York Times*, 20 November 1975, p. 50.

The *Sonata for Piano in Memoriam Ferruccio Busoni* (W162) was premiered, Tuesday, November 18, 1975, during a "Hear America First" program at the chapel of the Fifth Avenue Presbyterian Church, New York. The sonata is a "first-rate work ... played superbly by Ursula Oppens, who has already recorded it for Composers Recording Inc." Ericson comments on the relationship of Luening to Busoni.

B193. Ericson, Raymond. "League of Composers Marks Luening's 80th Birthday." *New York Times*, 27 November 1980, Section 3, p. 26.

Commenting on the fact that Aaron Copland is not the only American composer born in 1900, Ericson notes that "also 80 is Otto Luening, a major contributor to the American cultural scene as composer, educator, conductor, innovator, and promoter of his contemporaries' music." On Thursday, November 20, 1980, the League of Composers-International Society for Contemporary Music presented a concert at Carnegie Recital Hall. Luening's *Sextet* (W32) for flute, clarinet, horn, violin, viola, and cello, a "first-rate piece," was written when the composer was 18 years of age. The *Suite for Soprano and Flute* (W105) showed the composer in a "mildly experimental mood."

There was also the premiere of *Short Sonatas for Piano No. 5* (W234), *No. 6* (W235), and *No. 7* (W236).

B194. Ernst, David. *The Evolution of Electronic Music*. New York: Schirmer, 1977.

The author considers the historical significance of the collaborated compositions, especially *Rhapsodic Variations for Tape Recorder and Orchestra* (W159). Brief descriptions of several other compositions are included, with examples of *Fantasy in Space* (W148), *Low Speed* (W150), and *Synthesis for Orchestra and Electronic Sound* (W192).

B195. Ernst, David. *Musique concrete*. Boston: Crescendo Publishing Co., 1972.
Includes description of *Fantasy in Space* (W148), the flute being the only sound source, varied by reverberation.

B196. Escot, Pozzi. "Jarnach: One Beginning." *Sonus* 4 (Fall 1983): 8-11.
Within this tribute to Philipp Jarnach are Luening's comments on Jarnach's influence upon 20th century music, taken from the BMI brochure on Jarnach. **See also: B169.**

B197. "'Evangeline' par Otto Luening." *L'Evangeline* (Moncton, New Brunswick), 10 November 1948, p. 11.
In French. This is a description of *Evangeline* (W85), basically from a theater perspective.

B198. Ewen, David. "Evangeline." *Encyclopedia of the Opera*. New Enlarged Ed. New York: Hill and Wang, 1963.
Brief description of the opera by Luening, based on Longfellow's poem, premiered at Columbia University, May 5, 1948. "The music embodies various American references of the period, including Indian calls and Lutheran hymns." (See W85)

B199. Ewen, David. "Luening, Otto Clarence." In *American Composers: a Biographical Dictionary*, 424-428. London: Robert Hale, 1982.
One of the lognest biographies in current reference sources. Includes a biography, philosophical statement by Otto Luening, and a list of principal works.

B200. Ewen, David. "Music." In *The New International Year Book: a Compendium of the World's Progress for the Year 1948*, edited by Henry E. Vizetelly, 352-356. New York: Funk & Wagnalls, 1949.
One of two new American operas of 1948 was Otto Luening's *Evangeline* (W85), "found to be dramatically weak, though it did possess fine moments of vocal writing."

B201. Ewen, David. "Otto Luening." *American Composers Today*. New York: Wilson, 1949.
This biography includes a portrait of the composer, and several statements by Luening. Also a list of principal works. Ewen comments, "Luening has written many works, and in so many different styles that he has been described, in turn, as conservative and iconoclast."

B202.   Eyer, Ronald. "Works for Tape Recorder Played in Stokowski Concerts."
         Musical America 72 (15 November 1952): 8.
            A critical review of the premiere performances of *Low Speed* (W150),
         Invention in Twelve Tones (W149), and *Fantasy in Space* (W148), all
         occurring on October 28, 1952, at the Museum of Modern Art. The
         reviewer stated that tape music was still experimental.

B203.   *Famous Musicians at Work: Otto Luening*. Set #3. Pleasantville, N. Y.:
         Warren Schloat Productions, 1981. Filmstrip.
            In this filmstrip, Jane Beethoven visits Otto Luening in his music studio
         where he uses sophisticated tape recording equipment. Instead of rejecting
         the past, Luening strives to build upon all the knowledge and traditions he
         has inherited. It includes selections from *Moonflight* (W213).

B204.   Ferguson, Donald N. *Image and Structure in Chamber Music*. Minneapolis:
         University of Minnesota Press, 1964.
            Includes brief mention of Luening as a pioneer of electronic music, but
         also one who writes string quartets and sonatas. While Ferguson could not
         read the score to *Suite from King Lear* (W164), "Luening's vision and that
         of his colleague Vladimir Ussachevsky may well be longer than mine [i.e.
         Ferguson's]."

B205.   Feshbach, Sidney. "More News of Joyce in Zurich." *James Joyce Quarterly*
         20 (Fall 1982): 138-139.
            Reviews the chapter in *Odyssey of an American Composer*, in which
         Luening "recounts several interesting anecdotes of Joyce and himself." The
         composer appeared in at least two productions, under the stage name of
         James P. Cleveland. In 1958, Joyce's *Ulysses in Nighttown* (W179) was
         produced with the electronic music by Luening and Ussachevsky.

B206.   "Festival Music Flirts with Future." *Democrat and Chronicle* (Rochester, New
         York), 4 May 1962.
            Rhapsodic Variations for Tape Recorder and Orchestra (W159), in its
         Rochester premiere, "was not at all hard to take, even if it was more novelty
         than music." The indefinite sounds, rumbles, traffic simulations, and other
         sound were "carefully pitched to fit in with the orchestral music."

B207. Field, Connie Nisbet. "Flute Possibilities." *American Music* 1 (Winter 1983): 112-113.

Reviews the disc of this title, CRI SD 400. The *Suites for Solo Flute No. 3* (W186), *No. 4* (W196) and *No. 5* (W214) are "performed masterfully by Harvey Sollberger." **See D47a, D48a.**

B208. Fink, Robert, and Robert Ricci. *The Language of Twentieth Century Music: a Dictionary of Terms.* New York: Schirmer, 1975.

"Columbia-Princeton Electronic Music Center" (p. 16) is a brief history of the studios founded by Luening and Ussachevsky. Other citations within the dictionary include "Electronic Music" (p. 26), and "Tape Music" (p. 91). "Musique concrete" (p. 55-56) is principally about Pierre Schaeffer and Edgard Varèse.

B209. Finn, Robert. "Electronic Pioneer Was of Pseudo-Art." *Cleveland Plain Dealer*, 21 February 1969.

Otto Luening was a PBK Visiting Scholar on Feb. 20-21, 1969, at the Cleveland Institute of Music. He advocated the training of musicians in the electronic music field. He had earlier demonstrated excerpts from his own works.

B210. "First Performance of Luening Song Cycle." *Musical Courier* 144 (15 December 1951): 7.

The *Dickinson Song Cycle* (W125) received its first New York performance on December 11, 1951, this also being the debut of soprano Stephanie Turash. The soloist had given a preview in August of 1951 at the Composers Conference in Bennington, Vermont.

B211. "First Performances." *American Composers Alliance Bulletin* 6, no. 2 (1957): 21.

The *Suite for Bass and Piano* (W155) was performed by Robert Gladstone, double bass, and Alvin Brehm, piano, on January 22, 1957, in New York. Includes comments from the *New York Herald Tribune* (January 23, 1957): "Mr. Luening's Suite was concise, rhythmic and developed to the saturation point ..." **See: B115.**

B212. "First Performances." *American Composers Alliance Bulletin* 6, no. 4 (1957): 24.

Lists performance of *Love's Secret* (W140), April 29, 1957, Everett Anderson, baritone, in Town Hall, New York.

Otto Luening

B213. "Foreign Performances of Works of Native Born American Composers During 1960." *National Music Council Bulletin* 21 (Winter 1961): 30-32.

Includes electronic compositions, in Rome and various locations in the Netherlands; *Short Sonata for Flute and Piano No. 1* (W110), in Italy and over RAI, Severino Gazzelloni; one of the *Short Sonatas for Piano*, Italian Radio, Delia Calepai; and the joint Luening-Ussachevsky composition, *Suite from King Lear* (W164), on August 12, at the International Composers Conference in Stratford (Ontario).

B214. "Four Composers Discuss Modern Music." *National Music Council Bulletin* 20 (Fall 1959): 6-9.

In excerpts from an address presented at the Composers Symposium, January 11, 1959, during the convention of the American Symphony Orchestra League, Luening comments on the direction of modern music, his concerns about the decline in string playing and recitals in the United States. The responsibility for training young composers rests with our institutions. Other composers speaking during the convention were Gunther Schuller, Robert McBride, and Alan Hovhaness.

B215. Frank, Peter, compiler. "A Discography of Electronic Music on Recordings." *BMI* (Summer 1970): 14-22.

Includes 13 works by Luening and six collaborated compositions with Ussachevsky.

B216. Frankenstein, Alfred. "First Middlebury Conference." *Modern Music* 23 (Fall 1946): 300-301.

A description of the first annual Composers' Conference and Chamber Music Center, held at Middlebury College, Middlebury, Vermont, during August, 1946. Luening, then at Columbia University, met with younger composers, and analyzed several scores.

B217. Free Library of Philadelphia. *The Edwin A. Fleisher Music Collection of Orchestral Music in the Free Library of Philadelphia: a Cumulative Catalog, 1929-1977.* Boston: G. K. Hall, 1979.

Lists six works (p. 519) by Luening, with descriptions and premiere data where available. *Concertino for Flute* (W49), *Prelude to a Hymn Tune by William Billings* (W108), *Serenade for Three Horns and Strings* (W62), *Suite for string orchestra* (W111), *Symphonic Poem, op. 15 (Symphonic Fantasia No. 1)* (W56), and *Two Symphonic Interludes* (W96).

B218.   "French Opera 'Evangeline' Set for Today at SLI." *Tech News*, 28 October 1955.
        Preview of the concert at Southwestern Louisiana Institute on October 28, including French-Canadian music, and Otto Luening conducting his opera, *Evangeline* (W85). **See also: B40.**

B219.   Fugazza, Gian Felice. "Elettronica, Musica." In *Dizionario Enciclopedico Universale della Musica e dei Musicisti. La Lessico*, 2:120-131, edited by Albert Basso. Torino: UTET, 1983.
        In Italian. Includes descriptions of the Columbia-Princeton Electronic Music Center, early tape music of Luening and Vladimir Ussachevsky, influences of Ferruccio Busoni, and a brief description of the collaborative period of Luening and Ussachevsky. Includes bibliography. For biography, see **B591**.

B220.   Fuhrmeister, Chris. "Symphony Provides Breaks from Troubles of World." *The Caledonian-Record* (St. Johnsbury, Vermont), 1 November 1971.
        Review of concert October 30, 1971. "Stepping quietly through time, the musicians next number was *Synthesis for Orchestra and Electronic Sound* (W192) by Otto Luening. No one including this writer, knew quite what to make of the thing. The first segment was sheer dissonance. It sounded as if someone had gathered all the second violin parts from unknown symphonies together to create the piece. The second segment of the piece included a tape recording of electronic sound which the orchestra coupled with its own notes. The tape ran alone for a bit before the orchestra joined in. Since there is no score to electronic music, Director Carter had to use a stop watch to bring his group in at the right moment. The percussion section did an excellent job of following and supplementing the erratic beat of the electronic music."

B221.   Fuller, Donald. "Style in Recent Chamber Music." *Modern Music* 21 (March-April 1944): 164-169.
        The League of Composers presented a program, including works by Otto Luening.

B222.   Fuszek, Rita M. *Piano Music in Collections: an Index*. Detroit: Information Coordinators, 1982.
        Gay Picture (W166) is in a collection edited by Isadore Freed.

B223. Gagne, Cole, and Tracy Caras. *Soundpieces: Interviews with American Composers.* Metuchen, N. J.: Scarecrow, 1982.

While there is no interview per se with Luening, he is mentioned in the interviews with Henry Brant (p. 55), Charles Wuorinen (p. 384), and others.

B224. Galkin, Elliott W. "Res Musica." *High Fidelity/Musical America* 35 (April 1985): MA18.

Res Musica, an organization devoted to contemporary American music, founded by Vivian Rudow, performed *Potawatomi Legends for Chamber Orchestra* (W240) on December 2, 1984, with Luening as guest conductor. The music is reminiscent of "Farwell pentatonicism, Stravinsky bitonality, Copland's cowboy music, and Virgil Thomson's pandiatonic humor--all fused together by a craftsmanship wise and worldly."

B225. "A Gallery of Lifelong Achievers." *Music Educators Journal* 66 (April 1980): 47.

Included are a brief biography and portrait of the co-founder of the American Grand Opera Company in Chicago, and a key person in founding the American Music Center (1940), and the Columbia-Princeton Electronic Music Center (1959).

B226. "Gallery of Music." *BMI* (May 1971): 10.

In the series, a Gallery of Music in Our Time, a concert on March 7, 1971, included music of Dlugoszewski, Wuorinen, and Luening. *New York Times* critic Don Henahan describes Luening's *Sonata for Violin Solo No. 3* (W220) as a "freely serial piece in eight movements" with several "pleasing contrasts in mood, tempo and color. **See also: B273.**

B227. Geesaman, Virginia. "Twentieth-Century Literature for Unaccompanied Violin, 1900-1970." Diss., University of Iowa, 1973.

The annotated list of compositions covers *Elegy for Violin* (W195), *Meditation for Violin Solo* (W209), and *Sonata for Violin Solo, no. 2* (W211). Includes composer index, and examples of Luening's *Elegy*, compared with other contemporary solo violin music.

B228. Gerschefski, Edwin. "Henry Cowell." *Modern Music* 23 (Fall 1946): 255-260.

In a biography of Cowell, Luening is mentioned as one who "was attracted to the refreshing possibilities offered contemporary American composers by the hymn and fuguing style of several generations back. Since then nearly every composer has devoted some attention to the idiom," including Cowell.

B229. Gifford, Virginia Snodgrass. *Music for Oboe, Oboe D'Amore, and English Horn : a Bibliography of Materials at the Library of Congress.* Westport, Conn.: Greenwood Press, 1983.

Five compositions of Luening are listed, by title, with publication date and call number; divided by number of instruments.

B230. Glanville-Hicks, Peggy. "American Composers." *New York Herald Tribune,* 14 January 1952, p. 12.

Review of *Suite for Cello and Piano* (W136), performed January 13, 1952. "One of Luening's welcome assets is that he does not give a steady diet of either dissonance or consonance but, realizing the contrast and tension characteristics of each, plays them off for all they are worth."

B231. Glanville-Hicks, Peggy. "The Composers' Forum." *Pan Pipes of Sigma Alpha Iota* 45 (January 1953): 16-17.

Along with Wallingford Riegger, Henry Cowell, Peter Mennin, and Louise Talma, Luening was a member of an active reading committee which earnestly sought out young and talented composers.

B232. Glanville-Hicks, Peggy. "Luening, Otto." In *Grove's Dictionary of Music and Musicians.* 5th ed., edited by Eric Blom, 5:420-421. London: Macmillan; New York: St. Martin's Press, 1954.

A short biography and selective list of works.

B233. Glanville-Hicks, Peggy. "Music in the Making." *New York Herald Tribune,* 3 March 1953, p. 15.

Reviewed *Louisville Concerto* (W143), performed on March 1, 1953, by David Broekman and the Local 802 Orchestra. Descriptions from three perspectives included comments by reviewer, composer, and Paul Bowles, another critic.

B234. Glanville-Hicks, Peggy. "Rehearsal Concerts." *New York Herald Tribune,* 13 October 1952, p. 13.

The concert of 12 October 1952 included Luening's *Pilgrim's Hymn for Chamber Orchestra* (W133). Article only mentions that music of Luening was performed, without giving the specific title.

B235. Glanville-Hicks, Peggy. "Tapesichord: the Music of Whistle and Bang." *Vogue* 122 (July 1953): 80-82.

Description of the history of electronic music, including developments in France, and in the United States, Luening, Ussachevsky and John Cage.

While Otto Luening used flute sounds, Ussachevsky played the piano, laughed, sang, and clapped. Reviews concert of October 28, 1952, of Luening's *Fantasy in Space* (W148) *Low Speed* (W150) and *Invetnion in Twelve Tones* (W149) **See also: B553.**

B236. Gleam, Elfreda Sewell. "A Selected Graded List of Compositions for Unaccompanied Violin, With Preparatory Studies." Diss. Ball State University, 1979.

Studies 10 compositions for solo violin, including Luening's *Meditation for Violin Solo* (W209). Includes suggested bowings, fingering, some interpretation, and exercises for the student preparing to perform the works.

B237. Gojowy, Detlef. Rev. of *The Odyssey of an American Composer* by Otto Luening. *Orchester* 32 (October 1984): 892.

B238. Goldberg, Albert. "New Sounds and New Works in Los Angeles Premieres." *Musical America* 75 (January 1955): 42.

Alfred Wallenstein conducted the premiere of the Luening/Ussachevsky work, *A Poem in Cycles and Bells For Tape Recorder and Orchestra* (W158), on November 18, 1954. Goldberg viewed the music as "patently contrived." **See also: B239.**

B239. Goldberg, Albert. "Tape Recorder Used as Concert Soloist." *Los Angeles Times*, 19 November 1954, p. 8.

In his column "The Sounding Board," Goldberg reviews the premiere of the Luening/Ussachevsky work, *A Poem in Cycles and Bells for Tape Recorder and Orchestra* (W158). "The result, while undeniably novel, was not as radical as might have been expected." Flute tones are exploited in the early segment of the work, with some interesting background effects of reverberation, with later sections using the piano beyond its normal range. In Goldberg's opinion there were no startling sounds in this work.

B240. Goodman, Alfred. "Luening, Otto." *Die Musik in Geschichte und Gegenwart*, supplement, 2:1174-1175. Basel: Barenreiter, 1979.

In German, this brief biography is followed by a selective works lists and a brief bibliography.

B241. Graham, Mollie. "Finds Very Little 'Music' in Concert of Electronics." *Stratford Beacon-Harold* 13 August 1960, p. 6.

Reviews a concert which occurred during the International Conference of Composers, Stratford, Ontario, Canada, on August 12, 1960. Includes comments by Otto Luening on electronic music, and a review of the *Suite from King Lear* (W164).

B242. "Grant to Aid Study of New Music Form." *New York Times*, 26 June 1955, p. 51.

Barnard College received a Rockefeller Grant of nearly $10,000, enabling Otto Luening and Vladimir Ussachevsky to evaluate recent developments in electronic music. Funds would be used to visit radio stations and universities in Europe.

B243. Greene, David Mason. "Luening, Otto Clarence." *Greene's Biographical Encyclopedia of Composers*. Garden City, N.Y.: Doubleday, 1985.

This general biography is followed by a brief list of recordings.

B244. Griffiths, Paul. *The Thames and Hudson Encyclopedia of 20th Century Music*. London: Thames and Hudson, 1986.

Includes a brief biography of the composer ("Luening, Otto," p. 111) and references to him from "Electronic Music," "Columbia-Princeton Electronic Music Center," and "Ussachevsky, Vladimir."

B245. Grimes, Ev. "Conversations with American Composers." *Music Educators Journal* 72 (January 1986): 24-29.

This interview was part of a dissertation. Luening gives his views on education, the music industry, and directions he feels the country should move in.

B246. Gudger, William. "New Composition is Full of Good Humor." *Evening Post* (Charleston, S. C.), 31 May 1985, p. 5A.

Otto Luening, the "dean of American composers" at age 84, was be present for the premiere of *Opera Fantasia* (W257). Using melodies from popular operas of the 19th century, the "work is full of good humor and good tunes and is cast in a style that varies between neo-classical and neo-Romantic." Both violinist and pianist performed with a "flair for the dramatic, which is obviously inherent in this composition."

B247. Hadley, Benjamin. "Luening, Otto." *Britannica Book of Music*. Garden City, N. Y.: Doubleday/Britannica Books, 1980.

A brief biography emphasizes Luening's achievements in electronic music, the composer being "notable for his innovative experiments in composition employing tape."

B248.   Haggin, B. H. "Music." *Nation* 164 (31 May 1947): 667.
          Review of Luening conducting the premiere of Virgil Thomson's
          opera *The Mother of Us All*.

B249a.   Hall, David. "CRI: A Sonic Showcase for the American Composer."
          American Composers Alliance Bulletin 11, no. 2-4 (December 1963): 21-29.

B249b.   Hall, David. "CRI: A Sonic Showcase for the American Composer."
          Library Journal 88 (1 March 1963): 1826-1829.
          This description of Composers Recordings Inc. includes a review of
          two discs with music by Luening (CRI 103, CRI 112), the second including
          two compositions in collaboration with Ussachevsky. These were *A Poem
          in Cycles and Bells for Tape Recorder and Orchestra* (W158) and the *Suite
          From King Lear* (W164) The article concludes with a discography. The
          article appearing in *Library Journal* was revised for the *ACA Bulletin*.
          See: D16a, D25a, D50a, D51a.

B250.   Hall, David. "Recording". In *Dictionary of Contemporary Music*, edited by
          John Vinton. New York: Dutton, 1974.
          Discusses the use of tape for editing, speed pitch fluctuation, and
          timbre alteration.

B251.   Hannigan, Barry Thomas. "Compositional Trends in Music for Piano Solo
          Written Between 1950 and 1960 and an Annotated Catalog of Works from
          that Period." Diss., Eastman School of Music, 1980.
          Includes descriptions of the *Piano Prelude* (1952) (spurious work),
          Short Sonata for piano no. 2 (W172), and *Sonata for piano* (W162).

B252.   Hansell, Sven Hostrup. *A Provisional List of Electronic Music
          Compositions*. Urbana: University of Illinois Experimental Music Studio,
          1966.
          Descriptions of over fifteen electronic compositions by Luening, with
          performance data. *Ulysses in Nighttown* (W179) premiered in 1958. Others
          described are including *Fantasy in Space* (W148), *Invention in Twelve
          Tones* (W149), *Low Speed* (W150), *A Poem in Cycles and Bells for Tape
          Recorder and Orchestra* (W158), and *Rhapsodic Variations for Tape
          Recorder and Orchestra* (W159)

B253. Harman, Carter. "Composers Recordings, Inc." *Association for Recorded Sound Collections* 6 (1974): 26-29.

A representative history of the record company founded by Otto Luening, Douglas Moore, and Oliver Daniel, which has become the largest company dealing exclusively in contemporary music.

B254. Harman, Carter. "Luening, Otto." In *Dictionary of Contemporary Music*, edited by John Vinton. New York: Dutton, 1974.

"Luening is among the dozen or so most important composers of the formative years in modern American music." Includes a brief biographical sketch and highlights, with a list of principal compositions and writings. Four articles elsewhere in the dictionary relate to Luening. **See also: B67, B97, B170, B250, B333.**

B255. Harman, Carter. "Luening, Otto." In *Sohlmans Musiklexikon*, editor, Hanse Astrand. Stockholm : Sohlmans Forlag, 1975-1978.

In Swedish, mostly a translation of the biography in *Dictionary of Contemporary Music*, edited by John Vinton. (New York: Dutton, 1974.) **See: B254.**

B256. Harman, Carter. "Music Moves into the Future." *BMI* (Summer 1970): 4-13.

The subtitle is "The sound and means: electronic... the possibilities: limitless ... the history of a revolution." This brief history of electronic music includes references to Luening's "An Unfinished History of Electronic Music" (**B29a-b**), photographs of Luening, Ussachevsky, and others, with brief descriptions of *Rhapsodic Variations for Tape Recorder and Orchestra* (W159), *Low Speed* (W150), *Invention in Twelve Tones* (W149), and *Fantasy in Space* (W148).

B257. Harman, Carter. "Need for More Training Centers." *New York Times*, 2 May 1948, Section 2, p. 7.

Luening comments on the need for a national network of opera workshops. Conducting the premieres of Gian-Carlo Menotti's *The Medium* and Virgil Thomson's *The Mother of Us All* gave him the experience for commenting on the need for workshops. "After all, few of us can have a Leonard Bernstein career." (Luening)

B258. Harrand, Joe. "Electronic Music Pioneer Lectures at U.W. Sunday." *Capital Times* (Madison, Wisconsin), 7 November 1964, p. 9.

Otto Luening, who had lived in Madison, Wisconsin, as a boy, returned after 52 years. His visit to the University of Wisconsin would be capped by a recital on Sunday Nov. 8. Includes photograph and comments of composer.

B259. Harrison, Jay S. "Music and the Machine." *New York Herald Tribune*, 29 October 1952, p. 26.

Review of the October 28, 1952 concert of the American Composers Alliance, at the Museum of Modern Art. Works of Luening included *Fantasy in Space* (W148), *Invention in Twelve Tones* (W149), and *Low Speed* (W150). Harrison describes methods of production used by Luening and others. "It is the sound of echo, the sound of tone heard through aural binoculars. It is vaporous, tantalizing, cushioned. It is in the room, yet not a part of it. It is something entirely new."

B260. Harrison, Jay S. "Riegger Quartet is Introduced at Composers and Conductors' Concert." *New York Herald Tribune*, 24 January 1949, p. 12.

Review of *Short Sonata for Flute and Piano no. 1* (W110), played by John Wummer on January 23, 1949, observing the "sweetness of its diatonic harmonies and the nostalgic charm of its folk-like theme and variations."

B261. Harrison, Jay S. "Soprano in Debut." *New York Herald Tribune*, 13 December 1951, p. 25.

In a review of Stephanie Turash, in her New York debut, singing Luening's *Dickinson Song Cycle* (W125) with a "rich voice." The song cycle is "short, pointed and of a directness of sentiment rarely encountered these days."

B262. Harrison, Jay S. "5 Maestroes Lead 1 Philharmonic." *New York Herald Tribune*, 2 April 1960, p. 1, 6.

Harrison reviews performances of *Concerted Piece for Tape Recorder and Orchestra* (W180), with Leonard Bernstein conducting the New York Philharmonic, on March 31, and April 1 and 3, 1960. This is a critical review, describing the piece as split between the two composers, Luening writing the first 4 minutes, and Ussachevsky the last. "It is no credit to the individuality of either man that you have no idea where one left off and the other took over." He goes on to state that tape recorder/ electronic music rarely has personality, and considers their music to have "outlandish sonorities."

B263. Harrison, Lou. "Mostly Chamber Music." *Modern Music* 23 (Spring 1946): 123-125.

The Three-Choir Festival at Temple Emanu-el, directed by Lazare Saminsky, performed several works, including one by Otto Luening.

B264.   Harrison, Lou. "Reflections at a Spa." *Modern Music* 23 (Fall 1946): 296-297.
        Reviewed six concerts of music at the Yaddo Festival in September, including Luening's *Pilgrim's Hymn for Chamber Orchestra* (W133) and *Prelude for Chamber Orchestra* (W135).

B265.   Harth, Sidney. "No Tape Recorder Fan." *Louisville Times*, 31 March 1954.
        In a letter to the editor, the concertmaster of the Louisville Orchestra reacted to the premiere of *Rhapsodic Variations for Tape Recorder and Orchestra* (W159). "Let us hope that the tape recorder is not here to stay." He states it cannot be a replacement for humans, since it cannot change tempo, wait, restart, take a bow, or sign an autograph. "The whole ghastly affair of the personality-minus monster called to mind phrases of George Orwell's *1984*." Further reaction is by Calvin Bisha, a double bassist and a member of the audience. **See: B76, B183.**

B266.   Hastings, Baird. "At Long Last! The Mother of Us All." *American Record Guide* 40 (August 1977): 30-31.
        This 1947 opera by Virgil Thomson depicts the story of Susan B. Anthony. "Since its premiere at Columbia University under the direction of Otto Luening, I have seen numerous productions of the opera, and have never failed to enjoy it and to feel its poetic and humane messages."

B267.   Hauserman, Jan. "What's Electronic Music? Composer Explains It." *Erie Daily Times*, 22 October 1963.
        This preview of a concert in Erie, Pennsylvania, on October 22-23, 1963, includes comments and a photograph of Otto Luening. It describes his *Synthesis for Orchestra and Electronic Sound* (W192), to be premiered that night. **See:B36.**

B268.   Heckman, Donald. "Electronic Music." *American Record Guide* 35 (January 1969): 356-361.
        The author reviews 15 recordings, including the *Concerted Piece for Tape Recorder and Orchestra* (W180), by Luening and Ussachevsky (CRI 227), written in 1960 for Leonard Bernstein and the New York Philharmonic. It "unfolds in ... [a] conservative fashion; the preordained tape elements function in relatively reserved and unconflicting interrelationship with a traditional symphony orchestra."

B269.   "He's Electronic Music Pioneer." *Press* (Cleveland), 18 February 1969.
        Announcement of Luening's visiting lectures 20-21 February, to Case Western Reserve University, sponsored by PBK.

B270. Helm, Everett. "American Music." In *Larousse Encyclopedia of Music*, edited by Geoffrey Hindley, 433-444. London; New York: Hamlyn, 1965, reprinted 1974.

Within this one volume work is brief mention of Luening as a pioneer in electronic music. In English.

B271. Henahan, Donal. "Concert: 3 Premieres in Composers Series." *New York Times*, 16 May 1984, Section C, p. 22.

On May 14, 1984, The American Composers Orchestra premiered two works, plus a New York premiere for the third. Luening's *Symphonic Fantasia No. 4* (W216) was reviewed as cleverly orchestrated, bright, and laconic.

B272. Henahan, Donal. "The Human Electronic Musician." Rev. of *The Odyssey of an American Composer* . *New York Times*, 15 February 1981, Section 7, p. 8.

"When the history of the arts in the 20th century is written, by some word processor perhaps yet unborn, Otto Luening's name is sure to find a place on the data chip devoted to electronic music." But Henahan notes that this is but one facet of the music of Otto Luening, occupying but one chapter of the autobiography, *The Odyssey of an American Composer* . **See: B21.**

B273. Henahan, Donal. "Y.M.-Y.W.H.A. Halls Offer Diversified Music Bills." *New York Times*, 9 March 1971, p. 25.

The March 7, 1971 performance of Luening's *Sonata for Violin Solo No. 3* (W220), was played with "gusto" by Max Pollikoff, being a "freely serial piece in eight movements" with several "pleasing contrasts in mood, tempo and color." **See also: B226.**

B274. Hentoff, Nat. "Counterpoint." *Downbeat* 20 (29 July 1953): 8.

"Luening's *Fantasy in Space* (W148), for example, is most successful because of its firm structure involving a basic melodic line to which Luening taped other lines and accompanying harmonic figures in a pungently cohesive fusing." **See also: B553.**

B275. "Here & There." *High Fidelity/Musical America* 35 (August 1985): MA 12, 27.

Otto Luening received the American Eagle Award from the National Music Council for his contribution to American Music.

B276.   "Here & There." *Musical America* 107 (May 1987): 7.
          New York's Horace Mann School celebrated its centennial by commissioning Otto Luening to compose two symphonic fantasias, being no. 7 (W262) and no. 8 (W263), premiered in February, 1987, by the Horace Mann Orchestra, with Henry Bloch conducting.

B277.   Herz, Gerhard. "Current Chronicle: Louisville Kentucky (list of commissioned works)" *Musical Quarterly* 41 (1955): 76-85.
          Listed are Luening's *Louisville Concerto* (W143) and the joint composition *Rhapsodic Variations for Tape Recorder and Orchestra* (W159).

B278.   Hill, Donna Jean. "American Songs: An Introduction." *American Composers Alliance Bulletin* 7, no. 3 (1958): 10-11.
          Luening is mentioned as one of the users of William Blake's texts. Following this is an article, "Songs Available Through ACA," (*ACA Bulletin* 7, no. 3 (1958): 14)

B279.   Hiller, Lejaren A. "Musical Forms and Genres: Electronic Music." *New Encyclopaedia Britannica*, 24:600-605. Chicago: Encyclopaedia Britannica, 1985.
          Otto Luening and Vladimir Ussachevsky were the "only continuing effort" in electronic music in the United States. They were joined in 1959 by Milton Babbitt.

B280.   Hiller, Lejaren A., and Leonard M. Isaacson. *Experimental Music*. New York: McGraw-Hill, 1959.
          "Luening is perhaps the best-known experimentalist in this field in the United States." There are brief descriptions of *Suite From King Lear* (W164), *Theater Piece No. 2* (W165), and Luening's relationship with Ussachevsky.

B281.   Hinson, Maurice. *Guide to the Pianist's Repertoire*. 2nd ed., rev. and enlarged. Bloomington: Indiana University Press, 1987.
          Includes descriptions and difficulty levels for *Eight Pieces for Piano* (W66), *Five Intermezzi* (W91), *Six Piano Preludes* (W95), *Eight Piano Preludes* (W99), *Dance Sonata for Piano* (W77), *Sonata in Memoriam Ferruccio Busoni* (W162), three *Short Sonatas*, which are *No. 1* (W119), *No. 3* (W172), *No. 4* (W208), and other compositions.

B282.   Hinson, Maurice. *The Piano in Chamber Ensemble : an Annotated Guide*.
         Bloomington: Indiana University Press, 1978.
             The following works are among those described: *Sonatas for Violin
         and Piano No. 1* (W26), *No. 2* (W46), and *No. 3* (W129); *Suite for Cello
         and Piano* (W136); *Variations on Bach's Chorale Prelude Liebster Jesu wir
         sind heir* (W128); *Suite for Bass and Piano* (W155); *Short Sonatas for
         Flute and Piano* (W110, W222, W204); *Three Nocturnes for Oboe and
         Piano* (W145); *Trio for Violin, Cello and Piano* (W42); *Trio for Flute,
         Cello and Piano* (W193); and *Trio for Flute, Violin and Piano* (W152).

B283a.   Hipsher, Edward Ellsworth. *American Opera and its Composers*.
         Philadelphia: Theodore Presser, 1934.

B283b.   Hipsher, Edward Ellsworth. *American Opera and its Composers*. New
         York: Da Capo, 1978.
             Biography of Luening and description of *Evangeline* (W85). Da Capo
         is a reprint of the 1927 edition.

B284.   Holland, Bernard. "Louisville's Sound Celebration." *New York Times*, 29
         September 1987, p. C19.
             At a nostalgic concert of previous Louisville commissions, *Rhapsodic
         Variations for Tape Recorder and Orchestra* (W159) was performed. The
         concert "reenacted one of the first (1954) meetings of the tape recorder
         and orchestra, but the Luening-Ussachevsky collaboration seems now less
         an exploration of new sound than an attempt to reconcile electronics with
         the pastoral calm of Mr. Luening's orchestra."

B285.   Holmes, Thomas B. *Electronic and Experimental Music*. New York:
         Charles Scribner, 1985.
             The author includes photographs of the RCA synthesizer, and a
         description of the history of the Columbia-Princeton Electronic Music
         Center, and the influence of Otto Luening, not only in the Center, but
         upon electronic music.

B286.   Honegger, Marc. *Dictionnaire de la Musique*. [Paris]: Bords, 1970.
             "Luening, Otto" (2:653-654), in French, is a brief biography, with
         major instrumental and electronic compositions listed.
             "Etats-Unis" (3:351-356), by Nicolas Slonimsky, mentions Luening and
         Ussachevsky in connection with Varèse and electronic innovations in
         music.
             "Bande Mangetique" (3:75) by G. Brelet, gives a history of the
         collaborated compositions created at Columbia University.

B287.   "Honors and Awards." *BMI* (July 1965): 16.
         June 15, 1965, the composer's 65th birthday was celebrated in
Wisconsin, where the legislature passed a joint resolution, and in Munich,
where the composer was residing, the mayor hosted a reception in
Luening's honor.

B288.   Hopkins, Robin. "Luening Gives Union Hint of Music Future." *Wisconsin
         State Journal*, 9 November 1964.
         On Sunday, November 8, 1964, Luening concluded his return to
Wisconsin with a recital, which included *Sonority Canon for Two to
Thirty-Seven Flutes* (W191). It was described as "roof-raising" and
demanding a great deal more than the traditional conception of flute
sound."

B289.   Hovland, Michael. *Musical Settings of American Poetry.* Westport, Conn.:
         Greenwood Press, 1986.
         Listed are nine settings of poetry by Emily Dickinson, one to poetry
of Howard Moss, and eight to poetry of Walt Whitman. **See: W125, W137,
W60, W68, W74, W80, W83, W98, W103, W199, W272.**

B290.   "How New York Critics See New Works by Living Composers." *Music
         News* 41 (April 1949): 28.
         Excerpts of reviews by New York critics. Includes the premiere
review of *Pilgrim's Hymn for Orchestra* (W134), and Harrison's review of
Short Sonata for Flute and Piano No. 1 (W110) Both performances
occurred on January 23, 1949. **See: B260.**

B291.   Howard, John Tasker. *Our American Music.* 4th ed. New York: Crowell,
         1965.
         Biographical description of Otto Luening with several quotations
from reviews.

B292.   Hughes, Allen. "5 Composers Tell of Works at Concert." *New York Herald
         Tribune*, 3 February 1958, p. 12.
         A 'Music In Our Time' concert had five composers explain their
music. Otto Luening described *Sonata for Cello Solo No. 2 Composed in
Two Dayturnes* (W175) as being opposite of nocturnes.   Hughes
summarizes that these pieces are "witty parodies of a cellist's daily
setting-up exercises."

B293.   Hughes, Allen. "Colgate Glee Club Sings in Town Hall." *New York Times*, 24 April 1967, p. 38.

Works by Luening, Randall Thompson, and Vincent Persichetti were performed, with premieres of compositions by Kenneth Gaburo and Halim El-Dabh.

B294.   Hughes, Allen. "'Music in Our Time' Closes 1961 Series." *New York Times*, 1 May 1961, p. 35.

Review of performance of *A Day in the Country* (W184) for violin and tape, heard April 30. It "pitted the voice of an auctioneer against a country-fiddler kind of violin solo."

B295.   Hunt, Morton M. "The Next Sound You Hear." *Playboy* 9 (September 1962): 95.

Within a general discussion of tape music, subtitled "...May well be a Synthetic Creation of that Electronic Frankentstein the Tape Manipulator," are descriptions of the Columbia-Princeton Electronic Music Center, its RCA Electronic Music Synthesizer, and the composers associated with it, among them Otto Luening, Vladimir Ussachevsky, and Edgard Varèse. Includes comments by Luening.

B296.   "In the News." *BMI* (October 1966): 9.

Otto Luening received a citation for distinguished service to music at the 33rd annual awards dinner of the National Association for American Composers and Conductors, at New York in May, 1965. Includes photograph of composer.

B297.   "Information Department." *American Composers Alliance Bulletin* 6, no.4 (1957): 21-22.

The *Suite for Bass and Piano* (W155) was performed in Austin, Texas. Includes excerpts from the April 25, 1957 edition of the *Austin American*. **See also: B116.**

B298.   "Information Department." *American Composers Alliance Bulletin* 7, no. 1 (Fall 1957): 18.

Luening's birthday was celebrated in June during a program of "Weekend with the Masters," by station CFCF in Montreal.

B299.　"Information Department." *American Composers Alliance Bulletin* 7, no. 3 (1958): 26-29.

The New York Federation of Music Clubs and Community Opera presented an all-ACA opera program, February 17, 1958, included scenes from *Evangeline* (W85).

Otto Luening, retiring from the chairmanship of the music department, was on a sabbatical as Composer-in-Residence at the American Academy in Rome.

B300.　"Information Department." *American Composers Alliance Bulletin* 8, no. 2 (1959): 20.

Announcement of the $175,000 Rockefeller Foundation grant for the construction of the Columbia-Princeton Electronic Music Center, to be jointly managed by Otto Luening, Vladimir Ussachevsky, Milton Babbitt, and Roger Sessions.

B301.　"Information Department." *American Composers Alliance Bulletin* 9, no. 2 (1960): 17-18.

The New York press covered the premiere of *Concerted Piece for Tape Recorder and Orchestra* (W180).

B302.　"Les Interpretes a la Premiere mondiale de l'opera Evangeline." *L'Evangeline* (Moncton, New Brunswick), 6 May 1948, p. 1.

In French. Premiere review of *Evangeline* (W85) with descriptions of performers.

B303.　"Les Interpretes de l'opera Evangeline." *L'Evangeline* (Moncton, New Brunswick), 11 May 1948, p. 1.

Photographs of the premiere of *Evangeline* (W85) with descriptions in French. These photographs are also found in **B421**.

B304a.　Jacobs, Arthur. "Luening, Otto." *A New Dictionary of Music*. Chicago: Aldine Publishing Co., 1961.

B304b.　Jacobs, Arthur. "Luening, Otto." *A New Dictionary of Music*. London: Cassell, 1961.

Brief entry for Luening (p. 216-217), with three works named. Originally published in 1958 by Penguin.

B305.　Jacobs, Arthur. "Luening, Otto." *The New Penguin Dictionary of Music*. 4th ed. Harmondsworth, England: Penguin, 1977, reprinted 1978.

Brief biography.

B306.   Jacoby, Hugh William. *Contemporary American Composers Based at American Colleges and Universities*. Paradise, Calif.: Paradise Arts, 1975.
This includes a brief biography listing awards and major works, and the organizations which Luening helped to found, or has been active in.

B307.   Jarrett, Alfred Roosevelt. "'New Music' in the U.S.A., 1960-1966." Thesis. Howard University, 1967.
Composers discussed include Vladimir Ussachevsky, Otto Luening, and Halim El-Dabh.

B308.   Joffe, Matthew S. "Luening: Six Short Sonatas for Piano, Nos. 1-3, Nos. 5-7." *American Record Guide* 45 (November 1981): 25-26.
Dwight Peltzer, an apparent specialist in new music, performs admirably, in the reviewer's opinion, executing a "clean accurate sound with no trace of a cold machine gun approach," on this Serenus recording, SRS 12091. **See D32a-D37a, W119, W172, W173, W234-W236.**

B309.   Johnson, Lawrence B. "Symphony Ends Schermerhorn Festival." *Milwaukee Sentinel*, 1 March 1982.
Luening's "melodic *Short Symphony* (W237) set a new standard for terseness" during the Schermerhorn American Composers Festival, February 28, 1982.

B310.   Johnson, Lawrence B. "University of Wisconsin: Luening premiere." *High Fidelity/Musical America* 30 (August 1980): MA19-20.
Potawatomi Legends for Chamber Orchestra (W240) premiered April 13, 1980, at the University of Wisconsin--Parkside, in Kenosha, the composer conducting. It is described as a tone poem in eight short movements. Includes a photograph of Luening during rehearsal.

B311.   "Joint Commission." *New York Herald Tribune*, 21 March 1954.
Includes a description of the commissioned work, *Rhapsodic Variations for Tape Recorder and Orchestra* (W159). It had been scheduled for premiere the previous night by the Louisville Orchestra.

B312.   Joslyn, Jay. "Symphony Excels in Year's Debut." *Milwaukee Sentinel*, 5 January 1976, p.16.
Luening's *Wisconsin Symphony* (W230) was premiered January 4, 1976 by the Milwaukee Symphony. "The four movement composition is a musical history of the state from haunting primordial days to the inherent dedication to progress in the state's 'On Wisconsin.'" It included periodic use of electronic sound and Ivesian harmonies.

B313.   Kalipolites, Marcus. "Music in the Mountains opens on High Note." *The Times Herald Record* (Middleton, N. Y.), 12 July 1983, p. 32.

Review of festival "Music in the Mountains," with a chamber music concert July 9, 1983. Luening's *Sextet* (W32) for violin, viola, cello, flute, clarinet and French horn "shows the composer in a youthful neo-romantic vein. With its long-breathed flute solo, tremolo strings, seamless texture and plush harmonies shades of Puccini's operatic interludes come to mind." **See also: B390, B430.**

B314.   Kallman, Helmut, and Giles Potvin, Kenneth Winters. *Encyclopedia of Music in Canada*. Toronto ; Buffalo: University of Toronto Press, 1981.

Articles discuss *Evangeline* (W85), an opera based on Canadian themes, and its premiere, the International Conference of Composers (August 7-14, 1960, Stratford, Ontario), and Canadian born Ethel Luening, singer, and first wife of the composer.

B315.   Kammerer, Rafael. "New York Philharmonic Plays Avant-Garde Works." *Musical America* 80 (May 1960): 32.

This reviews performances of *Concerted Piece for Tape Recorder and Orchestra* (W180), with the New York Philharmonic conducted by Leonard Bernstein, in March and April of 1960.

B316.   Keats, Sheila. "Reference Articles on American Composers: an Index." *Juilliard Review* 1 (Fall 1954): 21-34.

Commentary on an article by Jack Beeson, "Otto Luening," *American Composers Alliance Bulletin* 3 (Fall 1953): 2-8. **See: B70.**

B317.   Kellogg, Virginia Katherine. "A New Repertoire: Works for Solo Violin and Tape." Diss. Eastman School of Music, 1975.

Describes *Gargoyles for Violin Solo and Synthesized Sound* (W183) in terms of the relationship of the violin and tape to each other, articulation of melodic material, and technical demands upon the violinist. Includes a glossary of terms associated with tape music, and a list of works for solo violin and tape.

B318.   Kennedy, Michael. *The Concise Oxford Dictionary of Music*. 3rd ed. London: Oxford University Press, 1980.

This edition includes articles on Milton Babbitt, Vladimir Ussachevsky, Electronic music, computers, and Musique concrete, in addition to a brief biography of Luening.

B319. Kennedy, Michael. *The Oxford Dictionary of Music*. London; New York: Oxford University Press, 1985.

In a biography of Luening is mentioned the music for the production of Shaw's *Back to Methuselah* (W168).

B320. Kenngott, Louise. "Sounding Board." *Milwaukee Journal*, 8 April 1979.

Preview of the lectures Otto Luening gave in April 1979 at the University of Wisconsin at Parkside. Includes several quotes by Luening.

B321. Kerner, Leighton. "Schuller Obeys the Berg principle." *Village Voice* (10 July 1978): 63-64.

Music for Orchestra (W51) waited 55 years for its first performance, "a performance that ate hungrily from the work's strong, lean, hymnic, upward-striving lines and from its sure sense of climax and response." It was performed at the American Composers Orchestra concert, in 1978, Gunther Schuller conducting.

B322. Kerr, Russell. "New York." *Musical Courier* 163 (June 1961): 17-18.

Max Pollikoff directed a program at Kaufmann Auditorium, April 30, 1961. *Duo Concertante* (W184), for violin and tape recorder, "subtitled *A Day in the Country*--ironically, one supposes, for it uses a fairly conventional violin part that alternates rustic, dancelike sections with sentimental movements in a continuous texture. Accompanying this was a recording (operated by the composer) in which the noise of a crowd, the sing-song of an auctioneer, and the like were heard." Included are photographs of Luening and Vladimir Ussachevsky operating tape equipment at McMillin Theatre.

B323. Kingman, Daniel. *American Music : A Panorama*. New York: Schirmer, 1977.

Commenting on electronic music (p. 516), the author observes that "the carefully crafted compositions--some of them large-scale, and by no means inexpressive--of composers such as Vladimir Ussachevsky and Otto Luening, and after them Mel Powell, Kenneth Gaburo, and especially Morton Subotnik, are representative of what is possible in the medium."

B324. Kirkpatrick, John. "Bennington's Festival of the Arts." *Modern Music* 18 (November-December 1940): 52-54.

The first summer festival of the Bennington School of the Arts was directed by Otto Luening. Fifteen composers' works were performed, including Luening's *Three Inventions for Piano*, part of *Eight Inventions for*

Piano (W114) and two compositions for voice and flute, *Evening Song* and *Morning Song*, from *Suite for Soprano and Flute* (W105)

B325.   Kirkpatrick, John. "The Challenge of the Harpsichord." *Modern Music* 23 (Fall 1946): 273-276.

"Many modern composers use the specific color of the harpsichord in combination with other instruments," among them Otto Luening.

B326.   "Kirkpatrick in Recital." *New York Times*, 21 November 1939, p. 18.

On November 20, 1939, Ralph Kirkpatrick, harpsichordist, gave a recital at the Carnegie Chamber Hall, consisting of twentieth century music. He accompanied Otto Luening on flute, in a performance of his *Short Sonata for Flute and Harpsichord* (W110).

B327.   Klein, Howard. "Carrozza Presents Accordion Recital." *New York Times*, 7 May 1962, p. 39.

Review of the May 6 performance of *Rondo for Accordion* (W189) by Carmen Carrozza. The Luening piece was "neatly handled and well conceived." Klein noted that Luening was becoming known for his electronic music innovations, but that he never quit writing music for traditional instruments.

B328.   Klein, Howard. "Ensemble Plays First Program." *New York Times*, 23 October 1962, p. 43.

The Group for Contemporary Music, sponsored by Columbia University and the Alice M. Ditson Fund, held its inaugural concert on October 22, 1962. Luening's *Trio for Flute, Cello and Piano* (W193) had "romantic overtones" with ideas developed in such a way that it displayed more continuity than the other compositions performed.

B329.   Klein, Howard. "Screech of Music is Heard at Cafe." *New York Times*, 18 June 1962, p. 21.

"Screeches, wails, crashes, twangs, roars, twiddlings and buzzings announced in the Cafe Figaro ... yesterday (June 17, 1962) that electronic music was here to stay." Included music of Milton Babbitt, Vladimir Ussachevsky, Edgard Varèse, and Luening's *Gargoyles for Violin Solo and Synthesized Sound* (W183).

B330.   Kobialka, Nancy. "Links to New York: Wisconsin's Contributions to Contemporary Music." *Music Library Association Newsletter* 63 (March-April 1986): 7-8.

Two composers, Otto Luening, and Michael Torke, joined music critic James Chute in a discussion during the 1986 Music Library Association Annual Conference, in Milwaukee. Excerpts from three works were heard: *Symphonic Interlude No. 2* (W96, No. 2); *Synthesis for Orchestra and Electronic Sound* (W192); *Wisconsin Suite* (W160).

B331.   Komorowski, Hans-Peter. *Die 'Invention' in der Musik des 20. Jahrhunderts.* Regensburg: Gustav Bosse, 1971.

Luening's composition for flute and tape, *Invention in Twelve Tones* (W149) is discussed. (p. 16, 21)

B332.   Kozinn, Allan. "A Composers' Cooperative That Works." *New York Times*, 14 February 1982, Section 2, p. 21.

During the 1930s, five American composers organized the objective of an "American music archive and distribution center [which] might further cause" of American music. These were Otto Luening, Quincy Porter, Aaron Copland, Howard Hanson, and Marion Bauer. "'The point was,' Luening recalls, 'that it was no good always talking about American music if nobody could their hands on it.'"

Luening led *New Music Quarterly Recordings* and New Music Publications. There is also a description of the American Music Center, and its relationship to the Research Libraries Information Network (RLIN)

B333.   Kriegsman, Alan and Sali Ann Kriegsman. "Dance." In *Dictionary of Contemporary Music*, edited by John Vinton. New York: Dutton, 1974.

Mentions Luening as a composer who wrote music for Doris Humphrey.

B334.   Krummel, Donald W., et al. *Resources of American Music History: a Directory of Source Materials from Colonial Times to World War II.* Urbana: University of Illinois Press, 1981.

Various special collections are named which hold primary sources of information relating to Otto Luening.

B335.   Krutz, Jon. "Otto Luening: an 85-year Investment in American Music." *Sinfonian* 35 (October 1985): 10-13+.

Biographical, highlighting musical career, with four photographs from his childhood to the 1980s. Includes interview, "Thought on Music in America," and an essay by Luening, "My Idea of a Good Sinfonian."

B336.   Kyle, Marguerite Kelly. "AmerAllegro." *Pan Pipes of Sigma Alpha Iota* 44 (January 1952): 38.

Includes news of premieres, publications and other selected performances of 1951. Noteworthy were premieres of *Two Byron Songs: (The Harp the Monarch Minstrel Swept* (W142) and *She Walks in Beauty* (W146)), *Legend for Oboe and Strings* (W144), and *Three Nocturnes for Oboe and Piano* (W145).

B337.   Kyle, Marguerite Kelly. "AmerAllegro." *Pan Pipes of Sigma Alpha Iota* 45 (January 1953): 60.

Includes lists of performances during 1952, and the announcement of his election to the National Institute of Arts and Letters cited as a composer "likely to have a permanent influence on American music." premiered, and *Tiger's Ghost* (W147) was performed over sixty times by Leonard de Paur's Infantry Chorus.

B338.   Kyle, Marguerite Kelly. "AmerAllegro." *Pan Pipes of Sigma Alpha Iota* 46 (January 1954): 50.

Luening was elected a life member of the National Institute of Arts and Letters in 1952 as "one of the composers of our time whose work is likely to have a permanent influence on American life." He also was elected Vice-President of the Institute in 1953. Performances of 1953 are listed, both live and radio broadcasts, including *Kentucky Concerto* (W143), *Fantasy in Space* (W148), *Invention in Twelve Tones* (W149), and *Low Speed* (W150)

B339.   Kyle, Marguerite Kelly. "AmerAllegro." *Pan Pipes of Sigma Alpha Iota* 47 (January 1955): 56.

Lists of significant events of 1954, including his joint commission with Vladimir Ussachevsky, *Rhapsodic Variations for Tape Recorder and Orchestra* (W159).

B340.   Kyle, Marguerite Kelly. "AmerAllegro." *Pan Pipes of Sigma Alpha Iota* 48 (January 1956): 60.

A list of performances during late 1954 and 1955. Alfred Wallenstein conducted the Los Angeles Philharmonic Orchestra in the November 18, 1954, premiere of *A Poem in Cycles and Bells for Tape Recorder and Orchestra* (W158).

B341.   Kyle, Marguerite Kelly. "AmerAllegro." *Pan Pipes of Sigma Alpha Iota* 49 (January 1957): 58.

A list of the 1956 performances of Luening's compositions, including *Incantation* (W153) (Luening-Ussachevsky), on March 13, during the "Today" program, and another collaborated work, the electronic sound score from *Carlsbad Caverns* (W161) for "Wide, Wide World" on CBS, May 12.

B342.   Kyle, Marguerite Kelly. "AmerAllegro." *Pan Pipes of Sigma Alpha Iota* 50 (January 1958): 61-62.

List of performances, recordings, and other significant events of 1957, including an October 3 lecture at Brown University, Providence, Rhode Island, on "New Directions in Music." During the Ninth Annual Convention of the Audio Engineering Society in New York, October 9, he was chairman of "Electronic Music." Lists other activities of the year, some with Ussachevsky.

B343.   Kyle, Marguerite Kelly. "AmerAllegro." *Pan Pipes of Sigma Alpha Iota* 53 (January 1961): 66.

A list of events of 1960, premieres included *Concerted Piece for Tape Recorder and Orchestra* (W180), and other selected performances including *Sonata for Violin Solo no. 1* (W177), and a live performance of *Rhapsodic Variations for Tape Recorder and Orchestra* (W159) at the Anglo-Uruguayan Cultural Institute in Montevideo.

B344.   Kyle, Marguerite Kelly. "AmerAllegro." *Pan Pipes of Sigma Alpha Iota* 55 (January 1963): 60.

A list of premieres, other selected performances, and lectures during 1962. Noteworthy among these were *Rhapsodic Variations for Tape Recorder and Orchestra* (W159), *A Poem in Cycles and Bells for Tape Recorder and Orchestra* (W158), and *Gargoyles for Violin Solo and Synthesized Sound* (W183). Luening gave lecture-demonstrations of electronic music throughout Europe in January of 1962, and major presentations were given in the USSR at the invitation of Soviet composers.

B345.   Kyle, Marguerite Kelly. "AmerAllegro." *Pan Pipes of Sigma Alpha Iota* 56 (January 1964): 69.

Events of 1963, including the premiere of *Synthesis for Orchestra and Electronic Sound* (W192), performances of *Sonority Canon for Two to Thirty-Seven Flutes* (W191) and *Rhapsodic Variations for Tape Recorder and Orchestra* (W159) (Houston), several new scores published, and the Doctor of Music degree conferred by Wesleyan University.

B346.   Kyle, Marguerite Kelly. "AmerAllegro." *Pan Pipes of Sigma Alpha Iota* 58 (January 1966): 73-74.

1965 marked the 65th birthday of the composer, and the 50th anniversary of his entry into the profession of music. Several premieres of both 1964 and 1965 are listed. These included *Suite for Flute Solo No. 3* (W186), *Three Duets for Two Flutes* (W188), *Elegy for Violin* (W195), and *Suite for High and Low Instruments* (W197).

Electronic music by Luening was placed in the Westinghouse Time Capsule buried at the conclusion of the World's Fair in New York, on October 17, a capsule to be opened in the seventieth century.

B347.   Kyle, Marguerite Kelly. "AmerAllegro." *Pan Pipes of Sigma Alpha Iota* 60 (January 1968): 82-83.

Lists performances of late 1966 and 1967, including the premiere of *Suite for Flute Solo No. 4* (W196) and *Trio for Three Flutists* (W205). Luening gave lectures and demonstrations at such colleges as Kalamazoo, Dickinson, Middlebury, and Mount Holyoke. He also wrote tributes for composers Quincy Porter, Henry Cowell, and Edgard Varèse in the Proceedings of the National Institute of Arts and Letters, 1966-1967.

B348.   Kyle, Marguerite Kelly. "AmerAllegro." *Pan Pipes of Sigma Alpha Iota* 63, no. 2 (1971): 68-69.

Lists premieres of 1968, 1969, and 1970. Noteworthy among these was *The Incredible Voyage* (W212), telecast October 13, 1969 on CBS TV's *The Twenty-First Century.* Also several other performances of 1970. On May 15, 1969, Luening served on a panel, "The New York Contemporary Music Scene," broadcast by WNYC Radio.

B349.   Kyle, Marguerite Kelly. "AmerAllegro." *Pan Pipes of Sigma Alpha Iota* 64, no. 2 (1972): 67.

Lists premieres, such as *Sonata no. 3 for Violin* (W220) and other selected performances and events of 1971. Luening lectured for the Madawaska Historical Society, August 18, 1971, on "Evangeline" (W85)

B350.   Kyle, Marguerite Kelly. "AmerAllegro." *Pan Pipes of Sigma Alpha Iota* 65 (January 1973): 62.

Events of late 1971 and 1972 are listed. *Introduction and Allegro for Trumpet and Piano* (W218) was premiered. *Lyric Scene for Flute and Strings* (W171) was the noteworthy performance. In August of 1972 he was composer in residence at the Johnson State Composers Conference in Vermont. He also received the Laurel Leaf from ACA.

B351.   Kyle, Marguerite Kelly. "AmerAllegro." *Pan Pipes of Sigma Alpha Iota* 69 (January 1977): 58.

Performances of 1976 included the 32nd Festival of Contemporary Music, February 18-26, at Louisiana State University.

Compositions performed included *If That High World* (W61), *Alleluia* (W130), *Psalm 146* (W219), *Lines from a Song for Occupations* (W199), *Sonority Canon for Two to Thirty-Seven Flutes* (W191), *Sonata for Trombone* (W154), and *Sonata for Piano* (W162)

B352.   Laderman, Ezra. "Music in Our Time." *Musical America* 78, no. 4 (March 1958): 24-25.

A review of the Feb. 2, 1958 concert of 'Music in Our Time.' Luening's *Sonata Composed for Cello Solo No. 2 Composed in Two Dayturnes* (W175) is a "musical prank that comes off." Study-like exercises are used. The second movement alternates a pizzicato motive and a sonorous chordal theme.

B353.   Landeck, Beatrice, and Elizabeth Cook, Harold C. Youngberg. "Listening to the Composer: Otto Luening." In *Making Music Your Own*, 6:200-201. Morristown, N. J.: Silver Burdett, 1964-65.

Brief biography and description of *Fantasy in Space* (W148) and the process of creating this composition. Includes photos. Luening was a "special contributor" to the 6th grade level volume and the "special consultant for basic music concepts" for the series. **See: D7f.**

B354.   Landsman, Jerome. *Annotated Catalogue of American Violin Music Composed Between 1947-1961*. Urbana, Ill.: American String Teachers Association, 1968.

Included is a brief biographical statement, followed by a description of *Sonata for Violin Solo No. 3* (W220).

B355.   Lang, Paul Henry. "Dictatorship of the Tube." *New York Herald Tribune*, 21 May 1961, Section 4, p. 13.

This is a very critical review of two concerts at McMillin Theatre, May 9 and 10, 1961. The Luening composition in the program was *Gargoyles for Violin Solo and Synthesized Sound* (W183). While Luening was not mentioned directly, the philosophy of the acceptance of his "new music" was.

Part of the continuing debate on electronic music. **See also: B66, B356, B357**. Also described in Luening's "Origins". **See: B22**.

B356. Lang, Paul Henry. "Electronic Game; Its Ground Rules." *New York Herald Tribune*, 18 June 1961, Section 4, p. 15.

Continuation of the debate on new electronic music. **See also: B66, B355, B357**. Luening was not mentioned directly. Also described in Luening's "Origins". **See: B22**.

B357. Lang, Paul Henry. "Music and Musicians: the Chaos Machine." *New York Herald Tribune*, 28 May 1961, Section 4, p. 11.

Response to Barzun's **(B66)** comments and letter to *NYHT* concerning the latter's comments on electronic music at Columbia University. The article stresses Varèse more than the other electronic composers. Luening is not mentioned directly in this article. Also described in "Origins". **See also B22, B73, B355, B356**.

B358. LaRue, Jan. "An Electronic Concert in New York." *Music Review* 22 (1961): 223-225.

A review of the May 9, 1961 concert at McMillin Theatre. "Otto Luening's *Gargoyles for Violin Solo and Synthesized Sound* (W183) disarmed the listener with its title: how could one better explore the character of gargoyles than with electronic music." Max Pollikoff performed live on the violin, a "contrast ... [which] seemed too divisive."

B359. Lantz, Russell A. "American Composers and Their Works: 1880-1934." Thesis. Ohio State University, 1934.

In this catalog of 600 composers is a selective list of about 25 works by Otto Luening (p. 119-120), classified.

B360. Levy, Marvin D. "Bennington Composers Conference." *Musical America* 75 (1 November 1955): 14.

At this conference composers were given opportunities to discover and explore the tape recorder. Otto Luening, recently returned from Europe "reported the variety of musical uses to which tape is being put."

B361. Lewis, Eugene. "A Challenge, Instead of a Sop." *Dallas Times Herald*, 1 January 1967, p. A29.

Review of a series of youth concerts by the Dallas Symphony Orchestra. Included Luening's *Synthesis for Orchestra and Electronic Sound* (W192). Includes criticism of Charles Blackman's selection of this music, and the conductor's response.

B362. "A List of American Operas." *American Composers Alliance Bulletin* 7, no. 4 (1958): 19-20+.

Coded description of *Evangeline* (W85), with duration, and availability of piano vocal score.

B363. "Louisville Orchestra in Novelty by Luening." *Musical Courier* 145 (1 May 1952): 18.

A program of exclusively 20th century music, on March 5, 1951, was controversial, producing several critical letters in local newspapers. Luening conducted his *Louisville Concerto* (W143). "The name has nothing to do with the contents, but expresses the fact that it was commissioned by the Louisville Philharmonic Society. The work, in three short movements, ... is skillfully orchestrated, and has ear-appealing melodies, but seems to lack serious substance. Yet the audience did not seem to mind."

B364. Lubin, Ernest. "Composers' Conference: Intensive Period of Study at Middlebury College. *New York Times*, 9 September 1950, Section II, p. 7.

Describes Composers' Conference lead by Luening. "Of the many works brought to light, a number of fine things deserve to be noticed ... Otto Luening's beautiful 'Andante and Variations'" [*Sonata for Violin and Piano, no. 3* (W129)] "The conference has a valuable contribution to make to our musical life."

B365. "Luening Concert Closes Series." *Ranger* (University of Wisconsin--Parkside), 1 April 1982, p. 7.

Three works of Luening would be performed at the University of Wisconsin--Parkside on April 2, 1982: *Coal Scuttle Blues* (W44), *Introduction and Allegro for Trumpet and Piano* (W218), *Trio for Violin, Cello and Piano* (W42). Biographical comments limited to pre-1960 achievements.

B366. "Luening Concerto and William Kapell to be Heard at Orchestra's Concerts." *Courier-Journal* (Louisville), 2 March, 1952.

Announces the premiere of the *Louisville Concerto* (W143), with Otto Luening conducting. Gives a brief biographical sketch of the composer.

B367. "Luening, Otto." In *Collins Pocket Dictionary of Music*. London: Collins, 1982.

Based on *Collins Pocket Encyclopedia of Music*, published in the United States as *The New College Encyclopedia of Music*, edited by J. A. Westrup and F. Ll. Harrison.

B368.   "Luening, Otto." In *Contemporary Authors*, 102:349-350. Frances C. Locher, editor. Detroit: Gale Research, 1981.

This biography traces both the personal and the professional facets of Luening, and includes comments from an interview of the composer, published in *Contemporary Authors*.

B369.   "Luening, Otto." In *Diccionario de la Musica Labor*, 2:1440. Barcelona: Labor, 1954.

A brief biography, in Spanish, covers Luening to his appointment at Columbia University; includes a short list of works.

B370.   "Luening, Otto." In *Dizionario Ricordi della musica e dei musicisti*. Milano: Ricordi, 1959.

A brief biography, in Italian, includes a selected list of works (p. 693).

B371.   "Luening, Otto." In *Enciclopedia Salvat de la Musica*. Barcelona: Salvat, 1967.

Brief biography in Spanish.

B372.   "Luening, Otto." In *Enciclopedia della musica*. Milano: Ricordi, 1972.

A brief biography, in Italian, includes a selected list of works.

B373.   "Luening, Otto." In *Encyclopedie de la Musique*. Paris: Fasquelle, 1961.

Brief biography in French.

B374.   "Luening, Otto." In *Encyclopedie van de Muziek*. Amsterdam: Elsevier, 1957.

Brief biography in Dutch; mentions the opera *Evangeline* (W85).

B375.   "Luening, Otto." In *Das Grosse Lexikon der Musik*, 5:168.   Freiburg: Herder, 1976.

This biography, in German, covers Luening to his co-founding of the Columbia-Princeton Electronic Music Center.

B376.   "Luening, Otto." In *International Cyclopedia of Music and Musicians*. 11th ed. Bruce Bohle, editor. New York: Dodd, Mead, 1985.

This brief biography includes a classified list of works, and a list of composers he taught.

B377.   "Luening, Otto." In *International Who's Who in Music*. 10th ed. Cambridge, England: International Who's Who in Music, 1985.

A brief entry includes biographical and directory type information.

B378. "Luening, Otto." In *Larousse de la Musique*. Paris: Larousse, 1957.
In French. Brief biography, covering Luening's career up to *Evangeline* (W85). **See also: B99.**

B379. "Luening, Otto." In *Mala Encyklopedia Hudby*, edited by Marian Jurik. Bratislava: Obzor, 1969.
In Czech; brief biography with reference to the article on "Ussachevskij, Vladimir."

B380. "Luening, Otto." In *La Musica*. Guido M. Gatti, Alberto Basso, editors. Torino: UTET, 1971.
Brief biography, in Italian, with a selective classified list of works.

B381. "Luening, Otto." In *Der Musik Brockhaus*. Mainz: Schott, 1982.
Brief biography in German, listing major works. Emphasis is on the Columbia University period.

B382. "Luening, Otto." In *Musikkens Hvem Hvad Hvor*, edited by Ernst Bramsen. Kobenhavn: Politikens Forlag, 1961.
Brief biography in Danish; list major compositions, including some electronic music.

B383. "Luening, Otto." In *New Columbia Encyclopedia*, edited by William H. Harris, Judith S. Levey. New York: Columbia University Press, 1975.
A brief biography of the American flautist and composer.

B384. "Luening, Otto." In *New Encyclopedia Britannica*, 7:548. 15th ed. Chicago: Encyclopedia Britannica, 1985.
This brief biography names major works of the composer, and includes a photograph.

B385. Luening, Otto. Personal interview by Joan Thomson, 15 December 1978. Tape Recording, Oral History, American Music Collection of Yale University.
Joan Thomson interviewed the composer for about 1 1/2 hours, in New York City, discussing electronic music.

B386. Luening, Otto. Personal interview by Vivian Perlis, 5 May 1982. Videorecording, Oral History, American Music Collection of Yale University.
Vivian Perlis interviewed the composer for about 2 1/2 hours, in New York City. The content is biographical and musical.

B387.   Luening, Otto. Personal interview by Margaret Fairbank Jory, 1967.
         Recording. Oral History, American Music Collection of Yale University.
             This interview was acquired from Margaret Fairbank Jory, occurring
         in New York City, with a duration of 1 1/2 hours. The content is
         biographical.

B388.   "Luening, Otto." In *Who's Who in America*, 2:2036. 43rd ed. 1984-1985.
         Chicago: Marquis Who's Who, 1984.
             The brief biography of the composer, conductor, and flutist includes
         his professional employment and honors.

B389.   "Luening, Otto." In *Who's Who in American Music: Classical*. New York:
         R. R. Bowker, 1985.
             A directory of information about the composer (p. 364).

B390.   "Luening, Stokes in concert." *The Daily Freeman* (New Paltz, N. Y.), 4 July
         1983, p. 6.
             Preview of festival "Music in the Mountains," at New Paltz, N. Y.,
         with a chamber music concert July 9, 1983, featuring Luening's *Sextet*
         (W32) for violin, viola, cello, flute, clarinet and French horn, with the
         composer as a guest, sponsored by the "Meet the Composer" program.
         Includes brief biography and photograph of Luening. **See also: B313,
         B430.**

B391.   "Luening-Ussachevsky Tape Work Premiered." *Musical America* 75 (15
         December 1955):921.
             Howard Shanet conducted *Rhapsodic Variations for Tape Recorder
         and Orchestra* W159), with the Columbia University Orchestra, at
         McMillin Theater, on December 3, 1955. Robert Whitney had premiered
         the work in early 1954 with the Louisville Orchestra. The work represents
         the first use in this country of a tape recorder and orchestra
         simultaneously. The sounds used were flute, piano, and percussion. "The
         work is the most musically fascinating piece of its kind to be produced to
         date." Its moderate difficulty level for the orchestra presents a
         composition feasible for nonprofessional groups.

B392.   "Luening Work Played." *New York Times*, 24 January 1949, p. 15.
             A new version of *Pilgrim's Hymn for Orchestra* (W134) was
         premiered on January 23, 1949. This is a critical review of the composition
         in its new arrangement for full orchestra.

189

B393.   Lust, Patricia. *American Vocal Chamber Music, 1945-1980*. Westport, Conn.: Greenwood Press, 1985.

The *Suite for Soprano and Flute* (W105), composed in 1936-1937, "contains much chromatic movement, glissandi, and trills."

B394.   Lyons, James. "Modern Americans, domestic and domesticated." *American Record Guide* 23 (September 1956): 2-4.

In reviewing *Symphonic Fantasia No. 1* (W56), on Composers Recordings CRI-103, Lyons notes that "Luening has been a champion of electronic esthetics (with Ussachevsky), but he can make nice music the old fashioned way, also, as these works attest." **See: D51a.**

B395a.   Machlis, Joseph. *Introduction to Contemporary Music*. New York: Norton, 1961.

B395b.   Machlis, Joseph. *Introduction to Contemporary Music*. 2nd ed. New York: Norton, 1979.

B395c.   Machlis, Joseph. *Introduction to Contemporary Music*. New York: Dent, 1980.

First edition describes *Rhapsodic Variations for Tape Recorder and Orchestra* (W159), a collaboration of Luening and Ussachevsky, plus major tape works by Otto Luening, including *Fantasy in Space* (W148), *Invention in Twelve Tones* (W149), *Low Speed* (W150).

In the second edition, Luening's influence is readily evident from the fifteen index entries as a teacher. Machlis also includes a brief history of the Columbia-Princeton Electronic Music Center. The dictionary within the text gives a very brief biography, listing major works.

B396.   Magers, Roy V. Rev. of *The Odyssey of an American Composer*, by Otto Luening. *Music Educators Journal* 69 (March 1983): 84-85 + .

The book's "merits lie to a considerable extent in what [Luening] tells us about others and about the state of the musical world in the first half of this century." Positive review in that anyone reading the biography will never again associate Otto Luening only with electronic music. Magers finds the book informative, at and times, amusing.

B397.   "Many Attended Symphony." *New York Times*, 13 April 1936, p. 15.

Two Symphonic Interludes (W96), as well as attending composer Otto Luening, were "well received" by the audience, on April 11, 1936.

B398.   Marcus, Genevieve. "New Concepts in Music from 1950 to 1970: a Critical Investigation of Contemporary Aesthetic Philosophy and its Translation into Musical Structures." Diss., UCLA, 1973.
         The author discusses the influence of Otto Luening and Vladimir Ussachevsky upon twentieth century music, including such works as *Rhapsodic Variations for Tape Recorder and Orchestra* (W159) (by Luening and Ussachevsky), and *Gargoyles for Violin Solo and Synthesized Sound* (W183) by Luening. The American style is compared to European schools. Includes index.

B399.   Maris, Barbara English. "American Compositions for Piano and Tape-Recorded Sound." Diss., Peabody Conservatory of Music, 1976.
         There are several references to articles by Luening, and his appearances on the "Today" show. Maris briefly discusses the historical significance of the collaborated compositions (e.g., *Rhapsodic Variations for Tape Recorder and Orchestra* (W159) and *Gargoyles for Violin Solo and Synthesized Sound* (W183)).

B400.   Martin, John. "Juilliard: Premieres by Humphrey and Limon in Festival." *New York Times*, 1 April 1956, Section 2, p. 8.
         Preview and description of music to be performed later in April, by Jose Limon and his dance company. Included would be the premiere of *Theater Piece No. 2* (W165), with music by Otto Luening. The piece was subtitled "a concerto for light movement, sound and voice." It was tentatively scheduled for April 17, and rescheduled for April 20 **See: B165.**

B401.   Mason, Elizabeth B., and Louis M. Starr. *The Oral History Collection of Columbia University*. New York: Oral History Research Office, 1979.
         Lists several oral histories, including that of Luening, the transcript covering 607 pages, discusses his family background, early music education, teaching career at various campuses, the development of electronic music, and impressions of Aaron Copland, Leonard Bernstein, Randall Thompson, and John Cage. Luening is also discussed in the oral history of Vladimir Ussachevsky.

B402.   McCoy, Guy. "Otto Luening." In *Portraits of the World's Best Known Musicians*. Philadelphia: Theodore Presser, 1946.
         Portrait on p. 119 with brief description.

B403.   McGeer, Ada. "Balanced Program by Honolulu Symphony." *Honolulu Advertiser*, 12 March 1956.

A review of the Honolulu Symphony's performance of Luening's *Louisville Concerto* (W143). Following Bach's *Violin Concerto in E Major*, "its linear construction gave it a certain distinction but it was overshadowed by the great classic. The American tunes incorporated in harmonies and reproduced in a straight-forward manner did something to mitigate its over-simplification."

B404.   McGregor, Jean. "Yaddo Group Presents Contemporary Music; Composers Critics Attend." *The Saratogian*, 16 September 1946.

Luening conducted his *Prelude to a Hymn Tune by William Billings* (W108), and *Pilgrim's Hymn for Chamber Orchestra* (W133). The Yaddo Music Group considered it a "high honor" to perform these. Includes a brief biography of the composer.

B405.   McInerney, John. "Juilliard School: Festival of Contemporary Music." *High Fidelity/Musical America* 32 (August 1982): MA26-27.

During the 2nd annual festival, Jose Serebrier led the Juilliard Philharmonia in performances of *Symphonic Fantasia no. 3* (W215) and *Symphonic Interlude no. 3* (W228). "Neither established much momentum; the former seemed a vigorous instruction, the latter is a vague ternary relying on a motive passed around the orchestra like a lost child."

B406.   McLellan, Joseph. "Noteworthy Odyssey." Rev. of *The Odyssey of an American Composer*, by Otto Luening. *Washington Post*, 16 January 1981, p. C9.

This review of *The Odyssey of an American Composer* highlights some of the events in the life of Otto Luening, such as his "uncommonly varied list of accomplishments." The review credits the composer with having "a skill with words comparable to his mastery of musical forms." See: B21.

B407.   McPhee, Colin. "Records and Scores." *Modern Music* 17 (March-April 1940): 179-181.

Luening's *Suite for Soprano and Flute* (W105) was among the then recent recordings of New Music. "Although a little thin in musical content, [it] is so charmingly performed that it is very agreeable to listen to."

B408.   McPhee, Colin. "Scores and Records." *Modern Music* 19 (March-April 1942): 190-192.
Luening's *Suite for String Orchestra* (W111) (Boosey & Hawkes) should also be "just the thing for schools and colleges."

B409.   McPhee, Colin. "Scores and Records." *Modern Music* 22 (November-December 1944): 58-59.
"Songs by American composers continue to blossom." *Coal Scuttle Blues* (W44) by Luening/Bacon is a "sedate and professional melange of boogie and blues that is far from the groove."

B410.   Mead, Rita H. *Henry Cowell's New Music, 1925-1936: the Society, the Music Editions, and the Recordings.* Ann Arbor, Mich. : UMI Research Press, 1981.
In a revision of her dissertation, Mead discusses the history of the *New Music Quarterly*, which began publishing music in 1927 under the leadership of Henry Cowell, with the *New Music Quarterly Recordings* under the direction of Otto Luening from 1937 to 1942. Also discussed are four songs with text by Walt Whitman: *A Farm Picture* (W80), *Here the Frailest Leaves of Me* (W83), *Only Themselves Understand Themselves* (W104), and *Hast Never Come to Thee* (W103).

B411.   Miller, Hugh Milton. *History of Music.* 3rd ed. rev. & enl. New York: Barnes & Nobles, 1960.
A brief biographical sketch describes Luening as a "prominent experimentalist in the media of electronic and tape-recorder music." As a teacher Luening has exerted influence on younger composers, and is also known for non-experimental songs and chamber music.

B412.   Miller, William Hugh. *Everybody's Guide to Music.* Philadelphia; New York: Chilton, 1961.
Brief mention of *Incantation* (W153) and *Rhapsodic Variations for Tape Recorder and Orchestra* (W159), description of the Luening-Ussachevsky collaboration, and methods of taping.

B413.   "Milwaukee Sym.: Luening prem." *High Fidelity/Musical America* 26 (May 1976): MA27-28.
The *Wisconsin Symphony* (W230) was premiered in Otto Luening's native community. The four movements were "representative of epochs." While not writing an anthology of tunes, the composer exerts "considerable skill in shaping provocative variations in the manner and boldness of Charles Ives."

B414.   "Miss Turnley Heard in Program of Songs." *New York Times*, 4 April 1951, p. 35.

Review of the April 3 performance by Margaret Turnley, which included Luening's *The Harp the Monarch Minstrel Swept* (W142) and *She Walks in Beauty* (W146).

B415.   Moles, Abraham A. *Les Musique Experimentales*. Paris: Editions du Cercle d'Art Contemporain, 1960.

Includes a description of Columbia University, in French, with photographs of the Columbia-Princeton Electronic Music Center, and Ussachevsky in the Columbia University laboratory.

B416.   Monson, Karen. "Res Musica's Program Disappointing." *Baltimore Sun*, 3 December 1984, p. B5.

Review of the December 2, 1984 performance of *Potawatomi Legends for Chamber Orchestra* (W240), with Otto Luening as guest conductor. The reviewer was disappointed with the concert , indicating that the Luening work "sounded more like a score for an old John Wayne film than an evocation of Indian life in rural Wisconsin." **See: B224.**

B417.   Moog, Robert A. "The Columbia-Princeton Electronic Music Center: Thirty Years of Explorations in Sound." *Contemporary Keyboard* 7, no. 5 (May 1981): 22-31.

Reviews history of electronic music, beginning with the 1951 developments of Luening and Ussachevsky at Columbia, concerts of 1952 to the formation in the late 1950s of the Columbia Princeton Electronic Music Center. Includes several photographs. Brief biographies of several composers involved with the CPEMC and a joint interview; participants include Luening, Ussachevsky, Peter Mauzey, and Milton Babbitt.

B418.   Moore, David W. "Composers Recordings: At the Quarter-Century Mark, Carter Harmon [i.e. Harman] and Otto Luening talk about CRI's Past, Present and Future." *American Record Guide* 43 (February 1980): 6-8.

In twenty-five years CRI produced 400 recordings. Includes comments of Carter Harman. Luening spoke of the founding of CRI, during his period at Bennington College, his current activity in the company, and CRI's attitude toward the avant-garde. The composer stated that "one important function that CRI serves is connected with our 25 years of life. We really have become a sort of archive of American music," this being CRI's most valuable contribution, a "library of contemporary American music."

B419. Moore, David W. "CRI on Cassette." *American Record Guide* 49 (November/December 1986): 43-45.

Reviews the new CRI collections of recordings of Luening, Norman Dello Joio, George Rochberg, and Charles Ives. As one of the "grand old men of today's music," Luening's works are so varied that large collections are few. The *Sonata for Piano* (W162) "reflects classically neat outlines no less than in its wide variety of expression the influence of its dedicatee, Busoni." *Legend for Oboe and Strings* (W144) is "more clearly American ... in its personality," while *Kentucky Rondo* (W143) is a "spoof on country fiddle tunes." This is followed by *Symphonic Fantasia No. 1* (W56), and a collaborative work with Ussachevsky, *A Poem in Cycles and Bells for Tape Recorder and Orchestra* (W158), "crudely produced in mono sound, but historically important." **See: D16b, D17b, D25b, D38b, D51b.**

B420. Moore, David W. "Rev. of *Third Short Sonata for Flute and Piano*, 1976, Luening." *American Record Guide* 50 (Fall 1987): 70.

The *Third Short Sonata for Flute and Piano* (W204) was in a "tempting program of flute music," recorded on CRI SD 531. The three-movement work is a "compact, amusing piece, unexpected in its turns, as one learns to anticipate from this perennially fresh composer." **See: D31a.**

B421. Moore, Douglas. "Columbia University Festival Contemporary American Music." *Pan Pipes of Sigma Alpha Iota* 41 (December 1948): 113-114.

A description of the festival is contained, with photographs of Luening conducting his opera *Evangeline* (W85).

B422. Mootz, William. "Luening-Ussachevsky Variations are Performed." *Courier-Journal/Louisville Times*, 21 March 1954.

Review of the premiere of *Rhapsodic Variations for Tape Recorder and Orchestra* (W159), a novelty. "In their *Rhapsodic Variations*, the composers have re-evaluated their conception of orchestral balances. The strings are used primarily to form a base of sound above which the woodwinds and brass carry independent material. Around and above all this, the tape-recorder envelops the music in waves of unorthodox sound. The composers have electronically distorted and mixed their original sound track to arrive at different orchestral colors and textures in much the same way a painter mixes his colors on a palette."

Otto Luening and Vladimir Ussachevsky could not be "dismissed as playboy pranksters," since too many musicians were experimenting like these two.

B423. Moss, Arnold. "Classic or Potboiler? Condensed Version of 'Methuselah' Arriving After Successful Tour." *New York Times*, 23 March 1958, Sec. 2, p. 1, 3.

Preview of the play *Back to Methuselah*, rewritten by Moss, including a history of the original work by George Bernard Shaw. The Theatre Guild would be performing this work. Moss tells how he worked with the play's text. Music was composed by Luening and Ussachevsky (W168).

B424. "Mrs. Slater to Perform." *The Colgate Maroon*, 27 October 1966, p. 2.

Vivian Slater will perform on November 1, 1966, *Variations for Harpsichord or Piano* (W120). This was also performed the previous Wednesday as part of the Otto Luening Festival.

B425. "Music by Americans Played at Concert." *New York Times*, 14 January 1952, p. 15.

Review of the January 13, 1952 performance of *Suite for Cello and Piano* (W136), being the "strongest work" of the evening; Luening "always seems to know where he is headed, musically speaking."

B426. *Music for Today & Tomorrow*. Videorecording. Milwaukee, Wis.: WITI-TV, 1981.

This videocassette includes a thirty minute interview with Otto Luening, August Wegner, and the chair of the Music Dept. at the University of Wisconsin-Milwaukee.

B427. "Music in Our Time." *Musical America* 84 (April 1964): 58.

The fourth concert in the 'Music in Our Time' series included *Duo for Violin and Viola* (W194). "As frequently occurs in works for two solo strings, Otto Luening's *Duo for Violin and Viola* implies more than it states. The brief multimovement work conveys through an aphoristic tonal language an enormous range of values, from familiar to unfamiliar, from serious to humorous."

B428. "'Music in Our Time' Gives Electronic Opera." *Musical Courier* 161 (June 1960): 25.

The *Sonata for Violin Solo No. 1* (W177), performed April 30, 1960, contains seven short movements, the final movement approaching a "country dance in spirit." The other movements were coherent, based on rhythmic patterns.

B429.   "Music in Our Time Series Will Begin Sunday, 5:30 p.m." *East Hampton Starr*, 25 July 1957, p. 1.
         Preview of performance of *Sonata for Viola Solo* (W176), to be performed July 28, 1957. In addition to hearing the concert sponsored by Max Pollikoff, there would be an informal discussion on new music with composers Otto Luening, Atilio (Teo) Macero, and Charles Wuorinen. **See: B147.**

B430.   "Music in the Mountains Starts Concert Series." *The Hudson Valley Newspapers*, 29 June 1983, p. 18.
         Preview of festival "Music in the Mountains," at New Paltz, N. Y., with a chamber music concert July 9, 1983, featuring Luening's *Sextet* (W32) for violin, viola, cello, flute, clarinet and French horn, with the composer as a guest, sponsored by the "Meet the Composer" program. Includes brief biography and photograph of Luening. **See also: B313, B390.**

B431.   "Music is All American: Organ Recital at Notre Dame Sunday is Most Unusual." *South Bend Tribune*, 16 July 1921.
         Announcement of a recital by William Middelschulte, including Luening's *Introitus* (W40), to be performed on July 18 at the Church of the Sacred Heart, University of Notre Dame.

B432.   "Music of American Given at Times Hall." *New York Times*, 23 January 1950, p. 16.
         A concert, January 22, 1950, at the meeting of the National Association for American Composers and Conductors, featured music of ten contemporary American composers. Luening's "Indian Legend", from *Evangeline* (W85), and Charles Ives' *Walking* were the only two works which came off at all convincingly."

B433.   "NAACC Concert, Times Hall, Jan. 22." *Musical America* 70 (February 1950): 278-279.
         "A quantity of dissonant tonal music" was presented January 22, 1950, at the meeting of the National Association for American Composers and Conductors. Ruth Krug sang songs by selected composers, but "only Mr. Luening's contribution, "Indian Legend", from *Evangeline* (W85), approximated an attractive vocal line."

B434.   "National Music Council Meets at Spoleto--Over 100 Leaders Expected to Attend." *National Music Council News* 1, no. 3 (Winter 1985): 1.
Preview announcement of meeting in Charleston, S. C., June 2-5, 1985. On June 4, Otto Luening would be presented the American Eagle Award. *Opera Fantasia* (W257) would be premiered at Charleston, S.C.

B435.   Nelson, Wayne A. "Edgard Varèse and the Electronic Medium." Thesis. University of Montana, 1979.
Describes the various schools of electronic music, including that of Otto Luening and other Americans.

B436.   "New Group." *International Musician* 50 (August 1951): 13.
Paul Wolfe formed a new orchestra in New York; he later invited oboist Robert Bloom to perform Luening's *Legend for Oboe and Strings* (W144). There is a brief description of the composition, and a photograph of Luening, Wolfe, and Bloom discussing this new concerto.

B437.   "New Humphrey and Limon Works In Juilliard Festival." *Musical America* 76 (May 1956): 14, 32.
In a program, April 20-22, 1956, Doris Humphrey choreographed *Theater Piece No. 2* (W165), also called a "Concerto for Light, Movement, Sound and Voice," with a score by Luening. "Luening's score contains some weird and boldly experimental effects." This premiere was conducted by the composer.

B438.   "New Luening Opera to Have Debut May 5." *New York Times*, 6 April 1948, p. 27.
Evangeline (W85) is scheduled to premiere May 5, 1948 at the Brander Matthews Theatre, Columbia University. Performances will be on May 5-7 and 10-12, the latter at the Festival of American Music. Describes the opera's origin and Luening's research in Acadian folk music since the original version was composed in 1930.

B439.   "New Music Quartet at Castle Hill; All Evening Concerts from Now On." *Ipswich Chronicle* (Ipswich, Mass.), 10 July 1952.
Legend for Oboe and Strings (W144) was performed on July 4 and 5, 1952, by Robert Bloom, oboe, with Alan Carter conducting the Vermont Chamber Orchestra. Article includes a brief resume of Luening's career up to 1952. **See also B590.**

B440.   "'New Music' Recital to be heard at UConn." *Hartford Courant*, 21 March
         1971, p. 6F.
                  Otto Luening would speak on "The Role of New Music at the
         American University," on March 29, 1971. On March 28, the Group for
         Contemporary Music would perform new works, in a series sponsored by
         University of Connecticut professor Charles Whittenberg and Museum
         Director Paul Rovietti.

B441.   "The New Theatrical Medium." in *Eastman School of the Dance and
         Dramatic Action presents 'Sister Beatrice* (W59)." [Rochester, N.
         Y.:Eastman, 1926]
                  The program notes for 15-16 January, 1926, give a brief description
         of the musical content of *Sister Beatrice* (W59). It was for organ, being
         suggestive of early Gregorian music, with the play being set in the
         fourteenth century.

B442.   "New York." *Music Journal* 25 (April 1967): 60-61.
                  Review of a "Music in Our Time" concert of Feb. 27, 1967, a
         "grab-bag of current styles," Luening's *Suite for Flute Solo No. 4* (W196)
         "seemed understated in such overstated surroundings. Its seven short
         movements would not be demanding for the fingers or musicianship of
         many flute students, nor their audiences' appreciation."

B443.   "The Newest 'New Festival'; a Discography of Music by Alliance
         Composers." *American Composers Alliance Bulletin* 9, no. 2 (1960): 13-17;
         9, no. 3 (1960): 17-25.
                  Includes announcement of the future recording of *Concerted Piece
         for Tape Recorder and Orchestra* (W180), Leonard Bernstein conducting
         the New York Philharmonic. Discography by composer: A-L in no. 2 and
         M-Z in no. 3.

B444.   Newlin, Dika. "Electronic Music." *Lexicon Universal Encyclopedia*. New
         York: Lexicon Publications, 1986.
                  In an article tracing the history and development of electronic music
         are the historic concerts of the early 1950s of Luening and Ussachevsky,
         with reference to other articles on Milton Babbitt, Mario Davidovsky, and
         Charles Wuorinen.

B445.   "Notes for NOTES." *NOTES* 42 (September 1985): 36.
                  Luening has recently received the American Eagle Award from the
         National Music Council for his significant contributions to American music.

B446.   "L'opera Evangeline." *L'Evangeline* (Moncton, New Brunswick), 6 May 1948, p. 3.
         In French. Description from the poetic perspective. Includes excerpt about the review of *Evangeline* (W85) which was translated by Philip Robert. **See: B509.**

B447.   "Orchestral List: Part II." *American Composers Alliance Bulletin* 10, no. 4 (December 1962): 22.
         A list of Luening's compositions with orchestra, including dates of composition, medium of performance, publisher, and durations.

B448.   "Orchestras." *Musical America* 84 (December 1964): 283.
         The first concert of the Arlington (Virginia) Civic Symphony's 20th season featured *Lyric Scene for Flute and Strings* (W171), composed to celebrate the 100th anniversary of Ferruccio Busoni, a former teacher of Luening.

B449.   "Orchestras in New York." *Musical America* 69 (February 1949): 265.
         The first performance of the *Pilgrim's Hymn for Orchestra* (W134) in a new version for large orchestra was conducted by Stokowski. It was written in 1946 for chamber orchestra and performed at the Yaddo Festival. "Essentially a chamber work, ... it is also too casually constructed, and too slight in content, for a symphonic program."

B450.   "Organized Noise." *Jerusalem Post*, 23 December 1953.
         Review of recording, "Demonstration Examples of Sound Material," recorded by the engineers of Galei Zahal. Included compositions for the tape recorder by Otto Luening and Vladimir Ussachevsky. The tape was presented before an audience, the reviewer concluding that the hypnotic repetition was "possibly a charming method of treating a 'normal' melody, but an opiate when used for the composition of noises."

B451.   Orgill, Roxane. "Composer Reviews a Life in Art." *Milwaukee Journal*, 12 November 1981.
         Review of concert November 11, 1981 at the Wisconsin Conservatory of Music, featuring music of Otto Luening.   Includes very brief biographical note. The premiere of *Soundless Song* (W52) was "melodious music that explores and juxtaposes unrest and calm." Texts are by Luening. Soprano Marlee Sabo's "intense, well-prepared performance added to the music's directness."

The reviewer enjoyed *Sextet* (W32), describing it as having "one foot in the past -- snatches of melodies in the flavor of Brahms and Sibelius and Bach -- and one foot in the present -- underlying dissonant harmonies."

Also performed were *Variations on Bach's Chorale Prelude Liebster Jesu wir sind hier* (W128), and the *Suite for Flute Solo No. 4* (W196), a piece which "investigates the colors of the flute," performed well by Janet Millard.

B452.   Orgill, Roxane. "Foss, Orchestra, Moderns: the Blend Seems Right." *Milwaukee Journal*, 1 March 1982.

The critic thought it had been difficult to tell whether the Milwaukee Orchestra, its director Lukas Foss, and contemporary music were compatible. The Schermerhorn American Composers Festival of February 28, 1982 "dispelled any doubts." It included the premiere of Luening "concise and simple" *Short Symphony* (W237).

B453.   Osborne, Bruce. "Electronic Music Comes to K." *Kalamazoo Gazette*, 24 October 1966.

Review of lectures by Otto Luening, October 17-18, 1966, at Kalamazoo College. "Electronic music was something to joke about until this Monday evening, where I've found it a subject of great interest. Dr. Luening was right: Electronic music adds color to the timbre palette that, in the hands of a true artist, can be rendered extremely effective." Luening distinguished two types of electronic music, that which results from the manipulation of sounds originally produced via natural means, and manipulation using sounds formed in the machines.

Luening played tape recordings of *Fantasy in Space* (W148), and *A Poem in Cycles and Bells for Tape Recorder and Orchestra* (W158). **See also: B476.**

B454.   "Otto Luening." *Compositores de America = Composers of the Americas* 7 (1961): 50-62.

Included is a brief biography, in Spanish and English, facsimile of his *Invention in Twelve Tones* (W149), plus a "Classified Chronological Catalog of Works by the United States Composer" (p. 52-62). Subdivided by medium, with headings in Spanish and English; some titles are not included in *Odyssey*. **See: B21.**

B455.   "Otto Luening." *Contemporary Music Catalogue, with 1976-1979 Supplement*, 34. New York: C. F. Peters, 1975.

This selected works list includes a brief biography of the composer, plus a statement by Luening on his philosophy of music.

B456.　"Otto Luening." *Contemporary Music 1982 Catalogue*, 60-62. New York: C. F. Peters, 1982.

This selected works list includes a brief biography of the composer, plus a statement by Luening on his philosophy of music.

B457.　"Otto Luening, Friends Return." *Kenosha News*, 24 April 1981, p. 10.

Announces Luening would begin his third visit to the University of Wisconsin at Parkside as composer-in-residence, with a concert, May 3, 1961. Works to be performed--*Sextet* (W32), *Sonata for Bassoon and Piano* (W151) and various songs, *The Harp the Monarch Minstrel Swept* (W142), *She Walks in Beauty* (W146), *A Roman's Chamber* (W69), *Wake the Serpent Not* (W75). Includes photograph of Luening during a previous lecture at UW-P.

B458.　"Otto Luening to Present Lecture and Concert at Bowdoin, Sept. 30." Joseph D. Kamin, Director of Public Relations. Bowdoin College News Service. 21 September 1981.

This two page press release announced the visit of Luening to Bowdoin, Bates, and Colby Colleges.

B459.　"Otto Luening to Speak at UW-P." *Kenosha News*, 23 March 1979, p. 18.

Announces Luening's visit to the University of Wisconsin at Parkside, the concert and lectures of April 1-3. Works would include *Fanfare for a Festive Occasion* (W200), *Sonata for Double Bass* (W174), *Fantasia Brevis for Clarinet and Piano* (W101), *Low Speed* (W150), *Fantasy in Space* (W148), and *Suite for cello and piano* (W136). Gives brief biography and photograph.

B460.　"Otto Luening; zur Autobiographie des amerikanischen Komponisten." Rev. of *Odyssey of an American Composer*. *Neue Zuricher Zeitung* 302 (29 December 1980): 11.

See B21.

B461.　Page, Tim. "Violinist Presents 20th-Century Program." *New York Times*, 2 November 1983, Section C, p. 22.

Dinos Constantinides, a professor at Louisiana State University, performed violin music at Carnegie Recital Hall on Thursday, October 27, 1983. "It was gratifying to hear some rare material by Otto Luening and Ernst Krenek, two distinguished octogenarians."

B462.   Paranov, Moshe. "The Music School and Music of Our Time." *Music Journal* 7 (November-December, 1949): 5, 37-38.

The director of the Julius Hartt School of Music in Hartford, Conn. outlines the purposes and results of his school's recent Institute of Contemporary American Music. The first institute included music of Luening. Each session had a full-length concert, short address by the guest composer, and an open forum.

B463.   Parmenter, Ross. "Electronic Studio Here Aided by Large Grant." *New York Times*, 18 January 1959, Section 2, p. 9.

This describes the $175,000 grant from the Rockefeller Foundation, early experiments by Otto Luening and Vladimir Ussachevsky, and their contact with Roger Sessions and Milton Babbitt.

B464.   Parmenter, Ross. "New Work Performed at 'Y' Concert." *New York Times*, 26 March 1959, p. 26.

In a 'Music in Our Time' concert of March 25, 1959, *Song, Poem and Dance for Flute and Strings* (W178) was performed. The "song poem" was "successfully songful and poetic," while the "rather trivial dance movement let the work peter out innocuously."

B465.   Paulson, John C. "Electronic Pioneers." *The Instrumentalist* 41 (June 1987): 40+.

Begins with the early history of electronic music, the Luening-Ussachevsky collaborations (*Rhapsodic Variations for Tape Recorder and Orchestra* (W159) and *A Poem in Cycles and Bells* (W158), etc.), and the establishment of the Columbia-Princeton Electronic Music Center. Brief biographies of and comments by Otto Luening, Vladimir Ussachevsky, Mario Davidovsky, Milton Babbitt, Pril Smiley, and Russell Pinkston. Includes photographs of all but Smiley.

B466.   Paulson, John Charles. "The History, Current Status and Possible Future of Electronic Music as Exemplified by the Works of Vladimir Ussachevsky." Thesis. University of Utah, 1976.

The early chapters describe the evolution of electronic music, and the development of the Columbia-Princeton Electronic Music Center. There are interviews with Vladimir Ussachevsky, Otto Luening, Mario Davidovsky, Pril Smiley, Alice Shields, and Milton Babbitt. The following collaborated compositions of Luening and Ussachevsky are described: *Rhapsodic Variations for Tape Recorder and Orchestra* (W159), *A Poem in Cycle and Bells for Tape Recorder and Orchestra* (W158), and *Concerted Piece for Tape Recorder and Orchestra* (W180). Also described is the sound track for the *Incredible Voyage* (W212), narrated by Walter Cronkite, with music by Luening and Ussachevsky, with the assistance of Shields and Smiley.

B467.   Pavlakis, Christopher. *The American Music Handbook*. London: Collier; New York: Free Press, 1974.
    Very brief biography, with a discography; also the relationship of Luening to Silver Burdett's series *Making Music Your Own*. **See: B353, D7f.**

B468.   Pellerite, James J. *A Handbook of Literature for the Flute*. Revised. Bloomington, Ind.: Zalo Publications, 1965.
    Sonatina for Flute and Piano (W36) is described as a Grade III-IV difficulty, "a short sonatina in one movement containing various contrasting sections; lyrical but fragmentary structures; written within a medium range of the flute."

B469.   Pellman, Samuel Frank. "An Overview of Current Practices Regarding the Performance of Electronic Music." Thesis. Cornell University, 1978.
    Luening is referred as one of the "few venturesome composers" of electronic music. There are also numerous references to "Reel vs. Real," by Elliott Carter and Vladimir Ussachevsky, *American Symphony Orchestra League Newsletter*, 11, no.5-6 (1960): 8.

B470.   "Perfomance Will be a 'First,' 'Evangeline' Readied for Stage." *Times Record* (Brunswick, Maine), 21 April 1986.
    Preview of *Evangeline* (W85) to be performed at Bowdoin College, May 2-3, 1986. Includes comments about *Evangeline* by Otto Luening: "'The story of 'Evangeline' is a timeless theme about the impersonality of governments and uprooting of families for political reasons," Luening says. "The impact of wars and sectarian strife on innocent human beings should never be forgotten." Also includes review comments from a *New York Times* critic of a 1985 performance by an eleven member choir in New York: "... There is some wonderful music in 'Evangeline' including passages that would make or enhance the reputation of virtually any composer working today. The final act begins with a ravishing evocation of moonlight, and the joyful paean to summertime belongs in the repertory of first-class American choral music."
    This was to be the first full staging with a narrator for the opera. **See also: B509.**

B471. Peterson, R. Dale. "A Brief History and Description of Electronic Music Including an Analysis of Davidovsky's *Synchronisms No. 1, 2,* and *3.*" Thesis. University of Cincinnati, 1972.

Covers the history of electronic music, the influence of Otto Luening and Vladimir Ussachevsky, and analyses of three compositions by Mario Davidovsky, himself a student of Luening. During 1958, Davidovsky was invited to work in the Columbia-Princeton Electronic Music Center. While in the United States he studied composition with Luening and Aaron Copland.

B472. Peyser, Joan. "Can the Mark II Sing 'Happy Birthday'?" *New York Times,* 3 May 1970. Section 2, p. 15.

Written on the tenth anniversary of the founding of the Columbia-Princeton Electronic Music Center, by Otto Luening, Vladimir Ussachevsky, Milton Babbitt, and others. Traces the development of the center from Ussachevsky's living room to Columbia University. Includes illustration of the founders in the center.

B473. "Phi Beta Kappa Adds 23 Members." *At Denison* (May 1967): 3.

Article about the initiation of members, including comments about Luening's visit to Denison University. He was speaker at the annual PBK convocation and dinner, speaking on trends in 20th century music and computer music, in a two day stay during the week of March 20-26, 1967. **See also: B534.**

B474. Pierreuse, Bernard. *Flute Literature.* Paris: Editions Musicales Transatlantiques, 1982.

Divided by number of performers and medium (flute, 2 flutes, or flute and piano), with index of composers to guide user to applicable sections. In French, German, Italian, and English.

B475. Pincus, Andrew L. "Two Birthdays and a Premiere at Tanglewood." *Berkshire Eagle,* 15 August 1980.

Tanglewood's Fromm Festival included a surprise birthday party to honor two guests, Otto Luening and Aaron Copland, each 80. Luening's *Symphonic Interludes No. 2* (W96, no. 2) and *No. 3* (W228) were "stirring and attractive ... richly scored and colored."

B476. "Pioneer to Review 20th Century Music." *Kalamazzo Gazette,* 16 October 1966.

Announcement/preview of lectures by Otto Luening, October 17-18, 1966, at Kalamazoo College. The topics presented would be: "The

Influence of Previous Masters on Present 20th Century Music;" "Electronic and Computer Music: Is it Here to Stay?"; "Music, a Science, an Art, and Sometimes Both;" and "Significant Trends in 20th Century Music." **See also: B453.**

B477.   Porter, Andrew. "Musical Events; Out of the Maze." *New Yorker* 60 (28 May 1984): 120-124.

Review of a May 21, 1984 concert by the American Composers Orchestra at Alice Tully Hall, New York City. Leonard Slatkin conducted the premiere of Luening's *Symphonic Fantasia No. 4* (W216), "a civilized unexacting five minutes of musical small talk by a man who has touched and influenced the music of our century at many points."

B478.   Poteet, Ewing. "Contemporary Music in Louisiana : Louisiana State University Festival." *American Composers Alliance Bulletin* 6, no. 2 (1957): 16-17.

Luening is one of the ACA composers whose works are performed during the Festival of Contemporary Music at Louisiana State University, Baton Rouge.

B479.   "Premiere Mondiale de L'opera 'Evangeline' Presentee a New York le Mois Prochain." *L'Evangeline* (Moncton, New Brunswick), 20 April 1948, p. 1.

In French. Preview and description of the premiere of *Evangeline* (W85), with notes on the career of Otto Luening. **See also: B197, B446, B509.**

B480.   "Premieres." *BMI* (April 1967): 14.

Review of the February 27, 1967 performance of *Suite for Flute Solo No. 4* (W196), as played by Luening on a wooden flute. This was in the 'Music in Our Time' series.

B481.   "Premieres." *BMI* (October 1970): 22.

Review of the performance of *Sonata for Violin Solo No. 2* (W211) as played by Max Pollikoff on May 21, 1970. Includes Theodore Strongin's comments in the *New York Times* and Carman Moore's in the *Village Voice*, both commenting on the piece's humor.

B482.   "Premieres." *Music Educators Journal* 64 (February 1978): 26-27.

The third *Short Sonata for Flute and Piano* (W204) premiered November 21, 1977, at the Manhattan School of Music, New York City.

B483.   "Premieres." *Music Educators Journal* 65 (November 1978): 73.
         Music for Orchestra (W51) premiered, May 23, 1978, at Alice Tully
Hall, New York City.

B484.   "Premieres." *Music Educators Journal* 67 (February 1981): 27.
         Songs, Old and New premiered 1 Dec. 1980, most likely a collection
of songs.

B485.   "Premieres Given in Concert Series *New York Times,* 9 March 1964, p. 36.
         Otto Luening's *Duo for Violin and Viola* (W194), "a set of
imaginative etudes cast as thumbnail sketches," was performed March 8,
1964, in a 'Music in Our Time' concert.

B486.   Prieberg, Fred K. *Lexikon der neuen Musik.* München (Munich): Verlag
Karl Alber Freiburg, 1958.
         In German. Pages 261-262 include a brief biography highlighting the
compositions up to 1957, and the collaborations with Vladimir
Ussachevsky.

B487.   Prieberg, Fred K. *Musik des Technischen Zeitalters.* Zurich: Atlantis
Verlag Karl, 1956.
         In German. Discusses the content of and reactions to performances
of *Low Speed* (W150), *Invention in Twelve Tones* (W149) and *Fantasy in
Space* (W148), *A Poem in Cycles and Bells for Tape Recorder and
Orchestra* (W158), *Rhapsodic Variations for Tape Recorder and Orchestra*
(W159), *Suite from King Lear* (W164), and *Theatre Piece No. 2* (W165).

B488.   Prieberg, Fred K. *Musik ex Machina.* Berlin: Verlag Ullstein, 1960.
         In German. In "Elektronische Musik in New York und Baden-Baden,"
p. 183-189, Prieberg discusses the content of and reactions to performances
of *A Poem in Cycles and Bells for Tape Recorder and Orchestra* (W158),
Of Identity (W157), *Rhapsodic Variations for Tape Recorder and Orchestra*
(W159), *Low Speed* (W150), *Invention in Twelve Tones* (W149) and
Fantasy in Space (W148). Also discusses the series "Music in Our Time"
by Max Pollikoff, *Suite from King Lear* (W164), *Theater Piece No. 2*
(W165), and the formation of the Columbia-Princeton Electronic Music
Center. See also: B24.

B489.   "Radio." *American Composers Alliance Bulletin* 2, no. 3 (1952): 14-15.
         Includes a chronology of radio performances of March 31, 1952 to
August 5, 1952. WJZ of New York broadcast *Prelude to a Hymn Tune by*

William Billings (W108) and *Two Symphonic Interludes* (W96) on June 7 of that year.

B490.   "Radio." *American Composers Alliance Bulletin* 2, no. 4 (Winter 1952-1953): 18-19.
Chronology of radio performances from July to December of 1952. Included *Legend for Oboe and Strings* (W144), *Invention in Twelve Tones* (W149), *Fantasy in Space* (W148), and *Low Speed* (W150).

B491.   "Radio." *American Composers Alliance Bulletin* 3, no. 1 (Spring 1953): 18-20.
Chronology of radio performances from June 1952 to March 1953.Included *Sonata for Violin and Piano no. 3* (W129), *Invention in Twelve Tones* (W149), *Fantasy in Space* (W148), and *Kentucky Concerto* (W143)

B492.   "Radio." *American Composers Alliance Bulletin* 3, no. 2 (Summer 1953): 26-28.
Chronology of radio performances from October 1952 to July of 1953. Included *Prelude to a Hymn Tune by William Billings* (W108), *Kentucky Concerto* (W143), , *Fantasy in Space* (W148), *Invention in Twelve Tones* (W149), and *Low Speed* (W150).

B493.   "Radio Performances." *American Composers Alliance Bulletin* 2, no. 2 (June 1952): 18-19.
Chronology of radio performances from January to April of 1952. Included selections from *Suite for Strings* (W111), *Symphonic Interlude no. 2* (W96, No. 2), *Fantasia for Organ* (W78), and *Alleluia* (W130)

B494.   Randel, Don Michael. "Luening, Otto." In *Diccionario Harvard de Musica*. Mexico: Editorial Diana, 1984.
Brief biography, in Spanish, p. 281.

B495.   Randel, Don Michael. "Luening, Otto." In *Harvard Concise Dictionary of Music*. Cambridge, Mass.: Harvard University Press, 1978.
Brief biography, p. 281-282.

B496.   Rathaus, Karol. "To Study With A Master." *Modern Music* 18 (March-April 1941): 164-167.
"Today, a large number of American composers of name and standing actively participate in music education," among them Otto Luening, then at Bennington College.

B497.	"Recital By the Luenings." *New York Times*, 23 March 1937, p. 27.
	On March 22, 1937, Ethel Luening, soprano, and Otto Luening, flute, assisted by Willard Rhodes, piano, gave a recital, with the second half of the program devoted to rarely heard compositions by contemporary Americans.	Works by Wallingford Riegger, Henry Cowell, Robert McBride, and Aaron Copland, were performed, in addition to Luening's *The Happy Sinner* (W107).

B498.	"Recital: Singer's Debut." *New York Times*, 30 April 1957, p. 25.
	The debut of bass-baritone Everett Anderson on April 29, 1957, included the premiere of *Love's Secret* (W140)."

B499.	Reis, Claire. *Composers in America*. New York: MacMillan, 1947.
	Brief biographical sketch with selected classified list of compositions.

B500.	"Reports from Member Organizations." Broadcast Music, Inc. (BMI)" *National Music Council Bulletin* 35 (1976): 16-18.
	The National Endowment for the Art commissioned the *Wisconsin Symphony* (W230), honoring Luening's 75th birthday, premiered by the Milwaukee Symphony, January 4, 1976, conducted by Kenneth Schermerhorn.	The American Music Center presented Luening with a "Letter of Distinction for Outstanding Contribution to American Music," on December 18, 1975, at the New York Public Library.
	CRI issued *Piano Sonata in Memoriam Ferruccio Busoni* (W162) and *Electronic Doubles of Chorale Fantasy and Fugue* (W224) as a tribute.	A manuscript of the opera *Evangeline* (W85) would be on display at the Kennedy Center for one year.	Luening spoke on "Communications" at the National Music Council annual meeting at the Gotham Hotel on Jan. 7, 1976.
	On February 8, 1976, Oliver Daniel gave a testimonial to Luening at a reception and concert at the National Arts Club.

B501.	Reti, Jean. "An International Conference of Composers." *Tempo*, no. 55-56, (Autumn-Winter 1960): 6-7.
	The conference, held in Stratford, Ontario, Canada, in August, had "new world vibrancy."	Edgard Varèse, the "father" of electronic music, joined a panel including Luening, Hugh LeCaine, Josef Tal, Luciano Berio, and Vladimir Ussachevsky.	The papers presented and music performed gave Reti the impression that electronic music was in its infancy--an idea rejected by the panel.

B502.   Rev. of *Accordion Revisited*. *Fanfare* 9, no. 2 (November-December 1985): 318-319.

Review of album by William Schimmel. Luening's *Rondo for Accordion* (W189) is "a sure-fire hit, a perpetual motion that recalls 'The Flight of the Bumblebee.'" Schimmel is praised as a true virtuoso. **See: D29a.**

B503.   Rev. of *Accordion Revisited*. *Keynote* (January 1986): 17.

William Schimmel, a virtuoso of the accordion, has commissioned new works for this instrument, including Luening's *Rondo for Accordion* (W189). The music "is, for the most part, entertaining; and Schimmel is a dynamite accordionist, making this the best new-music party record in years." **See: D29a.**

B504.   Rich, Alan. "Columbia Offers Electronic Concert." *Musical America* 81 (June 1961): 68.

At McMillin Theater, a program of May 9, 1961, included music of Mario Davidovsky, Bülent Arel, Charles Wuorinen, Halim El-Dabh, Vladimir Ussachevsky, Milton Babbitt, and *Gargoyles for Violin Solo and Synthesized Sound* (W183), by Otto Luening. This premiere included Max Pollikoff, violin.

"If nothing else was proved at this extraordinary concert, at least we now know that the term 'electronic music' can cover as wide a range of expression as 'symphony.'"

"Luening's work, a sort of dialogue between violin and taped sounds seemed ... unwilling to fulfill whatever possibilities there are in this new idiom." Rich was equally critical of Ussachevsky and Wuorinen.

B505.   Richards, Wendy Jo. "An Analysis of Three Works by Luening, Rochberg, and Wolff as Representative of Unaccompanied Solo Violin Literature Composed 1970-1979." Diss., University of Northern Colorado, 1983.

This analyzes *Sonata for Violin Solo No. 3* (W220), including over 25 musical examples. Also includes excerpts from an interview with the composer.

B506.   Riemann, Hugo. *Musik Lexikon*. Mainz: B. Schott's Sohne, 1959-1967.

In German. Includes a brief biography (2:108) with a selective list of compositions. "Elektronische Musik," (3:256-257) briefly mentions his associations with Milton Babbitt and Vladimir Ussachevsky.

B507.   Ringo, James. "Collaborations in Music." *American Composers Alliance Bulletin* 5, no. 3 (1955): 13-14.

Compares the collaborations of Otto Luening and Vladimir Ussachevsky with other such enterprises in history. Emphasizes *Rhapsodic Variations for Tape Recorder and Orchestra* (W159). Also describes Luening and Ernst Bacon jointly composing *Coal Scuttle Blues* (W44).

B508.   Robert, Philip. "At 85, Otto Luening is Still Composing." *Times Record* (Brunswick, Maine), 21 April 1986.

Preview of the performance of *Evangeline* (W85) at Bowdoin College. Gives brief biography of Luening. This article is largely philosophical in context. Includes photograph of composer.

B509.   Robert, Philip. "Opera Tells Acadian Story." *Times Record* (Brunswick, Maine), 21 April 1986.

Preview of *Evangeline* (W85) and its musical history. The opera was to be performed at Bowdoin College in May of 1986. Luening traveled to Nova Scotia to compose this. Include comments of the composer: "Even 231 years after the events portrayed, people are still being forcibly uprooted and families separated by war, sectarian strife and political decisions over which they have no control."

Also includes comments of Virgil Thomson from the *New York Herald Tribune*, and those from a 6 May 1948 article in a French language newspaper, *l'Evangeline*, of Moncton, New Brunswick: "'Today, we are assisting at the birth of a work which is able to portray as well or better than a poem our story, our sufferings, our people, for the music is not limited by the restrictions which language imposes ...'" **See also: B21, B446, B470, B568.**

B510.   Rockwell, John. "An Influential Musician at 80." *New York Times*, 15 June 1980, Section 2, p. 27+.

This brief biography, published on the composer's 80th birthday, discusses his pioneering in electronic music with Ussachevsky, and his widespread influence. "You name 'em, I've taught 'em."

Includes a photograph of the composer and several quotes.

B511.   Rockwell, John. "Music: Luening Tribute." *New York Times*, 2 March 1986, Section 1, p. 63.

A retrospective concert for Luening's 85th birthday was given, Friday, February 28, at McMillin Theatre. The concert included *Symphonic Fantasia No. 1* (W56), *Legend for Oboe and Strings* (W144), *Wisconsin Suite* (W160), and *Lyric Scene for Flute and Strings* (W171). Luening, who conducted the third work, was described as a "man full of compositional vigor."

B512.   Rogers, Bernard. "Rochester Twenty Years After." *Modern Music* 22 (May-June 1945): 262-263.
        In this twentieth festival, directed by Howard Hanson, 30 new works were presented. Luening's *String Quartet No. 2* (W53) "is a work of considerable sinew, built in craggy fashion."

B513.   "Rome Academy Elects." *New York Times*, 15 December 1949, p. 12.
        The American Academy in Rome announced on December 14 the election of four members to its board, one being composer Otto Luening. Founded in 1894, this academy is "devoted to furthering the arts and humanities in the United States."

B514.   Roos, James. "First Performances Thrill Chamber's Audience." *Miami Herald*, 26 October 1984, p. 12C.
        The International Festival of the Americas included a performance of *Potawatomi Legends for Chamber Orchestra* (W240), "Its tartly etched texture is flecked with the faint sound of rattles and chimes, and runs a gamut of Indian folklore in eight concise movements, from "Keeps of the Second Fire" to a charming "Love Song" for flute and a "Dance of Eagles, Crows and Woodpeckers." Luening conducted with rare economy of style and the players responded with a lucid, vibrant performance." **See also: B515.**

B515.   Roos, James. "The International Festival of the Americas: There was Carter, Luening, and Music from South of the Border." *High Fidelity/Musical America* 35 (April 1985): MA33, 40.
        "The art of Otto Luening or Elliott Carter ... remains esoteric to many audiences outside major musical centers." The festival, held in October of 1984, included a performance of *Potawatomi Legends for Chamber Orchestra* (W240), the composer conducting with "rare economy of style and the UM [University of Miami, Florida] faculty musicians responded with a lucid, vibrant performance." **See also: B514.**

B516.   Rosenstiel, Leonie. *Schirmer History of Music*. New York: Schirmer Books, 1982.
        Within his discussion of electronic music, Otto Luening and Vladimir Ussachevsky, among others, are mentioned. There are illustrations of the Columbia-Princeton Electronic Music Center.

B517.   Rossi, Nick, and Robert A. Choate. *Music of Our Time : an Anthology of Works of Selected Contemporary Composers of the 20th Century.* Boston: Crescendo, 1969.

Describes early Luening-Ussachevsky collaboration, brief biographies of each, history of the Columbia-Princeton Electronic Music Center's development and such significant works as *Rhapsodic Variations for Tape Recorder and Orchestra* (W159) and *Concerted Piece for Tape Recorder and Orchestra* (W180). It then gives an analysis of *A Poem in Cycles and Bells for Tape Recorder and Orchestra* (W158), including four musical examples from that work. The book contains three portraits of these two composers. Includes composers' comments of this and several other of their compositions, some collaborated, some individual.

B518.   Rudd, Michael. (R. Michael) "Stylistic Features and Compositional Activities in Organ Literature Since World War II." *Diapason* 59 (June 1968): 12.

"A surprise for performers of organ music exists in the *Fantasia for Organ* (W78)." Luening, not generally thought of as an organ composer, combines American hymn tunes and gospel hymns.

B519.   Rudd, Robert Michael. "Stylistic Trends in Contemporary Organ Music." Diss., Louisiana State University, 1967.

This includes analysis of *Fantasia for Organ* (W78), probably published in 1963, composed 40 years earlier. Six musical examples from this composition are included. The appendix has a brief biography of the composer.

B520.   Russcol, Herbert. *The Liberation of Sound: an Introduction to Electronic Music.* Englewood Cliffs, N.J.: Prentice-Hall, 1972.

Otto Luening is acknowledged as the "Grand Old Man of electronic music in America." Describes the Columbia-Princeton Electronic Music Center, the beginnings of electronic music, collaboration with Vladimir Ussachevsky, and various recordings.

Includes chronologies, quotes from several reviews, and discusses such major compositions as *Rhapsodic Variations for Tape Recorder and Orchestra* (W159), *A Poem in Cycles and Bells for Tape Recorder and Orchestra* (W158), and *Suite from King Lear* (W164). An Appendix has the "Documented History of the Cologne School," by Otto Luening, also published as the "Unfinished History of Electronic Music. **See also B29a-B29b**.

B521. Saabe, H. "Luening, Otto." In *Algemene Muziek Encyclopedie*, edited by J. Robijns, Miep Zijlstra, 6:107. Antwerpen: Uniebock, 1979-1984.
A brief biography, in Dutch.

B522. Sabin, Robert. "New Music." *Musical America* 75 (1 January 1955): 32.
During the Third Composers Forum, December 18, 1954, music of Louis Calabro and Robert Palmer was performed, with the succeeding discussion period moderated by Otto Luening.

B523. Saminsky, Lazare. *Living Music of the Americas*. New York: Crown, 1949.
Describes works such as *Sun of the Sleepless* (W63), *Evangeline* (W85), a *Sonata for Violin and Piano*, *Eight Inventions for Piano* (W114), and *String Quartet No. 2* (W53) the last of which Saminsky considered to be "ultra-radical."

B524. Schackleford, Rudy. "The Yaddo Festivals of American Music, 1932-1952." *Perspectives of New Music* 17 (1978): 92-125.
Of the nine total festivals, works of Luening were represented in seven: 1933, 1936, 1937, 1938, 1940, 1946, 1949. From 1933 Luening was on the Executive Committee for the Yaddo Music Group.

B525. Schiff, Nancy Rica. "The Art of Aging." *Psychology Today* 18 (January 1984): 32-41.
Luening was one of nine octogenarians interviewed. The journal commented on the composer's post retirement activities, Luening stating that "Turning people out at 65, 70, or 85 is a social waste." Includes photograph.

B526. "Scholar Speaks to Students." *The Red and Black*, 2 March 1967, p. 1.
On March 2, 1967 Otto Luening presented an "information introduction to the world of electronic music" to students of Washington and Jefferson College, Washington, Pennsylvania. Dr. Luening emphasized the traditional background which preceded present-day music, referring to such influential composers as Igor Stravinsky, Arnold Schoenberg, and Ferruccio Busoni. Includes photograph of composer. **See also: B546.**

B527. Scholes, Percy A. "Luening, Otto." In his *The Concise Oxford Dictionary of Music*. 2nd ed. Edited by John Owen Ward. London: Oxford University Press, 1964.
Includes a brief description as flautist, opera conductor, and composer.

B528.   Schonberg, Harold C. "Wired for Sound." *New York Times*, 7 May 1963, p. 47.

Review of a program, May 6, sponsored by the Columbia-Princeton Electronic Music Center. Included *Sonority Canon for Two to Thirty-seven Flutes* (W191). Reviewer was surprised that electronicists had widened their vision to include living performers. He referred to Otto Luening as "bringing four real, live flute players on stage and giving them a background of 33 recorded flutes."

B529.   Schonberg, Harold C. "Work by Luening in First Hearing." *New York Times*, 20 April 1959, p. 34.

On Saturday, April 18, 1959, the *Fantasia for String Quartet and Orchestra* (W170) was premiered at McMillin Theater. The reviewer felt the work was "well-made, though it [had] no particular individuality."

B530.   Schwartz, Elliott. "Directions in American Composition since the Second World War: Part I, 1945-1960." *Music Educators Journal* 61 (February 1978): 29-39.

Describes the evolution of electronic music, the Luening-Ussachevsky programs of 1952-1954, the founding of the Columbia-Princeton Electronic Music Center, associations with Milton Babbitt, Roger Sessions, and others, and comparing various schools of thought of electronic music. Portrait of Luening and several other composers in article.

B531.   Schwartz, Elliott. "Electronic Music: a Thirty-year Retrospective." *Music Educators Journal* 64 (March 1978): 36-41.

Within an article about electronic music is an annotated discography of 20 discs, two of which include compositions by Luening and Ussachevsky. *Tape Music: An Historic Concert*, Desto DC-6466, contains Luening's *Fantasy in Space* (W148) and Ussachevsky's *Sonic Contours*. The other disc contains the collaborated composition, *Rhapsodic Variations for Tape Recorder and Orchestra* (W159), Louisville 545-5. **See: D7b, D14b, D15b, D17d, D20b, D21b, D23b, D28a.**

B532.   Schwartz, Elliott. *Electronic Music : a Listener's Guide*. Rev. ed. New York: Praeger, 1975.

Within this general guide are a brief history of Otto Luening, Vladimir Ussachevsky, and the Columbia-Princeton Electronic Music Center, comments by Luening.

B533.   Seaman, Julian. "Visiting Critic Finds Concert Well Played: Praises Taste, Discipline Installed by Whitney." *Courier-Journal* (Louisville), 6 March 1952.

Review of *Louisville Concerto* (W143), heard for the first time. It was described as a "Viennese romp in a beer garden. Its tunes seemed to me banal and repetitious, and Mr. Luening's derivations only too transparent, yet the audience was long and fervent in its applause--so probably I was wrong."

B534.   Shakeley, Lauren. "Showcase." *The Denisonian* 17 March 1967, p. 2.

This article announces Luening's appearance at Denison University for the week of March 20-26, 1967; includes photograph. **See: B473.**

B535.   Shanet, Howard. *Philharmonic: A History of New York's Orchestra.* Garden City, N. Y.: Doubleday, 1975.

During the 1930s Luening assisted Hans Lange in conducting the Philharmonic Symphony Chamber Orchestra; he became Associate Conductor for the 1937-38 season. Repertoire lists of several seasons are in the appendix of this book.

B536.   Shavin, Norman. "No All-Modern Concerts for Orchestra Next Season." *Louisville Times*, 4 March 1952.

A February, 1952 all-modern concert had caused reaction. Article includes announcement of the premiere of Luening's *Louisville Concerto* (W143) and a brief description of the composer.

B537.   Sigmon, Carl. "Colin McPhee, March 1901-January 7, 1964." *American Composers Alliance Bulletin* 12 (Spring 1964): 15-16.

Within this obituary of McPhee are comments of Luening.

B538.   Simms, Bryan R. *Music of the Twentieth Century.* New York: Schirmer, 1986.

Briefly describes the compositional technique of Luening and Ussachevsky's tape music.

B539.   Sims, Jo Ann Margaret Lacquet. "Capturing the Essence of the Poet: a Study and Performance of Selected Musical Settings for Solo Voice and Piano of the Poetry of Emily Dickinson." Diss. University of Illinois, 1987.

Surveys 34 composers, including Otto Luening. Brief biographical sketch of Luening and other composers using settings of Emily Dickinson. More coverage is given to Ernst Bacon, Ned Rorem, and Aaron Copland.

Includes indexes of settings. With one exception, Luening set songs which no one else did. See: **W125.**

B540. "Six Composers Get $1,200 Each for Commissioned Works." *Louisville Times*, 10 March 1954.

Otto Luening and Vladimir Ussachevsky were two composers receiving a commission for *Rhapsodic Variations for Tape Recorder and Orchestra* (W159). Includes a brief description of the piece.

B541. Slonimsky, Nicolas. "Luening, Otto (Clarence)" In *Baker's Biographical Dictionary of Musicians*, 1398-1400. 7th ed. Revised by Nicolas Slonimsky. New York: Schirmer, 1984.

A brief but thorough overview of the composer, with several works listed with their premiere performances noted.

B542a. Slonimsky, Nicolas. *Music Since 1900.* New York: Norton, 1937.

B542b. Slonimsky, Nicolas. *Music Since 1900.* London: Dent, 1938.

B542c. Slonimsky, Nicolas. *Music Since 1900.* 2nd ed. New York: Norton, 1938.

B542d. Slonimsky, Nicolas. *Music Since 1900.* 3rd ed., rev. and enlarged. New York: Coleman-Ross, 1949.

B542e. Slonimsky, Nicolas. *Music Since 1900.* 4th ed. New York: Scribner, 1971.

The premiere of *Two Symphonic Interludes* (W96) occurred on April 11, 1936, Hans Lange conducting the New York Philharmonic.

Mentioned in the third edition are such events as the premieres of Virgil Thomson's *The Mother of Us All*, conducted by Otto Luening, the latter's opera, *Evangeline* (W85), and *Two Symphonic Interludes* (W96), for orchestra.

The fourth edition lists events involving Luening and Wallingford Riegger (p. 1111), *Evangeline* (W85) (p.853), *A Poem in Cycles and Bells for Tape Recorder and Orchestra* (W158) (p. 987), *Sonority Canon For Two to Thirty-seven Flutes* (W191) (p. 1135), and *Synthesis for Orchestra and Electronic Sound* (W192) (p. 1169), but no mention of *Rhapsodic Variations for Tape Recorder and Orchestra* (W159).

B543. Slonimsky, Nicolas. *Supplement to Music Since 1900.* New York: Scribner, 1986.

Describes the October 28, 1952 premieres of *Fantasy in Space* (W148), *Invention in Twelve Tones* (W149), and *Low Speed* (W150).

Rhapsodic Variations for Tape Recorder and Orchestra (W159), the "first score ever composed that combined electronic sounds with human musicians," was premiered March 20, 1954, by the Louisville Orchestra. *Symphonic Fantasia No. 4* (W216) premiered May 14, 1984, in New York.

B544.   Smith, Cecil Michener. "Contemporary Music, Chicago Style." *Modern Music* 17 (March-April 1940): 171-173.

One performance worthy of notice was Luening's *Prelude to a Hymn Tune by William Billings* (W108) by Civic Orchestra, Hans Lange, conductor.

B545.   Smith, Cecil Michener. "What Chicago Needs." *Modern Music* 13 (May-June 1937): 224-225.

Criticizes selection of music performed in Chicago area by various ensembles. Smith cites the fact that only 3 novelties were performed in two months, one being Luening's *Two Symphonic Interludes* (W96)

B546.   "Society Scholar Otto Luening Talks With Students from March 1 to 3." *The Red and Black*, 23 February 1967.

From March 1-3, 1967 Otto Luening would be the visiting scholar of Phi Beta Kappa at Washington and Jefferson College, Washington, Pennsylvania, speaking on "Significant Trends in Twentieth Century Music." Includes brief biographical highlights, association with Ussachevsky, and photograph. **See also: B526.**

B547.   "State-born Composer Will Visit Parkside." *Racine Journal Times*, 29 March 1979.

Announces Luening's visit to the University of Wisconsin at Parkside, the concert and lectures of April 1-3. Works would include *Fanfare to a Fellow Composer* (W200), *Sonata for Bass* (W174), Fantasia Brevis for Clarinet and Piano (W101), *Low Speed* (W150), *Fantasy in Space* (W148), and *Suite or Cello and Piano* (W136).

B548.   Steinfirst, Donald. "Electronic Music Topic at Concert." *Pittsburgh Post-Gazette and Sun-Telegraph*, 1 May 1960.

Review of lecture by Otto Luening and Vladimir Ussachevsky at the Carnegie Institute, 30 April 1960. "The possibilities of electronic combinations are endless. Sounds of unbelievable, otherworld quality emerge. Not all sounds were percussive, some being lyrical bells."

B549.   Stone, Kurt. "New York." *Musical Quarterly* 49 (1963): 371-375.
         Stone reviewed three "concerts brimful of contemporary American music and dance, on May 6, 7, and 8, at Columbia's McMillin Theatre." Concert of 1963 included Luening's *Sonority Canon for Four Live Flutes and Thirty-three Recorded Flutes* (W191).

B550.   Strongin, Theodore. "Arlie Furman Gives Violin Recital Here." *New York Times*, 8 February 1964, p. 14.
         On Feb. 7, 1964, Arlie Furman premiered *Elegy for Violin* (W195), composed in memory of Maurice Wilk. Written for solo violin, the piece is "broadly melodic, and restrained but strong in feeling." She also played *Gargoyles for Violin Solo and Synthesized Sound* (W183).

B551.   Strongin, Theodore. "Pollikoff's 'Music in Our Time' Presents a Madcap 'Archangel.'" *New York Times*, 28 February 1967, p. 30.
         Luening's *Suite for Flute Solo No. 4* (W196) is reviewed as "purposely off-balance, deceptively conservative," and being played by the composer on an old-fashioned wooden flute.

B552.   "Symphony Presents Impressive Program." *Capital Times* (Madison, Wisconsin), 18 October 1965, p. 4.
         The Madison Civic Symphony "gave a provocative reading to a startling dash of electronic daring," *Concerted Piece for Tape Recorder and Orchestra* (W180), the composer in the audience. The work was startling to the reviewer because it was not preceded by music of Alban Berg, but rather was inserted between Brahms' *Symphony No. 2 in D Minor* and Ravel's *Daphnis and Chloe*. The Luening/Ussachevsky work was "less like traditional music and more like sounds from outer space."

B553.   *Tape Recorder Music*. New York: Gene Buck, 1955.
         Program notes accompanying Innovations GB1. Describes *Fantasy in Space* (W148), *Invention in Twelve Tones* (W149), *Low Speed* (W150) and *Incantation* (W153). Includes chronology of early performances, photograph of Luening and Ussachevsky, and reprints of two articles: "Counterpoint," by Nat Hentoff (**B274**), and "Tapesichord," by Peggy Glanville-Hicks (**B235**) **See: D7e, D14d, D15c, D20c.**

B554.   "Tape Recorder is Featured in Orchestra's Saturday Matinee." *Courier-Journal* (Louisville), 14 March 1954, Sec 5, p. 4.
         Announces premiere of *Rhapsodic Variations for Tape Recorder and Orchestra* (W159), a "novelty of musical combinations."

B555.   "Tape Recorder Will be 'Soloist' in Composition Commissioned Here."
         Louisville Times, 11 March 1956.
             Announces premiere of *Rhapsodic Variations for Tape Recorder and
         Orchestra* (W159), descriptions of the composers, and the composition as
         described during an interview of Ussachevsky.

B556.   "Tapesichordists." *Time* 60 (10 November 1952): 95-96.
             Describes *Musique Concrete*, and the beginnings of the collaboration
         between Luening and Ussachevsky. Includes photographs of the two
         composers.

B557.   Taubman, Howard. "Our Own Composers; Stokowski Starts a New Move
         to Play Them." *New York Times*, 19 October 1952, Section 2, p. 7.
             Stokowski offered to conduct two concerts of contemporary
         American music at the Museum of Modern Art, October 26 and 28.
         Included would be music of Otto Luening and Vladimir Ussachevsky. **See:
         W148, W149, W150**.

B558.   Taubman, Howard. "Saratoga's Fortnight of Music." *New York Times*, 12
         September 1937, Section 11, p. 5.
             The Yaddo Festival, which had begun September 4, 1937, included
         music of several composers, including Luening. A portrait of the composer
         is also in the article.

B559.   Taylor, Timothy. "New Calliope Singers." *American Record Guide* 51
         (July/August 1988): 84.
             Luening's *Lines from a Song for Occupations* (W199) is a setting of
         Walt Whitman poetry which verges on prose. The music "sounds at times
         like Ives's in his artful manipulation of tonal idiom. A well-crafted moving
         work."

B560.   Temko, Peter M. "The Perception of Pitch Predominance in Selected
         Musical Examples of Avant-Garde Composers, 1945-1961. Diss., Florida
         State University, 1971.
             "The experiment was designed to seek data concerning the perception
         of predominant pitches in selected musical examples and to compare
         electronic and non-electronic pieces regarding the perception of these
         pitches." Included for analysis is *A Poem in Cycle and Bells for Tape
         Recorder and Orchestra* (W158), by Luening and Ussachevsky.

B561.   "Temple Emannu-El Presents Concert." *New York Times*, 6 December 1954, p. 32.

       So Gleams the Past (*Sun of the Sleepless* (W63)) was performed at a concert, December 5, 1954, commemorating three anniversaries.

B562.   "They Compose on Tape." *Pittsburgh Press*, 24 April 1960.

       Announcement of a Carnegie Institute program in series on contemporary music which would be the "most unusual of the lot." On 30 April 1960, Otto Luening and Vladimir Ussachevsky would explain and demonstrate their music. **See: B548.**

B563.   Thibodeau, Ralph. "Dello Joio at Del Mar." *American Musical Digest* 1, no. 6 (1970): 18.

       Norman Dello Joio was guest composer at the Third Contemporary Music Festival at Del Mar College, Corpus Christi, Texas. The "most futuristic piece" of the festival was Luening's *Gargoyles for Violin and Synthesized Sound* (W183), with Acgille [i.e. Achille] di Russo on violin. Excerpts from the *Corpus Christi Caller*. **See: B564.**

B564.   Thibodeau, Ralph. "Dello Joio's Performance 'Sound'." *Corpus Christi Caller*, 2 March 1970, p. 12A.

       Otto Luening's *Gargoyles for Violin and Synthesized Sound* (W183) is reviewed. "After some semblance of a dance on the Moog, the violin entered with a passionate recitative. The rest was chaos. It sounded suspiciously like an avant-garde gypsy fiddler playing at a Parisian sidewalk cafe, while high above the gargoyles of Notre Dame vomit amplified obscenities."

B565a.   Thomson, Virgil. *American Music Since 1910*. London: Nicolson, 1971.

B565b.   Thomson, Virgil. *American Music Since 1910*. New York: Holt, Rinehart and Winston, 1971.

       Includes a brief biography (p. 158-159) with a very short list of major works. Also discusses Vladimir Ussachevsky (p. 180-181), and the two composers' collaborations. Includes a photograph of the tenth anniversary of the Columbia-Princeton Electronic Music Center.

B566.   Thomson, Virgil. "Americanisches Divertimento." *Der Monat* 1 (March 1949): 98-102.

       Thomson discusses the state of American music, including comments on works by Otto Luening, Arnold Schoenberg, Igor Stravinsky, and others.

B567.   Thomson, Virgil. *The Art of Judging Music*. New York: Alfred A. Knopf, 1948.

In this book of his articles from the *New York Herald Tribune* is "Melodious and Skillful" written March 4, 1946 (p. 153-154). Reviews *Coal Scuttle Blues* (W44), by Luening and Bacon, and other music by Ernst Bacon. **See: B569.**

B568.   Thomson, Virgil. "Luening's *Evangeline*." *New York Herald Tribune*, 16 May 1948, Section 5, p. 5.

Thomson reviews the premiere of *Evangeline* (W85), "not an opera" .. but what Germans call Liederspiel, a song-cycle in costume. However, Thomson changed his attitude after listening to this a few times to describe Luening as "an original composer" whose music has very expressive and personal textures.

B569.   Thomson, Virgil. "Melodious and Skillful." *New York Herald Tribune*, 4 March 1946.

Reviews *Coal Scuttle Blues* (W44), by Luening and Bacon, and other music by Ernst Bacon. Reprinted in *The Art of Judging Music*. **See: B567.**

B570.   Thomson, Virgil. *Virgil Thomson*. New York: Alfred A. Knopf, 1966.

Thomson discusses his opera, *The Mother of Us All*, and Luening's role in its premiere performance.

B571.   Thorne, Francis. "The ACA Story." *BMI* no. 1 (1984): 32-33.

The Executive Director of the American Composers Alliance gives a concise history of the organization, with references to Luening as president during the 1950s, and a co-founder of Composers Recordings.

B572.   "The Threat is to Composers, Too." *New York Times*, 23, November 1970, Section 2, p. 17.

The "Music Mailbag" includes a joint letter of composers David Diamond, Benjamin Lees, Otto Luening, William Mayer, and Elie Siegmeister. "As composers, we strongly support conductor Izler Solomon's call to save our embattled orchestras.... Composers need more--not fewer--orchestras to give realism to their efforts." Includes a reply from Solomon, stating that the Indianapolis Symphony had not merged with the Cincinnati Symphony, but that this was "only one of several proposals."

B573.   "Three Choir Fete Ends at Emanu-El." *New York Times*, 5 May 1952, p. 19.

        The women's choruses of the University Singers and the Emanu-El Choirs sang Luening's *Sun of the Sleepless* (W63) and *If That High World* (W61) on May 4, 1952.

B574.   Three Composers." *New York Herald Tribune*, 14 November, 1953, p. 8.

        T.M.S. (probably Theodore Strongin) reviews concert of music of Luening, Jack Beeson, and Alan Hovhaness. Luening works included the premiere of *Two Preludes* (1953), a spurious work, and a performance of *Variations for Harpsichord* (W120). It was a positive review.

B575.   Tischler, Barbara L. *An American Music: the search for an American Musical Identity*. New York: Oxford University Press, 1986.

        Discusses Luening's varied styles, contrasting such works as *Sextet* (W32), *String Quartet No. 1* (W38), and *Rhapsodic Variations for Tape Recorder and Orchestra* (W159).

B576.   Toff, Nancy. *The Flute Book: a Complete Guide for Students and Performers*. New York: Charles Scribner's Sons, 1985.

        "Important work in flute compositions is centered at Columbia University. First of this 'school' is flutist-composer Otto Luening." Toff's Repertoire Catalog lists over twenty works by Luening which involve the flute.

B577.   Trimble, Lester. "Luening, Otto (Clarence)". *The New Grove Dictionary of American Music*. London: Macmillan, 1986.

        A biography highlighting the composer's career, and classified list of selected works.

B578.   Trimble, Lester. "'Electronic Opera': Music Taped, Drama Dadaesque." *New York Herald Tribune*, 2 May 1960, p. 12.

        A review of the *Sonata for Violin Solo No. 1* (W177), performed by Max Pollikoff on April 30, 1960. The sonata has "leanness and fine-lined lyricism," which Trimble has expected from an "expert flutist" such as Luening.

B579.   Trimble, Lester. "The Unsung American Composer." *New York Times*, 29 November 1981, Section 6, p. 74.

        Several composers, including Otto Luening, are described. The article includes a photograph of Luening. Its thesis is that it is easier to schedule or perform popular or rock music than it is for an American orchestra to schedule music by native composers.

B580.　Trimble, Lester. Rev. of *The Odyssey of an American Composer*, by Otto Luening. *Musical Quarterly* 69 (1983): 279-285.

This lengthy review compliments the writing of Otto Luening as unique. "More than an autobiography, it is a cultural-historical chronicle of three-quarters of a century of American life, seen through the sensibilities of a native-born participant." Trimble describes the style of the writing, from the dedication through the early experiences of Luening, including his exposure to Schoenberg, influences of World War I, life in Zurich, his return to the United States, and brief mention of events after 1932, leaving it for the reader to discover. His recommendation is that the volume be owned by every American composer, music educator, and others wishing to "know what the life of an American composer is *reaaly* like." **See: B21.**

B581.　"Turash, Soprano, Bows." *New York Times*, 12 December 1951, p. 51.

Stephanie Turash sang in Carnegie Recital Hall, in the New York premiere of the *Dickinson Song Cycle* (W125).

B582.　Tuthill, Burnet C. "Recordings of Serious Music by American Composers." *Pan Pipes of Sigma Alpha Iota* 42 (December 1949): 124-130.

Includes two items withdrawn from circulation, but in the American Music Center: *Four Songs for Soprano* (New Music 1211); *Suite for Soprano and Flute* (W105) (New Music NM 1513) **See: D8a, D12a, D13a, D24a, D49.**

B583.　"U. S. Music." *Jerusalem Post*, 19 August 1956.

Don Shapiro performed piano works by various composers on August 14 in Tel-Aviv. *Variations for Harpsichord or Piano* (W120) was performed. "The works by Ward, Luening, Haines and Goeb attested to the high technical standard of these composers but scarcely gave any proof of real originality."

B584.　"Union Card for a Tape Recorder." *Music Journal* 22 (May 1954): 17.

This is a premiere review of *Rhapsodic Variations for Tape Recorder and Orchestra* (W159), from its March 1954 performance. "When the number was over, and the last screeching sound had died away, there was polite applause. Music patrons and orchestra members heard it with mixed feelings." Includes comments by Luening, Ussachevsky, and concertmaster Sidney Harth. **See also: B76, B183, B265.**

B585.   "Urges Formation of Small Orchestras to Stimulate the American Composer." *Musical America* 36, no 14 (29 July 1922): 20.

Otto C. Luening (includes drawing of composer) suggests the organization of several small ensembles "so that American composers may have their compositions played." Includes further comments of Luening and a brief biography up to his period as composition teacher at the Chicago Musical Arts Studio.

B586.   Ussachevsky, Vladimir. "As Europe Takes to Tape." *American Composers Alliance Bulletin* 3 (1953): 10-11.

Ussachevsky was invited by the Radiodiffusion and Television Francaise to speak on American tape music during the First International Decade of Experimental Music. His demonstration including compositions by Otto Luening, John Cage, and Earle Brown.

B587.   Ussachevsky, Vladimir. "Columbia-Princeton Electronic Music Center." *Revue Belge de Musicologie* 13 (1959): 129-131.

In English; includes discography, list of scores, films.

B588.   Ussachevsky, Vladimir. "Music in the Tape Medium." *Juilliard Review* 6 (Spring 1959): 8-9, 18-,

Ussachevsky explains tape music (electronic music) and its development in various countries. Included are discussions of techniques use in the joint composition *Rhapsodic Variations for Tape Recorder and Orchestra* (W159), and Luening's *Fantasy in Space* (W148) and *Low Speed* (W150).

B589.   Ussachevsky, Vladimir. "La 'Tape Music' aux Etats-Unis." *Revue Musicale*, no. 236 (1957): 50-55.

In French; discusses tape music in the United States; includes mention of Luening, John Cage and Earle Brown; three compositions of Luening are described briefly: *Low Speed* (W150), *Invention in Twelve Tones* (W149), and *Fantasy in Space* (W148).

B590.   "Vermont Chamber Orchestra This Week at Castle Hill." *Ipswich Chronicle* (Ipswich, Mass.), 3 July 1952.

Announcement of Vermont Chamber Orchestra performance, with *Prelude to a Hymn Tune by William Billings* (W108) as the Luening work; this work was not performed. See **B439** for review of concert in which *Legend for Oboe and Strings* (W144) was performed July 4, 1952.

B591.   Vinay, Gianfranco. "Luening, Otto Clarence." In *Dizionario Enciclopedico Universale della Musica e dei Musicisti. Le Biographie*, edited by Albert Basso, 4:515-516. Torino: UTET, 1986.
In Italian. Brief biography with selective list of works.

B592.   "Violinist Feature of Philharmonic." *New York Times*, 12 April 1936, Section 2, p. 8.
Review of program including Luening's *Two Symphonic Interludes* (W96), which premiered on April 11, 1936, displaying originality, brevity, and good orchestral color, in the reviewer's opinion.

B593.   "Visiting Composer Featured on TV." *Racine Journal Times*, 8 May 1981.
Announcement of interview of Otto Luening on the Milwaukee Public Library "Public Conference Show." **See: B426.**

B594.   Waldrop, Gid W. "School News: 33 U. S. Composers Commissioned for Juilliard's 50th Anniversary." *Musical Courier* 152 (15 November 1955): 34.
One new score by Luening was commissioned for a festival, scheduled between February and April of 1956.

B595.   Walter, Arnold. *Aspects of Music in Canada*. Toronto: University of Toronto Press, 1969.
Compares Pierre Schaeffer with Otto Luening, the latter believing that "new sound material, however strange, could be put to legitimate musical uses." Also brief mention of the International Conference of Composers at Stratford in 1960.

B596.   "Walter Trampler: a True Virtuoso." *Times-Union* (Albany, N. Y.), 27 January 1972, p. 22.
Two violists, Walter Trampler and Karen Phillips, performed *Eight Tone Poems for Two Violas* (W223), by Luening, referred to as a "happy but not frivolous piece of writing, and the two players played it with great spirit and a sense of humour."

B597.   Ward, Robert. "New Electronic Media." *Juilliard Review* 5, No. 2 (1958): 17-22.
A panel discussion, held in December of 1957, with Jacques Barzun as moderator, included William Bergsma, Sergius Kagen, Otto Luening, Harry F. Olson, and Vladimir Ussachevsky. Excerpts from the music of Luening and others were played. Ward summarized by saying it is "the responsibility of the professional musician to study and become familiar with anything new in the area of sound."

B598.   Warner, A. J. "American Composers' Concert Given in Eastman Theater." *Rochester Times Union*, 25 November 1925.

    Symphonic Poem, retitled *Symphonic Fantasia No. 1* (W56) was premiered in the second concert of unpublished works by American composers. "It is essentially 'mental' music that has vitality and power, and was listened to with special curiosity."

B599.   Warner, A. J. "Orchestra Plays Mozart Symphony." *Rochester Times Union*, 13 January 1928.

    Review includes premiere of *Serenade* (W62), for three horns and strings, in which Luening "has been content to write diatonically an unassuming work that is not ungrateful to the ear. It is, one suspects, ingeniously done, while its content is light as air."

B600.   Watson, Jack M. and Corinne Watson. "Luening, Otto." *A Concise Dictionary of Music*. New York: Dodd, Mead, Co., 1965.

    A fairly brief biography.

B601.   Watt, Charles E. "Chamber Music Recital." *Music News* 14, no. 44 (3 November 1922): 9.

    A review of a recital, October 26, 1922. Otto Luening's *Trio for Violin, Cello, and Piano* (W42) had its first American performance at Kimball Hall, Chicago and "won immediate recognition. It is a work of extreme difficulty and the most modern construction." Luening also performed the American premiere of Philipp Jarnach's *Sonatina for Flute and Piano*. Luening's technique was "artistic in the extreme."

B602.   Watt, Charles E. "'Shanewis' at the Studebaker." *Music News* 14, no. 46 (17 November 1922): 19-21.

    Article contains subtitle: "Otto Luening an Effective Conductor." Within this positive review of the 2 November 1922 premiere of Charles Wakefield Cadman's opera, Watt stated that: "All this mass of material was handled with great technical skill as well as constant artistry by Mr. Luening, who easily proved himself a vital factor of the performance and a man and musician to be reckoned with for the future."

B603.   "The Week's News and Comment Concerning Music." *New York Times*, 12 April 1936, Section 9, p. 5-6.

    There is a portrait of Otto Luening, whose music would be performed that day by the Philharmonic-Symphony. Hans Lange would conduct *Two Symphonic Interludes* (W96).

B604.   Weinstock, Herbert. "United States: Music." *Encyclopedia Americana*, v. 27, p. 606-611 (1981) Danbury, Conn.: Grolier, 1981.
Luening and Ussachevsky are mentioned as leaders of the Columbia-Princeton Electronic Music Center. (p. 610)

B605.   Welch, Roy D. "The College, The Composer and Music." *Modern Music* 14 (November-December 1936): 18-23.
This examines the criticism of higher education in music. He defends the quality and content of various programs, past and present, from Horatio Parker and Edward MacDowell to contemporary teacher-composers, including Luening, then at Bennington.

B606.   Wentz, Brooke. "Otto Luening at 85: An Interview: An American Pioneer recalls Early, Adventurous Times." *High Fidelity/Musical America* 35 (November 1985): MA24-27.
Luening discusses such influential people in his musical life as his father, Arnold Schoenberg, Ferruccio Busoni, and Philipp Jarnach. Includes later experiences with Howard Hanson and Edgard Varèse.

B607.   Wentz, Brooke. "Vladimir Ussachevsky." *High Fidelity/Musical America* 36 (November 1986): MA24-26.
In an article written for the 75th birthday of Ussachevsky, Wentz includes a brief biography, an interview recounting the relationship with Otto Luening, *Rhapsodic Variations for Tape Recorder and Orchestra* (W159), and the beginnings of the Columbia-Princeton Electronic Music Center.

B608.   Westrup, J. A., and F. Ll. Harrison. *The New College Encyclopedia of Music*. Revised by Conrad Wilson. New York: Norton, 1976.
"Luening, Otto" (p. 329), gives a brief and succinct biography. "Ussachevsky, Vladimir" (p. 571), is a very sketchy statement, and "Electronic Music" (p. 188-189), gives a general definition and history with brief mention of Luening, Ussachevsky, and Milton Babbitt.

B609.   "What's New." *American Composers Alliance Bulletin* 11 (December 1963): 18-20.
Vladimir Ussachevsky was among the composers represented at the Festival of Contemporary Arts, at the University of Rhode Island, in the spring of 1963. Later that year, New York's educational television station, WNDT, broadcast on October 29 and November 2, a telecast of the Composers Workshop Series which presented Milton Babbitt, Otto

Luening, and Ussachevsky, interviewed by Gunther Schuller, in a discussion of electronic music and the techniques of its composition.

B610.   Wier, Albert E. "Luening, Otto." *Macmillan Encyclopedia of Music and Musicians in One Volume*, 1086. New York: Macmillan, 1938.
Brief biography up to the Bennington period.

B611.   Wiley, Charles H. "Chicago Symphony Delights Audiences." *Musical Leader* (Chicago), 27 March 1937.
Review article of March 11, 1937 performance. "Two Symphony Sketches by ... American composer Otto Luening, were ... heard and approved." **See: W96.**

B612.   Williams, Michael D. *Music for Viola*. Detroit: Information Coordinators, 1979.
In a classified list are found two works, the unaccompanied *Sonata for Viola Solo* (W176), and the *Suite for Cello and Piano* (W136).

B613.   Wiser, John D. "Music in the Mountains; Virgil Thomson is honored at SUNY Summer Series." *High Fidelity/Musical America* 33 (November 1983): MA25, 39-40.
In July of 1983, the State University of New York at New Paltz, honored Virgil Thomson in a summer series. "The opening chamber concert was flawed by poor individual preparation by most of the string players who diluted the effectiveness of ... an exuberant 1918 *Sextet* (W32) for winds and strings by Otto Luening."

B614.   "World Premiere of 'Theatre Piece No. 2'." *New York Times*, 21 April 1956, p. 10.
Theatre Piece No. 2 (W165) premiered April 20, 1956. "The new piece is an evocative and exciting experiment in the combined use of theatrical elements." Includes description of the story in *Theatre Piece No. 2*.

B615.   Wuorinen, Charles. "Conversations with Otto Luening." *Perspectives of New Music* 9-10 (1971): 200-208.
In an interview of August 1970, Luening recalls his own past, comments on the young composers of today, the situation at the universities, aleatoric vs. serial techniques, and the championing of new music.

B616.   Wuorinen, Charles. "Ussachevsky, Vlamidir (Alexis)." *The New Grove Dictionary of American Music*. London: Macmillan, 1986.

Brief biography of Vladimir Ussachevsky, with highlights of his collaboration with Otto Luening. Includes photograph of the two in 1952.

B617.   Wyatt, Lucius Reynolds. "The Mid-Twentieth-Century Orchestral Variation, 1953-1963: An Analysis and Comparison of Selected Works by Major Composers." Diss. Eastman School of Music, 1973.

This discusses *Rhapsodic Variations for Tape Recorder and Orchestra* (W159), by Luening and Ussachevsky, from eight perspectives: thematic materials, form, melodic style, harmony, tonality, rhythm and meter, orchestration, and recorded sound material.

B618.   "YMHA, New York." *Music Journal* 29 (May 1971): 67.

Luening's *Sonata for Violin Solo No. 3* (W220) was performed in the series Gallery of Music in Our Time. "Max Pollikoff, instigator of the series, gave Otto Luening's *Sonato* [i.e. *Sonata*] *No. 3 for Solo Violin* one of his typically incisive performances."

B619.   "Yaddo Presents 7th Music Period." *The Saratogian*, 14 September 1946.

Acknowledgment that Otto Luening was a composer-conductor at the festival.

B620.   Zinsser, John. "Composer of the Modern Symphony." *50 Plus* 25 (December 1985): 50-51.

Description of the avant-garde composer in a senior citizen publication. "Luening had a sparkle in his eye and a playful sense of humor that made it easy to forget that he was more that 60 years my senior." Includes photograph with his flute. Describes several aspects of his life.

Supplement

B621.   Good, Emily. "Otto Luening: an Appreciation." *NOTES* 46 (December 1989): 490-492.

Descriptive biography of Otto Luening. Discusses *Sextet* (W32), *Sonata in Memoriam Ferruccio Busoni* (W162), *Opera Fantasia* for violin and piano (W257), *Three Fantasias for Baroque Flute* (W265).

Appendix I: Alphabetical List of Compositions

Ah! Sunflower (W250)
Alleluia (W130)
An dem Traume for Sopran (W7)
Andante and Variations, for Violin
and Piano
See Sonata for Violin and Piano,
no. 3 (W129)
Andante for Piano (W97)
Anthem (W88)
Aria for Cello and Piano (W124)
At Christmastime (W20, no.1)
At the Last (W98)
Auguries of Innocence (W64)

Back to Methuselah (W168)
Bagatelles for Piano
See Two Bagatelles for Piano
(W54)
Bass with the Delicate Air (W116)
Behold the Tabernacle of God
(W87)
Bells of Bellagio (W206)
Birth of Pleasure (W65)
Blood Wedding (W117)
Broekman Fantasia for String
Orchestra (W202)

Canon in the Octave (W131)
Canonical Study for Piano (W121)
Canons for Harpsichord (W122)

Canons (3) for Two Flutes
See Three Canons for Two Flutes
(W255)
Canons (10) for Two Flutes
See Ten Canons for Two Flutes
(W232)
Carlsbad Caverns (W161)
Children's Pieces for Piano
See Ten Pieces for Five
Fingers (W132)
Choral Vorspiel zu Christus der ist
mein Leben (W29)
Chorale Fantasy for Organ (W43)
Christ is Arisen (W118)
Coal Scuttle Blues (W44)
Concerted Piece for Tape Recorder
and Orchestra (W180)
Concertino for Flute and chamber
Orchestra (W49)
Cum Sancto Spiritu (W15)

Dance Sonata for Piano (W77)
Dawn (W89)
Day in the Country (W184)
Dickinson Song Cycle (W125)
Diffusion of Bells (W187)
Divertimento for Oboe and Strings
(W269)
Divertimento for Brass (W268)
Divine Image (W139)

Happy Sinner (W107)
Harp the Monarch Minstrel Swept
  (W142)
Hast Never Come To Thee (W103)
  Hear the Voice of the Bard
    (W71, no. 1)
  See Songs of Experience (W71)
Here the Frailest Leaves of Me
  (W83)
Hymn to Bacchus (W58)

I Faint, I Perish (W84)
Ich denke Dein (W127)
If that High World (W61)
In Weihnachtzeiten (W20, no.1)
Incantation (W153)
Incredible Voyage (W212)
Infant Joy (W67)
Introduction and Allegro for
  Trumpet and Piano (W218)
Introitus (W40)
Inventions for Piano (8)
  See Eight Inventions for Piano
    (W114)
Invention in Twelve Tones (W149)

Kentucky Concerto (W143)
Kentucky Rondo (W143, no. 3)
King Lear (W164)

Laughing Song (W252)
Legend for oboe and Strings (W144)
Legend for Violin and Piano (W50)
Lily (W253)
Lines from a Song for Occupations
  (W199)
Lines from The First Book of
  Urizen and Vala (W247)
Little Miniature Pieces (W1)
Little Vagabond (W239)
Locations and Times (W68)

Louisville Concerto
  See Kentucky Concerto (W143)
Love's Secret (W140)
Low Speed (W150)
Lyric Scene for Flute and Strings
  (W171)

Maidens of Shang-Ti
  See Vocalise (W201)
Mañana (W93)
Meditation for Violin Solo (W209)
Mexican Serenades (W226)
Minuet for Cello and Piano (W21)
Moonflight (W213)
Music for Orchestra (W51)
Music for Piano--a contrapuntal study
  (W41)
Mysterium for Soprano or tenor
  (W22)

No Jerusalem But This (W245)
Noon Silence (See W20, no. 2)

Of Identity (W157)
One Step, for Piano (W23)
Only Themselves Understand
  Themselves (W104)
Opera Fantasia (W257)

Phantasy for Piano (W94)
Piano Preludes (6) (W95)
  See Six Preludes for Piano (W95)
Piano Preludes (8)
  See Eight Preludes for Piano
    (W99)
Piece for Organ (W10)
Piece for Piano (W3)
Piece for Piano (W24)
Piece for String Quartet (W5)
Pilgrim's Hymn for Children's Voices,
  Soprano, Alto, and (W137)

Sonata for Violin and Piano, no. 1 (W26)

Sonata for Violin and Piano, no. 2 (W46)

Sonata for Violin and Piano, no. 3 (W129)
also known as *Andante and Variations*

Sonatina for Flute and Piano (W36)

Song Without Words (W266)

Song, Poem and Dance for Flute and Strings (W178)

Songs of Experience (W71) includes:
Earth's Answer
Hear the Voice of the Bard

Sonority Canon for two to thirty-seven Flutes (W191)

Sonority Forms no. 1 for Orchestra (W225)

Sonority Forms no. 2 for Orchestra (W249)

Sonority Forms no. 1 for Piano (W246)

Sonority Forms no. 2 for Piano (W254)

Soundless Song (W52)

String Quartet no. 1 (W38)

String Quartet no. 2 (W53)

String Quartet no. 3 (W72)

Study in Synthesized Sound (W185)

Suite for Baroque Flute (W265)

Suite for Cello and Piano (W136)

Suite for Double Bass and Piano (W155)

Suite for Flute and Soprano (W272)

Suite for Flute Solo, no. 1 (W138)

Suite for Flute Solo, no. 2 (W156)

Suite for Flute Solo, no. 3 (W186)

Suite for Flute Solo, no. 4 (W196)

Suite for Flute Solo, no. 5 (W214)

Suite for High and Low Instruments (W197)

Suite for Horn (W267)

Suite for Soprano and Flute (W105)

Suite for String Orchestra (W111)

Suite for two Flutes and Piano with Cello ad lib (W231)

Suite for Violin Solo (W167)

Suite from King Lear (W164)

Sun of the Sleepless (W63)

Swing, swing and swoon (W106)

Symphonic Fantasia no. 1 (W56)
formerly Symphonic Poem

Symphonic Fantasia no. 2 (W115)

Symphonic Fantasia no. 3 (W215)

Symphonic Fantasia no. 4 (W216)

Symphonic Fantasia no. 5 (W238)

Symphonic Fantasia no. 6 (W259)

Symphonic Fantasia no. 7 (W262)

Symphonic Fantasia no. 8 (W263)

Symphonic Fantasia no. 9 (W271)

Symphonic Interlude no. 1 (W96)

Symphonic Interlude no. 2 (W96)

Symphonic Interlude no. 3 (W228)

Symphonic Interlude no. 4 (W260)

Symphonic Interlude no. 5 (W264)

Symphonic Poem
See Symphonic Fantasia no. 1 (W56)

Synthesis for Orchestra and Electronic Sound (W192)

Tango (W261)

Ten Canons for Two Flutes (W232)

Ten Pieces for Five Fingers for Piano (W132)

Theatre Piece No. 2 (W165)

Thema con Variazione (W27)

Theme with Variations (W2)
Three Canons for Two Flutes (W255)

Three Duets for two Flutes (W188)

Three Fantasias for Baroque Flute
  See Suite for Baroque Flute
  (W265)
Three Fantasias for Solo guitar
  (W182)
Three Nocturnes for Oboe and
  Piano(W145)
Three Songs for Soprano and Piano
  or small Orchestra (W20)
Three Swiss Folksongs (W28)
Tiger's Ghost (W147)
To Morning (W73)
To See the World in a Grain of
  Sand
  See Auguries of Innocence
  (W64)
Tone Poems (8), Violas
  See Eight Tone Poems for Two
  Violas (W223)
Transcience (W47)
Triadic Canons (W229)
Trio for Flute, Cello, and Piano
  (W193)
Trio for Flute, Violin, and Soprano
  (W57)
Trio for Flute, Violin, and Piano
  (W152)
Trio for Three Flutists (W205)
Trio for Trumpet, Horn, and
  Trombone (W217)
Trio for Violin, Cello and Piano
  (W42)
Trio for Women's Voices (SMzA)
  (W6)
Two Bagatelles for Piano (W54)
Two Songs for Soprano and Piano
  (W14)
Two Symphonic Interludes (W96)

Ulysses in Nighttown (W179)

Variations for Harpsichord or Piano
  (W120)
Variations on the National Air
  "Yankee Doodle" (W48)
Variations on Christus des ist mein
  Leben (W29) (Organ)
Variations on Christus des ist mein
  Leben (W34) (4 Horns)
Variations on Bach's Chorale Prelude
  Liebster Jesu wir sind hier (W128)
Vater unser im Himmelreich (W35)
Venilia (W20, no. 3)
Visored (W74)
Vocalise (SSAA) (W201)

Wake the Serpent Not (W75)
Waltz (W4)
When in the Languor Evening (W92)
Wie Sind die Tage (W39)
Wir Wandeln alle den Weg (W13)
Wisconsin Suite (W160)
Wisconsin Symphony (W230)

Young love (W76)

Appendix II: Classified List of Compositions

Chamber Music

Strings

Aria for Cello and Piano (W124)
Doppelfugue (W16)
Duo for Violin and Viola (W194)
Eight Tone Poems (W223)
Elegy for Violin (W195)
Fantasia and Dance in Memoriam Max Pollikoff (W251)
Fantasia for Cello (W203)
Fantasia for String Quartet and Orchestra (W170)
Fantasia for Violin no. 1 (W244)
Fantasia brevis for Violin, Viola, and Cello (W100)
Fugue for String Quartet (W37)
Gavotte for Cello and Piano (W18)
Legend for Violin and Piano (W50)
Mañana (W93)
Meditation for Violin Solo (W209)
Minuet for Cello and Piano (W21)
Opera Fantasia (W257)
Piece for String Quartet (W5)
Sonata for Cello, no. 1 (W55)
Sonata for Cello, no. 2, composed in Two Dayturnes (W175)
Sonata for Bass (W174)
Sonata for Viola Solo (W176)

Sonata for Violin Solo, no. 1 (W177)
Sonata for Violin Solo, no. 2 (W211)
Sonata for Violin Solo, no. 3 (W220)
Sonata for Violin and Piano, no. 1 (W26)
Sonata for Violin and Piano, no. 2 (W46)
Sonata for Violin and Piano, no. 3 (W129)
String Quartet no. 1 (W38)
String Quartet no. 2 (W53)
String Quartet no. 3 (W72)
Suite for Cello and Piano (W136)
Suite for Double Bass and Piano (W155)
Suite for Violin Solo (W167)
Three Fantasias for Solo Guitar (W182)
Variations on Bach's Chorale Prelude Liebster Jesu wir sind hier (W128)

Woodwinds

Bass with the Delicate Air (W116)
Fantasia for Clarinet (W243)
Fantasia brevis for Clarinet and Piano (W101)
Fantasia brevis for Flute and Piano (W79)

Fantasias on Indian Motives for Flute (W233)
Four Cartoons (W227)
Fourteen Easy Duets for Recorders (W207)
Fuguing Tune for Woodwind Quintet (W113)
Happy Sinner (W107)
Potawatomi Legends no. 2 for Flute (W233)
Serenade and Dialogue (W258)
Short Sonata for Flute and Piano, no. 1 (W110)
Short Sonata for Flute and Piano, no. 2 (W222)
Short Sonata for Flute and Piano, no. 3 (W204)
Sonata for Bassoon and Piano (W151)
Sonatina for Flute and Piano (W36)
Suite for Baroque Flute (W265)
Suite for Flute Solo, no. 1 (W138)
Suite for Flute Solo, no. 2 (W156)
Suite for Flute Solo, no. 3 (W186)
Suite for Flute Solo, no. 4 (W196)
Suite for Flute Solo, no. 5 (W214)
Ten Canons for two Flutes (W232)
Three Canons for two Flutes (W255)
Three Duets for two Flutes (W188)
Three Nocturnes for Oboe and Piano (W145)
Trio for Three Flutists (W205)
Variations on the National Air "Yankee Doodle" (W48)

Brass

Divertimento for Brass (W268)
Introduction and Allegro for trumpet and Piano (W218)
Sonata for Trombone and Piano (W154)
Suite for Horn (W267)

Trio for Trumpet, Horn, and Trombone (W217)
Variations on Christus des ist mein Leben (W34) (4 horns)

Other Chamber

Divertimento for Oboe and Strings (W269)
Duo for Flute and Viola (W256)
Easy March for Wind Instruments and Piano (W141)
Elegy for the Lonesome Ones (W109)
Entrance and Exit Music (W198)
Fantasia for Violin, Cello, and Piano (W242)
Green Mountain Evening (W270)
Mexican Serenades (W226)
Serenade for Flute and Strings (W163)
Serenade for Violin, Violoncello, and Piano (W248)
Sextet for Flute, Clarinet, Horn, Violin, Viola, Violoncello (W32)
Short Ballad for two Clarinets and Strings (W109)
Short Fantasy for Violin and horn (W86)
Short Fantasy for Violin and Piano (W112)
Song, Poem and Dance for Flute and Strings (W178)
Suite for High and Low Instruments (W197)
Suite for two Flutes and Piano with Cello ad lib (W231)
Triadic Canons (W229)
Trio for Flute, Cello, and Piano (W193)
Trio for Flute, Violin, and Soprano (W57)

Trio for Flute, Violin, and Piano (W152)
Trio for Violin, Cello and Piano (W42)

Piano Music

Andante for Piano (W97)
Bells of Bellagio (W206)
Canon in the Octave (W131)
Canonical Study for Piano (W121)
Canons for Harpsichord (W122)
Coal Scuttle Blues (W44)
Dance Sonata for Piano (W77)
Easy Canons for Piano (W123)
Eight Inventions for Piano (W114)
Eight Pieces for Piano (W66)
Eight Preludes for Piano (W99)
Fantasia no. 2 for Piano (W90)
Fantasia for Harpsichord or Piano (W126)
Fantasie Stücke for Piano (W9)
Five Intermezzi (W91)
Four Short Piano Pieces (W12)
Fuga a tre voci for Piano (W31)
Fugue for Piano (W17)
Gavotte for Piano (W19)
Gay Picture (W166)
Hymn to Bacchus (W58)
Little Miniature Pieces (W1)
Music for Piano--a Contrapuntal Study (W41)
One Step, for Piano (W23)
Phantasy for Piano (W94)
Piece for Piano (W3)
Piece for Piano (W24)
Short Sonata for Piano, no. 1 (W119)
Short Sonata for Piano, no. 2 (W172)
Short Sonata for Piano, no. 3 (W173)
Short Sonata for Piano, no. 4 (W208)

Short Sonata for Piano, no. 5 (W234)
Short Sonata for Piano, no. 6 (W235)
Short Sonata for Piano, no. 7 (W236)
Six Preludes for Piano (W95)
Six Short and Easy Piano Pieces (W70)
Slumbersong for Piano (W33)
Sonata for Piano in Memoriam Ferruccio Busoni (W162)
Song Without Words (W266)
Sonority Forms no. 1 for Piano (W246)
Sonority Forms no. 2 for Piano (W254)
Tango (W261)
Ten Pieces for Five Fingers for Piano (W132)
Thema con Variazione (W27)
Theme with Variations (W2)
Two Bagatelles for Piano (W54)
Variations for Harpsichord or Piano (W120)
Waltz (W4)

Organ Music

Choral Vorspiel zu Christus der ist mein Leben (W29)
Chorale Fantasy for Organ (W43)
Fantasia for Organ (W78)
Fugue for Organ (W221)
Introitus (W40)
Piece for Organ (W10)

Choral Music

Alleluia (W130)
Anthem (W88)
Behold the Tabernacle of God (W87)
Christ is Arisen (W118)

239

Cum Sancto Spiritu (W15)
Enigma Canon (W45)
I Faint, I Perish (W84)
Ich denke Dein (W127)
Lines from a Song for Occupations (W199)
Lines from The First Book of Urizen and Vala (W247)
Pilgrim's Hymn for Children's Voices, Soprano, Alto and Piano (W137)
Psalm 146 (W219)
So Gleams the Past (W63)
Sun of the Sleepless (W63)
Three Swiss Folksongs (W28)
Tiger's Ghost (W147)
Trio for Women's voices (SMzA) (W6)
Vater unser im Himmelreich (W35)
Vocalise (SSAA) (W201)
When in the Languor Evening (W92)

Solo Vocal Music

Ah! Sunflower (W250)
An dem Traume for soprano (W7)
At Christmastime (W20, no. 1)
At the Last (W98)
Auguries of Innocence (W64)
Birth of Pleasure (W65)
Dawn (W89)
Dickinson Song Cycle (W125)
Divine Image (W139)
Earth's Answer (W71, no. 2)
Eichwald (W8)
Farm Picture (W80)
For Like a Chariot's Wheel (W81)
Forever Lost (W102)
Fruhling (W30)
Gliding O'er All (W60)
Goodnight (W82)

Harp the Monarch Minstrel Swept (W142)
Hast Never Come To Thee (W103)
Hear the Voice of the Bard (W71, no. 1)
Here the Frailest Leaves of Me (W83)
If that High World (W61)
In Weihnachtzeiten (W20, no. 1)
Infant Joy (W67)
Laughing Song (W252)
Lily (W253)
Little Vagabond (W239)
Location and Times (W68)
Love's Secret (W140)
Mysterium for Soprano or Tenor (W22)
No Jerusalem But This (W245)
Noon Silence (See W20, no. 2)
Only Themselves Understand Themselves (W104)
Requiescat (W25)
Roman's Chamber (W69)
Septembermorgen, for Soprano or Tenor (W11)
She Walks in Beauty (W146)
Silent, Silent Night (W241)
Six Proverbs (W210)
Songs of Experience (W71)
Soundless Song (W52)
Suite for Flute and Soprano (W272)
Suite for Soprano and Flute (W105)
Swing, Swing and Swoon (W106)
Three Songs for Soprano and Piano or Small Orchestra (W20)
To Morning (W73)
To See the World in a Grain of Sand (W64)
Transcience (W47)
Two Songs for Soprano and Piano (W14)
Venilia (W20, no. 3)

Visored (W74)
Wake the Serpent Not (W75)
Wie Sind die Tage (W39)
Wir Wandeln alle den Weg (W13)
Young love (W76)

Electronic Music

Day in the Country (W184)
Dynamophonic Interlude (W169)
Fantasy in Space (W148)
Fugue and Chorale Fantasy with
    Electronic Doubles (W224)
Gargoyles for Violin Solo and
    Synthesized Sound (W183)
Invention in Twelve Tones (W149)
Low Speed (W150)
Moonflight (W213)
Sonority Canon for Two to
    Thirty-seven Flutes (W191)
Study in Synthesized Sound (W185)
Synthesis for Orchestra and
    Electronic Sound (W192)
Theatre Piece No. 2 (W165)

In Collaboration with Vladimir Ussachevsky

Back to Methuselah (W168)
Carlsbad Caverns (W161)
Concerted Piece for Tape Recorder
    and Orchestra (W180)
Incantation (W153)
Incredible Voyage (W212)
Of Identity (W157)
Poem in Cycles and Bells for Tape
    Recorder and Orchestra (W158)
Rhapsodic Variations for Tape
    Recorder and Orchestra (W159)
Suite from King Lear (W164)
Ulysses in Nighttown (W179)

In Collaboration with Halim El-Dabh

Diffusion of Bells (W187)
Electronic Fanfare (W181)

Orchestral Music

Broekman Fantasia for String
    Orchestra (W202)
Concertino for Flute and Chamber
    Orchestra (W49)
Fantasia for String Quartet and
    Orchestra (W170)
Fanfare for a Fellow Composer
    (W200)
Kentucky Concerto (W143)
Kentucky Rondo (W143a)
Legend for Oboe and Strings (W144)
Lyric Scene for Flute and Strings
    (W171)
Music for Orchestra (W51)
Pilgrim's Hymn for Chamber
    Orchestra (W133)
Pilgrim's Hymn for Orchestra (W134)
Potawatomi Legends for Chamber
    Orchestra (W240)
Prelude for Chamber Orchestra
    (W135)
Prelude to a Hymn Tune by William
    Billings (W108)
Rondo for Accordion (W189)
Rondo for Accordion and Chamber
    Orchestra (W190)
Serenade for Three Horns and String
    Orchestra (W62)
Short symphony (W237)
Sonority Forms no. 1 for Orchestra
    (W225)
Sonority Forms no. 2 for Orchestra
    (W249)
Suite for String Orchestra (W111)

Otto Luening

Symphonic Fantasia no. 1 (W56)
Symphonic Fantasia no. 2 (W115)
Symphonic Fantasia no. 3 (W215)
Symphonic Fantasia no. 4 (W216)
Symphonic Fantasia no. 5 (W238)
Symphonic Fantasia no. 6 (W259)
Symphonic Fantasia no. 7 (W262)
Symphonic Fantasia no. 8 (W263)
Symphonic Fantasia no. 9 (W271)
Symphonic Interlude no. 1 (W96a)
Symphonic Interlude no. 2 (W96b)
Symphonic Interlude no. 3 (W228)
Symphonic Interlude no. 4 (W260)
Symphonic Interlude no. 5 (W264)
Two Symphonic Interludes (W96)
Wisconsin Suite (W160)
Wisconsin Symphony (W230)

Stage Music/Opera

Back to Methuselah (W168)
Blood Wedding (W117)
Evangeline (W85)
Sister Beatrice--Incidental Music
    (W59)

Index

References for each item indexed are presented in the same order as found in the text: page numbers refer to the **Biography** section, followed by references to the **Works and Performances** section ("W"), the **Discography** ("D"), and the **Bibliography** ("B").

Otto Luening

Wummer, John W110b, B260
Wummer, Mildred W110c
Wuorinen, Charles p.16, W193a-b,
    B73, B147, B155, B223, B429, B444,
    B504, B615-B616
Wyatt, Lucius Reynolds B617
Wyton, Alec D10a

Y.M.-Y.W.H.A. B273
Yaddo Festival W72a, W101a, W108b,
    W111a, W133a, B78, B264, B404,
    B449, B524, B558, B619
Yaddo Orchestra W108b
Yaddo Records D27a-b, D43b, D57a
Yankee Doodle W48
Young Love W76
Young People's Concert (New York
    Philharmonic) B74
Youngberg, Harold C. B353

Ziehn, Bernhard p.4
Zijlstra, Miep B521
Zimmerman, Hans W32a
Zinsser, John B620
Zubryki, Robert W86a
Zurich p.4, W32a, B21, B205, B580
Zygman, Flora W36a

About the Author

RALPH HARTSOCK is the Senior Music and Audiovisual Materials Cataloger at the University of North Texas. He holds degrees from Weber State College and the University of Arizona, with additional study at the University of New Mexico. The author has served in catalog departments of the University of New Mexico, Northern Arizona University, and Clarion University of Pennsylvania before assuming his present post.